Producing Islamic Knowledge

How do Muslims in Europe acquire discursive and practical knowledge of Islam? How are conceptions of Islamic beliefs, values and practices transmitted and how do they change? Who are the authorities on these issues that Muslims listen to? How do new Muslim discourses emerge in response to the European context?

This book addresses the broader question of how Islamic knowledge (defined as what Muslims hold to be correct Islamic beliefs and practices) is being produced and reproduced in West European contexts by looking at specific settings, institutions and religious authorities. Chapters examine in depth four key areas relating to the production and reproduction of Islamic knowledge:

- authoritative answers in response to explicit questions in the form of *fatwas*.
- the mosque and mosque association as the setting of much formal and informal transmission of Islamic knowledge.
- the role of Muslim intellectuals in articulating alternative Muslim discourses.
- higher Islamic education in Europe and the training of imams and other religious functionaries.

Featuring contributions from leading sociologists and anthropologists, the book presents the findings of empirical research in these issues from a range of European countries such as France, Italy, the Netherlands and Great Britain. As such it has a broad appeal, and will be of great interest to students and scholars of Islamic studies, anthropology and religion.

Martin van Bruinessen holds the chair of Comparative Studies of Contemporary Muslim Societies in the Department of Religious Studies and Theology, Utrecht University. He was one of the founders and an academic staff member of the International Institute for the Study of Islam in the Modern World (ISIM), where he co-ordinated the research programme on the Production of Islamic Knowledge in Western Europe.

Stefano Allievi is Professor of Sociology at the University of Padua. He specialises in migration issues, sociology of religion and cultural change, with a particular focus on the presence of Islam in Italy and Europe.

Routledge Islamic studies series

This broad ranging series includes books on Islamic issues from all parts of the globe and is not simply confined to the Middle East.

Historians, State and Politics in Twentieth Century Egypt
Contesting the nation
Anthony Gorman

The New Politics of Islam
Pan-Islamic foreign policy
in a world of states
Naveed Shahzad Sheikh

The Alevis in Turkey
The emergence of a secular
Islamic tradition
David Shankland

Medieval Islamic Economic Thought
Filling the great gap in
European economics
S.M. Ghazanfar

The West and Islam
Western liberal democracy versus
the system of *shura*
Mishal Fahm al-Sulami

The Regency of Tunis and the Ottoman Porte, 1777–1814
Army and government of a North-African
eyâlet at the end of the eighteenth century
Asma Moalla

Islamic Insurance
A modern approach to Islamic banking
Aly Khorshid

The Small Players of the Great Game
The settlement of Iran's eastern
borderlands and the creation
Afghanistan
Pirouz Mojtahed-Zadeh

Interest in Islamic Economics
Understanding riba
Abdulkader Thomas

Muslim Diaspora
Gender, culture and identity
Edited by Haideh Moghissi

Human Conscience and Muslim-Christian Relations
Modern Egyptian thinkers on *al-ḍamīr*
Oddbjørn Leirvik

Islam in Nordic and Baltic Countries
Göran Larsson

Islam and Disability
Perspectives in theology and
jurisprudence
Mohammed Ghaly

Producing Islamic Knowledge
Transmission and dissemination in
Western Europe
*Edited by Martin van Bruinessen
and Stefano Allievi*

Producing Islamic Knowledge
Transmission and dissemination
in Western Europe

Edited by
Martin van Bruinessen
and Stefano Allievi

Routledge
Taylor & Francis Group

LONDON AND NEW YORK

First published 2011
by Routledge
2 Park Square, Milton Park, Abingdon, Oxon OX14 4RN

Simultaneously published in the USA and Canada
by Routledge
270 Madison Ave, New York, NY 10016

*Routledge is an imprint of the Taylor & Francis Group,
an informa business*

Typeset in Times New Roman by Glyph International
Printed and bound in Great Britain by CPI Antony Rowe,
Chippenham, Wiltshire

British Library Cataloguing in Publication Data
A catalogue record for this book is available from the British Library

Library of Congress Cataloging in Publication Data
Producing Islamic knowledge: transmission and dissemination in
Western Europe / edited by Martin van Bruinessen and Stefano Allievi.
    p. cm.
Includes bibliographical references and index.
1. Islamic religious education–Europe. 2. Islam–Europe.
I. Bruinessen, Martin van. II. Allievi, Stefano.
BP43.E85P76 2011
297.7'7094–dc22   2010005350

ISBN 978-0-415-35592-6 (hbk)
ISBN 978-0-203-84623-0 (ebk)

Contents

Preface

This book was conceived many years ago and took a long time in germinating. Early versions of most chapters were presented as work in progress at the Fourth Mediterranean Social and Political Research Meeting in Montecatini Terme in 2003, in a workshop convened by the editors and co-sponsored by ISIM, the International Institute for the Study of Islam in the Modern World. Most of the contributors continued their research in the following years, and the present chapters reflect the current state of research. One chapter (by Birt and Lewis) was commissioned later as an important complement to the others.

Much of the research on Muslims in Europe has, until recently, tended to be highly descriptive and little theorized. Questions of the integration of Muslims into the secularized European societies have loomed large in this literature, and especially since the train and underground bombings in Madrid (11 March 2004) and London (7 July 2005), European public discourse on Islam has had a heavy emphasis on radicalization and security threats. Islam and Muslims in Europe have increasingly come to be seen and studied as problems for Europe. The religious aspects of Muslims' lives have received relatively little attention.

Two prominent academics and public intellectuals of Muslim background, Bassam Tibi and Tariq Ramadan, have, apparently independently of one another and with rather different emphases, proposed the concept of Euro-Islam as the expression of universal Islamic values in a European cultural and political framework. For both, Euro-Islam is a project rather than the description of actual developments and both have implied that the way European Muslims are reshaping the relationship between Islam and society will bear upon the future of Islam in the Muslim-majority world as well. Social scientists have also come to speak of Euro-Islam or European Islam as a distinct regional variety (or a number of varieties) of Islamic practices, comparable to other regional varieties such as Turkish or South Asian or North African Islam, that they believe to see emerging. (Some have juxtaposed the concepts of Islam *in* Europe and Islam *of* Europe, the former referring to a transplanted Islam coloured by cultures of origin and the latter to a uniquely European elaboration of Islamic religious inspiration.) There has been little empirical work, however, on whether and how a European Islam is emerging.

The chapters in this volume represent an effort to fill some of this gap. They all address the broader question of how Islamic knowledge (defined as what Muslims hold to be correct Islamic beliefs and practices) is being produced and reproduced in West European contexts by looking at specific settings, institutions and religious authorities. Mosques and mosque associations figure prominently as sites of production of Islamic knowledge in several of the chapters, notably Morgahi's on the modernizing traditionalist organization Minhajul Qur'an and Amiraux' chapter on the Parisian mosque led by the remarkable imam (or rather, *recteur*) Larbi Kechat. Both chapters discuss a wide range of relevant activities in and around the mosque and engage questions of how religious authority is constituted. The delicate relationship between imams and mosque or association committees as competing authorities is also discussed in van Bruinessen's introductory overview.

The training of imams in Europe, rather than 'importing' them, often for short periods only, from migrants' countries of origin, has often been hailed as an important step in the creation of a European Islam, and most European countries aspire to gain control of the process of imam education. Birt and Lewis provide an interesting overview of the Muslim seminaries in Britain, the European frontrunner in Islamic higher education.

Fatwas are perhaps the most explicit formulations of Islamic knowledge in response to specific and context-related questions, and properly studied they potentially offer important insights into the dynamics of Islamic thought and the legitimation of locally specific Islamic practices. The two chapters dealing with fatwas, by Caeiro and Mariani, focus on different types of authorities serving different constituencies. The European Council for Fatwa and Research, studied by Caeiro, is the major institution involved in the development of Islamic legal thought specifically relevant to Muslims in a minority situation, and its fatwas appear to be conceived as building bricks for a European Islam. The two media-savvy preachers whose online and offline fatwas and other activities are studied by Mariani, Omar Bakri and Amr Khaled, represent very different styles of Islam, hard-line Islamism versus 'Islam light', but both have successfully targeted constituencies that are not easily reached by mainstream institutions. With its effort to understand mediated communications within the larger framework of these preachers' relations with their followers, Mariani's work is also a major contribution to understanding the role of the new media in the production of Islamic knowledge.

The ulama, men whose credentials include training in an established institution of Islamic education, remain the most influential figures of religious authority. In the chapters by Morgahi, Amiraux, Caeiro and Mariani we encounter various types of ulama, who have established their authority in a variety of ways, and whose contributions to Islamic discourse and practices have taken an even wider range of forms. Besides the ulama, authority figures of a new type have emerged, however, the Muslim intellectuals: men (and occasionally women) whose main education is in another discipline than traditional Islamic studies but who are strongly committed to Islam and have acquired sufficient knowledge to speak confidently about matters of religion and its social relevance. Amr Khaled, an accountant by training, represents one type of Muslim intellectual (in Mariani's chapter); we encounter several others in the chapters by Morgahi and Amiraux as speakers addressing young Muslim audiences. Muslim intellectuals of a rather different type, who nonetheless have also made a significant impact on shaping European Muslim discourses, are the Traditionalists who constitute the subject of Sedgwick's chapter.

Allievi's chapter focuses on the European context within which, and in response to which, European Muslim discourses develop. It is at once a critique of the production of knowledge *about* European Islam and of the role of the observer in shaping the observed. Van Bruinessen surveys what we know about how 'ordinary' Muslims produce their Islamic knowledge – with a special emphasis on non-discursive modes of knowledge and the disciplining practices that produce those.

The editors wish to thank Muhammad Khalid Masud, former academic director of ISIM, for his stimulating intellectual input in the research programme on production of Islamic knowledge in Western Europe, and the Robert Schuman Centre of the European University Institute for providing the setting for the first discussions out of which this book emerged. We also thank the other participants in the original workshop and later seminars, whose contributions to the discussions gave important feedback on the research presentations and helped to improve the chapters. Finally we thank Sanaa Makhlouf for her essential editorial support.

The Editors

Contributors

Stefano Allievi is Professor of Sociology at the University of Padua. He specializes on migration issues, the sociology of religion and cultural change, focusing particularly on Islam in Europe. His publications include numerous books in Italian and the edited volumes *Muslim Networks and Transnational Communities in and across Europe* (with Jorgen Nielsen, Brill, 2003) and *Muslims in the Enlarged Europe* (with Brigitte Maréchal, Felice Dassetto, and Jorgen Nielsen, Brill, 2003). His most recent research, directed on behalf of the Network of European Foundations, is *Conflicts over Mosques in Europe: Policy Issues and Trends* (Alliance Publishing Trust, 2009).

Valérie Amiraux is a permanent senior research fellow in sociology at the CNRS, affiliated with the CURAPP (University of Amiens). She is currently on leave and is professor of sociology at the University of Montreal, where she holds the Canadian Chair of Research for the Study of Religious Pluralism and Ethnicity. Her current work focuses on the use of law by religious minorities in the European context. She is also developing a new project on pluralism and radicalization in Québec and Europe. Her publications include the edited volume *Politics of Visibility: Young Muslims in European Public Spaces* (with Gerdien Jonker, Bielefeld, Transcript, 2006), numerous articles, and two special issues of *The American Behavioral Scientist* on anti-dicrimination policies in a comparative perspective (co-edited with Virginie Guiraudon, 2010).

Jonathan Birt is a visiting lecturer at the Markfield Institute of Higher Education in Leicestershire, UK and holds an M.Phil. in Social Anthropology from the University of Oxford. He has written over a dozen academic articles on aspects of Muslim life in Britain. He is a co-editor of a forthcoming volume on *British Religion and Secularism: Islam, Society and the State*, due to be published in 2010 (Markfield: Kube).

Martin van Bruinessen holds the chair of Comparative Studies of Contemporary Muslim Societies in the Department of Religious Studies and Theology, Utrecht University. He was one of the founders and an academic staff member of the International Institute for the Study of Islam in the Modern World (ISIM), where he coordinated the research programme on the Production of Islamic Knowledge in Western Europe. His most recent publications include the edited volumes *Sufism and the 'Modern' in Islam* (with Julia D. Howell, I.B. Tauris, 2007), *The Madrasa in Asia* (with Farish A. Noor and Yoginder Sikand, Amsterdam University Press, 2008), and *Islam and Modernity* (with M. Khalid Masud and Armando Salvatore, Edinburgh University Press, 2009).

Alexandre Caeiro was a Ph.D. fellow at the International Institute for the Study of Islam in the Modern World (ISIM) in Leiden, the Netherlands, from 2004 to 2008. His Ph.D. dissertation tries to understand and contextualize ongoing Muslim attempts to device a fiqh for minorities. Since March 2009 Caeiro has been a research fellow at the newly established Erlangen Centre for Islam and Law in Europe (EZIRE) at the Friedrich-Alexander University in Erlangen-Nürnberg, Germany. His publications include 'The Social Construction of shariᶜa: Bank Interest, Home Purchase, and Islamic Norms in the West', *Die Welt des Islams*, 44 (2004), and 'The Shifting Moral Universes of the Islamic Tradition of *ifta*: A Diachronic Study of Four *adab al-fatwa* Manuals', *The Muslim World*, 96 (2006).

Philip Lewis lectures on 'Islam in the West' in the Department of Peace Studies, Bradford University and advises the city's Anglican Bishop on Christian–Muslim Relations. A particular research focus is the training and formation of Islamic religious personnel in Britain and their capacity for collaboration with Christian priests and secular agencies. Among his latest publications are *Young, British and Muslim* (Continuum, 2007) and 'For the Peace of the City: Bradford, A Case Study in Developing Inter-Community and Inter-Religious Relations', in Stephen R. Goodwin (ed.), *World Christianity in Muslim Encounter* (Continuum, 2009).

Ermete Mariani holds a degrees in Arabic Language and Civilization from the University of Venice and Comparative Politics of the Arab and Muslim World from the Institut d'Études Politiques in Paris and is completing his Ph.D. dissertation on the 'political ecology' of the new media in Arab countries at the Institut d'Études Politiques in Lyon. For the past six years he has coordinated the research unit on politics and security in the Muslim World of Italy's main private news agency, Adnkronos International. He has published numerous journalistic articles, video reports and essays about Middle Eastern politics and the production of Islamic discourse on the Internet.

M. Amer Morgahi is a Ph.D. candidate at the Free University, Amsterdam, and a former junior research fellow at ISIM. His Ph.D. project is titled 'Religion, Recreation, and Devotion: A Comparative Study of the Minhajul Qurᶜan Movement among South Asian Youth in Europe'. His further research interests concern new developments among traditionalist Barelwi groups in Europe more generally.

Mark Sedgwick is an associate professor at Aarhus University, Denmark, where he is the coordinator of the Arab and Islamic Studies Unit. By training a historian, he is the author of *Against the Modern World: Traditionalism and the Secret Intellectual History of the Twentieth Century* (New York: Oxford University Press, 2004). His other books deal with Sufism and with Islam in the modern world.

1 Producing Islamic knowledge in Western Europe

Discipline, authority, and personal quest

Martin van Bruinessen

What is Islamic knowledge?

In this chapter, I shall be using the term 'Islamic knowledge' for whatever Muslims consider to be correct or proper belief and practice – in the widest meaning of those words, and including non-discursive, embodied forms of knowledge. Since Muslims hold different views of what is properly Islamic, there cannot be a single, unified and universal knowledge (though some Muslims make such claims for their particular conception of it), and Islamic knowledge is inherently contested. What makes it Islamic is not necessarily its congruence with some broadly accepted standard of orthodoxy and orthopraxy, but its reference to the ongoing series of debates that constitutes Islam as a living tradition. I find Talal Asad's conception of Islam as a discursive tradition, as he first formulated it in a paper on the anthropology of Islam (1986), very useful, though I would broaden the understanding of tradition to include non-discursive elements as well. Not everything Muslims do is Islamic; Muslims engage in many activities and debates that are not informed by any relation with Islamic tradition. The 'local knowledge' of Muslim communities similarly includes much that has nothing to do with their 'Islamic knowledge', although the latter may also contain numerous elements that are local. As Asad writes, '[a] practice is Islamic because it is authorized by the discursive traditions of Islam, and is so taught to Muslims – whether by an ‛alim, a khatib, a Sufi shaykh, or an untutored parent' (Asad 1986: 15). This obviously includes much belief and practice that in the opinion of at least some other Muslims is non-Islamic, such as Sufi ritual, shrine visits, and certain healing practices; the legitimation by some form of authority deemed to be Islamic is the crucial aspect. I would even argue for the inclusion of rituals such as the Alevi *cem* and *semah*, even though these appear to be alien to the mainstream scriptural tradition of Islam and are widely perceived as having pre- or extra-Islamic origins. Both are embedded in a complex of myths and concepts that clearly relate to the broader Islamic tradition, and they share this feature with the rituals of various other heterodox communities that have been present as a counterpoint to the dominant melody of Sunni Islam.

My interest in this chapter is in the processes by which Muslims, and especially young Muslims growing up in the West, acquire or themselves produce Islamic knowledge. In the existing literature on this subject one encounters – I simplify for the sake of the argument – two different models of production and dissemination of Islamic knowledge. One is the religious market model, in which on the supply side there is a variety of religious specialists or religious movements and associations involved in producing and marketing Islamic knowledge, and on the demand side a public of potential consumers who more or less critically make a choice out of what is on offer. The second model, found especially in the literature on individualization, assigns a more active role to (at least some) young Muslims in rejecting the Islam of their parents and established institutions and constructing their own forms of Islamic knowledge in an eclectic and creative process.[1] In the first model, there is a strict distinction between producers and consumers of religious knowledge; in the second, everyone is to some degree involved in its production. My interest here is not so much in how religious specialists arrive at authoritative formulations of Islamic knowledge in the context of European secular societies (the chapters by Caeiro, Mariani and Sedgwick do engage with this, however) as in how 'ordinary' Muslims, aided or not by such specialists, develop their Islamic knowledge.

It hardly needs to be emphasized that the context in which Islamic knowledge is being produced and reproduced is likely to have a significant impact on the process of knowledge production and the specific forms of knowledge that emerge. Even those who would reject all sources of religious authority apart from the Qur'an and *hadith* will need to access these sources with specific questions in mind that derive from the encounter with the wider society around them. A wide range of persons and institutions of religious authority is available in Western Europe, or can easily be accessed through the new media. Moreover, most European governments have been making deliberate efforts to regulate the form and content of religious education.

So how is it that Muslims in Europe, especially second- and third-generation immigrant Muslims, acquire their knowledge of Islam? Whom do they seek out as teachers, counsellors or role models, and on what grounds? What is the impact of their linguistic competence on the type of knowledge demanded or acquired? To what extent does the life-world of young Muslims in Western Europe give rise to new questions, new values, new practices, new interpretations?

Learning Qur'an and prayer

For the most basic forms of Islamic knowledge, concerning the technicalities of ritual purification (*wudu'*), prayer (*salat, namaz*) and fasting (*sawm*), the process of knowledge acquisition appears quite straightforward. Children learn the details through emulation of their parents or, more frequently, explicit instruction by a teacher, often a mosque's imam. This is one of the few areas of expertise in which the authority of the mosque imam is not seriously questioned. Virtually all mosque organizations have Qur'an courses, where children are taught to recite and perhaps to read (though not necessarily to understand) sufficient verses and invocations for use in prayer and where they are taught the other essentials of worship. Yalçin-Heckmann (1998: 171) reports that a surprisingly high percentage of the Turkish parents in Germany whom she interviewed acknowledged the need for such Qurʿan courses. Those who actually sent their children to the courses in the neighbourhood were considerably fewer, however, though still more than half. (Note that this proportion is considerably higher than the 25 per cent of Turkish Muslim men who, according to various surveys, regularly perform the five daily prayers. Parents apparently want their children at least to know how to pray, even if they don't do so themselves.)

The reasons given by parents for their failure actually to send their children to Qurʿan courses were either lack of time or, more significantly, the perception that religious organizations were involved in politics (Yalçin-Heckmann, ibid.). Similar observations of Muslim parents' attitudes towards Qurʿan courses in Britain and France were earlier reported by Daniele Joly and Rémy Leveau, respectively (both in Gerholm and Lithman 1988). This indicates that in at least some parents' perception the teaching of the basic ritual obligations cannot be separated from other dimensions of Muslim discourse and practice. On the other hand, it is true that the Qurʿan courses of the Süleymanci movement, which are known for their thoroughness and strictness, are also attended by many Turkish children whose parents are not followers or sympathizers of this movement. In her study of the Süleymanci movement, Gerdien Jonker estimated that 60–70 per cent of the children following these courses in Berlin were from families that were not themselves Süleymanci, and that of all children who did take part in Qurʿan courses the vast majority did so with the Süleymancis.[2]

The Süleymanci movement concentrates on children in the age group of 10–13 years, which is considered the best age to mould their personalities – 'a branch should be bent when it is still green', as was explained to Jonker. The training is more systematic than in other Muslim communities and involves rote learning of Qurʿanic verses, the Arabic alphabet, and a basic catechism (*ilmihal*) with detailed instructions on the proper performance of prayer. The courses are in six stages, in which memorization is gradually complemented by understanding of grammar and the meaning of the verses memorized. Only few children, however, follow through beyond the first or second stage. Disciplining in the proper movements and utterances is considered as more important than discursive understanding: the moral person is shaped by such bodily disciplining, not by the intellectual grasping of subject matter that is privileged in Western didactic methods (Jonker 2002: 184–9). The Süleymanci movement is perhaps unique, at least among Turks, in the detailed training given in these courses; in other movements, children learn more through emulation of adults, simply taking part in prayer and gradually improving their performance. The acquisition of proper dispositions, embodied rather than discursive knowledge, is the aim of all Qurʿan courses.

A considerable proportion of children of Muslim parents never attend Qurʿan courses, and many of those who do attend a course give up before the course is completed. The data from surveys that ask questions about actual performance are inconsistent but suggest that only a minority of young Muslims performs the prayers regularly. However, significant numbers turn to a more strict Islamic practice later in life. Such 'internal' conversions (including conversions of practising Muslims to another pattern of religious practice) are a fascinating phenomenon that has not received much scholarly attention yet.[3] Proselytizing movements such as Tablighi Jamaʿat, Hizb ut-Tahrir, and the Salafi movement (about which more below) have contributed much to such 'internal' conversions as well as conversions of non-Muslims to Islam. In these movements, the basics of prayer and Qurʾan recital are mainly acquired through peer learning and participation in congregational prayer, besides simple written manuals; Salafi groups offer also more systematic instruction. Numerous Islamic websites offer detailed instructions for prayer, which appear to be directed at nominal Muslims as well as new converts, and simple prayer instruction booklets can be found in many shops that cater to a Muslim clientele.

The actual performance of *salat*, as John Bowen has argued in one of the few anthropological analyses of Muslim prayer, besides producing and expressing pious self-control and discipline, may also involve various forms of boundary creation. Differences in the performance of *salat* may be read as signs of social distinctions; in his Indonesian examples this concerns distinctions between reformists and traditionalists, or boundaries between sectarians and the mainstream community, besides of course the primary distinction between believers and non-believers (Bowen 1989).[4] These distinctions appear, however, irrelevant to the basic Qurʾan courses offered in most Western European mosques.

There exist, of course, some differences between the four Sunni schools (*madhhab*), and between traditionalists and reformists, concerning minor details of the movements to be made in *salat*, notably concerning the position of the hands, the prescribed time of the early morning and afternoon prayers, as well as the actions and events that bring about ritual pollution and necessitate renewal of *wuduʿ*. As long as most parents send their children to a mosque of their own national background, they are not even confronted with the existence of such minor differences. Mosques with North African congregations teach according to the Maliki *madhhab*, Turkish and Pakistani mosques according to the Hanifi *madhhab*. It appears to be language rather than the difference in *madhhab* that keeps the congregations separate. Most Kurds from Turkey, for instance, are not Hanafis but Shafiʿis, but Kurds and Turks worship in the same mosques and send their children to the same Qurʾan courses. The differences between the two schools of law tend to be played down, unless there are other reasons to emphasize them. Turkish and Kurdish Naqshbandis or Nurcus often feel more strongly united by their common adherence to a particular Sufi order or pious movement than they feel divided by the difference in *madhhab*. There exists a small distinctly Kurdish Islamic association that controls a few mosques in Europe, but the reasons for its establishment were political rather than religious, and Kurdish ethnicity rather than the Shafiʿi madhhab is its reason of existence.[5]

Within communities of the same national origin there may, however, exist grave differences between traditionalists and the various reformist movements. In Europe, this is perhaps most strikingly so among South Asians, among whom the reformist Deobandis and Ahl-i Hadith do have different conceptions of proper ritual practice than the traditionalist Barelwis. Among these South Asian Muslim denominations the performance of *salat* is one of a whole array of markers of distinction. Barelwis and Deobandis in Britain and increasingly else-where too have their separate institutions and do not mix socially, so that there has been relatively little active contestation between them over ritual practice. The active proselytization by newer religious movements such as Tablighi Jamaᶜat, Hizb ut-Tahrir and various Salafi groups, which are in various degrees critical of existing attitudes and practices, has been making dents in the bounda-ries of these well-established mainstream groups (as well as those of other nation-alities). This has given rise to some dissension over ritual practice when recruits to these movements insisted on 'correcting' the practice of other members of their congregation.

In matters of performance of the *salat*, it has been especially Salafis who have given rise to much unease by claiming that the way most other Muslims pray deviates from that of the Prophet and needs therefore to be corrected.[6] A hand-book on prayer by the late Salafi scholar Nasir al-Din al-Albani (d. 1999), *Sifat salat al-nabi*, 'The Prophet's prayer', has been at the root of much unease because it argues that several details of the concrete forms of prayer that have been taught from generation to generation are based on dubious hadith. Al-Albani is known to his followers as the greatest expert on hadith, who single-handedly reviewed hundreds of thousands of hadith, sifting out the dubious ones. On the basis of what he has determined to be the most reliable hadith, he indicates, among other things, different positions of the hands and different forms of supplication than the widely accepted ones as the only correct forms. On the performance of other prayers than the regular five daily ones, such as *tarawih* prayers (in the evenings of the month Ramadan, after the evening prayer) and the *tahajjud* prayer (performed at night, after a few hours of sleep and well before the dawn prayer), his descrip-tions deviate considerably from established practice. Translated in many languages and warmly adopted by recruits to Salafism, this book has provoked much discussion and disagreement.[7]

Mosques, imams, mosque committees

The mosque is the most visible Muslim institution, and the imam officiating in the mosque the most easily visible Muslim authority in Western Europe. The real importance and influence of imams has been much exaggerated, especially in the perception of European authorities. Especially in Germany and the Netherlands, with their tradition of moral leadership by church ministers, there has been a tendency to perceive imams as the Muslim equivalent of priests and ministers and to attribute to them pastoral functions that they usually do not have in the countries of origin. The imams were often considered to be the most appropriate and representative spokespersons for their communities (or even for all Turks, all Moroccans, etc.), and they became favourite targets for government programmes aiming at the integration of Muslims. Interestingly, in neighbouring Belgium, where the Protestant church tradition is absent, imams were never given the same importance and it was teachers of religion in schools who were given the central role (Boender and Kanmaz 2002).

The very fact that European governments and non-governmental institutions took the imams more seriously than their societies of origin appears to have given the imams some extra leverage (Landman 1992; Buffin 1998; Reeber 2000). To the extent that they became middlemen in their own right and/or assumed pastoral functions – which very much depended on the individual imam's abilities – they gained some power vis-à-vis the board of the mosque association that employed them. Apart from some exceptional personalities who acquired a reputation for their learning or for taking a courageous political stand, most imams are in a precarious position that makes it hard for them to exert real authority.

Those who did reach positions of authority and/or engage in a wider range of activities than those associated with worship in the mosque often prefer other titles than that of imam. Thus the leading religious authority of the Great Mosque of Paris, Dalil Boubakeur, styles himself '*recteur*' (rector) of the mosque, a title adopted by several others including Larbi Kechat (see Amiraux in this volume). Their positions are, it is true, significantly different from that of the simple prayer leaders also attached to the same mosques, who continue to be called imam; but another authority who is definitely in the same league with these '*recteurs*', Tareq Oubrou, emphatically takes pride in the title of imam (Oubrou 2009). Turkish Muslims do not generally use the term imam (except in communicating with Europeans) but address the mosque official as '*hoca*' (teacher), a term that carries more respect. In Diyanet mosques, the imam is known by the appropriately bureaucratic title of '*din görevlisi*' (religious functionary), which implies a range of functions besides officiating at worship.

The reported research findings concerning the respect the imams enjoy in their own communities appear to be contradictory. On the one hand, educated inform-ants frequently complain of the ignorance of most imams and the irrelevance of their *khutba*s (sermons) to the life-world of Muslims in Europe (e.g. Canatan 2001, *passim*). The demand for a better imam education, more explicitly geared to European conditions, often comes from these circles (as well as, partially for other reasons, from European authorities, who believe that modern-educated imams are the keys to the social and cultural integration of Muslim communities in the wider society). On the other hand, there are also increasingly numerous reports about imams who do inspire the younger generation, whose knowledge in matters of religion is taken seriously, and who have been able to make young men change their behaviour. These are not necessarily the imams whose sermons are more 'relevant' to Western society. An interesting example is described exten-sively by Martijn de Koning in his dissertation on young Moroccans in a mosque in the city of Gouda (de Koning 2008). Here it was a young imam, fresh from Morocco, who taught very strict rules about right and wrong Muslim behaviour and made no effort to adapt his teaching to the context, who succeeded in drawing youth into the mosque and changing their public behaviour. The imam was less popular with the mosque committee, and after a conflict he had to leave – showing once again where power in the mosque resides.

Many Muslims clearly hold the average imam here in low esteem, much like the position of the average imam in Muslim countries. They expect him to perform the necessary ritual functions and teach children the basics of Islam, and they may ask his opinion in simple matters of belief and practice, but if they don't like his answers, they are likely to look for a more respected authority. The low esteem is reflected in the low salaries paid to mosque imams, and this in turn makes the position unattractive to more highly educated young men. People educated in Europe expect better salaries, which is one reason why imams keep being recruited from the countries of emigration, where even a low European salary represents a financial improvement. The organizing committees of mosques and larger religious associations, who select and employ imams, moreover do not usually want too independent-minded imams serving their mosques. Often it is only persons educated in the country of origin who are willing to accept the conditions of employment offered. Anecdotal information suggests that at least some imams, once they have gained immigrant status, have left their positions when they found the possibility of more profitable employment.

This is partly why one early Dutch experiment in imam training for the Turkish community failed. It was well known that many pious Turkish parents sent their children to religiously oriented schools in Turkey to protect them from the danger of negative influences – sex, drugs, petty crime – they perceived present in the secondary-school environment in the Netherlands. Both state *imam-hatip* schools and private institutions run by the Süleymanci and Nurcu movements attract significant numbers of such migrant children.[8] The Dutch imam school was set up in response to this pattern; it provided *imam-hatip* type education, with Dutch- and Turkish-medium instruction and with Dutch as well as Turkish teachers. The school was plagued by various difficulties, as was to be expected, but the major problem was that none of its graduates wanted to become an imam; they all had set their ambitions higher.[9]

Given this reportedly low esteem for the position, it is surprising to hear that according to a survey of the mosques in Rotterdam, twenty out of thirty imams had academic degrees from faculties of theology in their home countries.[10] Not every mosque has its own full-time imam, but the committees administering the larger mosques clearly make an effort to recruit highly educated persons as their imams – at least in part because they expect the imam to be more than just a prayer leader and Friday preacher. All over Europe it is observed that more is expected of the imam there than in the countries of origin.[11] Michel Reeber, who interviewed imams and mosque communities in France, notes that his questions about the minimal requirements of an imam almost invariably yielded the same five qualities: 'a certain distance from worldly life, knowledge of the Qurʿan and its interpretation, availability and approachability, skills as an orator, and juridical and spiritual insight' (Reeber 2000: 197). An academic degree from a theological faculty clearly lends credibility to one's claims to knowledge of the Qurʿan and Islamic legal and doctrinal thought. It is no guarantee, however, for insight in the dilemmas faced by young Western-educated Muslims or for the ability to adapt Islamic thought to new and unknown conditions. Nor is there a guarantee that an academically trained imam will be capable of acting as the interface between European authorities and his mosque community or the Muslims in general, as those authorities would like him to. Imams who do have these additional skills, however, can become quite influential.

Real power in the mosque is not in the hands of the imam but of the organizing committee or, if the mosque belongs to a larger association (such as Milli Görüs or Diyanet in the case of Turkish Muslims), the executive board of that association. The imam is supposed to have more specialized knowledge than the members of the board, but it is the latter who call the shots – as is clear in the case of conflict, when it is the imam who has to go.[12] In the relatively rare cases where a mosque changed hands from one Islamic movement to another, this commonly meant that another imam was brought in. The governments of Turkey and Morocco attempt to keep control over their (ex-)subjects by keeping control over the appointment of imams, and they do this through mosque organizations. Turkey is more successful in this respect than other countries and has signed an agreement with Germany concerning its dispatch of religious personnel. Its Directorate of Religious Affairs (Diyanet) controls the largest Turkish mosque associations in Europe, and the imams appointed to those mosques are selected and directly salaried by Diyanet.

The imam owes his religious authority not only to his formal studies and knowledge of Islam (the extent of which cannot usually be judged by the *jamaᶜat*) but also to endorsement by the mosque committee or association. He can, however, considerably improve his position vis-à-vis the committee if he succeeds in establishing a good rapport with the *jamaᶜat* and convincing them of his knowledge and wisdom. Delivering remarkable *khutba*s is no doubt one of the best ways of doing this, but only few imams appear to be capable of doing so. An active role in personal counselling, mediating in family conflicts, and similar pastoral activities may also contribute to the imam's standing. Initiating, or participating in, other activities in and around the mosque can be another way of strengthening the bond between the *jamaᶜat* and the mosque and thereby also increasing the imam's influence and authority.

In everyday practice, the imam is the nearest source of Islamic knowledge for most Muslims, imparting his knowledge through explicit teaching (in Qurᶜan courses and occasionally discussion sessions), preaching, personal counselling and answering questions, guiding major rituals (such as the hajj and sacrifice), and his personal example of Muslim life style. To what extent his explicit and implicit teaching is adopted by the members of the congregation into their own conceptions of proper Islamic practice depends on their perceptions of his learning but on contextual factors as well. The mosque committee exerts pressure on the imam to act and speak in a certain way, and both the committee and the imam respond to pressures from a variety of actors in the European environment.[13] Whether he wants it or not, the imam has to respond to many questions that arise in the interaction between Muslims and their non-Muslim environment, and the political context imposes certain restraints and allows certain freedoms that may be different from those in the country of origin. Even at the basic level of communication between the imam and the congregation, the production of Islamic knowledge is a process of negotiation between various actors with differing interests.

Imam training in Europe

Because members of the congregation, mosque committees, and the various European stakeholders with whom they interact (local and national governments, partners in inter-religious dialogue, non-governmental institutions and organizations) have felt the need for imams and religious teachers in general to respond more adequately to local conditions and to express Islamic ideas in a way that is meaningful in the European context, there have been many initiatives to establish imam training institutes in Europe. Especially since 9/11, many governments have been wary of imams trained abroad who continue to teach in Arabic (or Turkish, or Urdu), for reasons of both security and integration policy. At least part of the congregations also would prefer imams who understand Western society well enough to engage with it meaningfully.

The first Muslim seminaries in Europe were established by the Muslim communities themselves: South Asian Muslims in Britain may have been the earliest, followed by North African Muslims in France, and Turks in the Netherlands, Germany and Austria.[14] Many of the students in these institutions were primarily motivated by the desire to know more about Islam, not by any particular wish to become imams. Other youth of Muslim background enrolled for similar reasons in the Middle Eastern and Islamic Studies departments of European universities. Various universities and professional schools, moreover, responding to the perceived need for European-trained imams, established courses for teachers and pastoral workers with a partly Islamic, partly professional curriculum. So far, few graduates of these various institutes appear to have become imams, though several have become chaplains in hospitals, prisons, or the armed forces. Chaplains, like religious teachers in schools, are civil servants with more security of tenure and better pay than the average imam. Seminaries and 'imam training' courses therefore vie for the official recognition of their diplomas that opens this segment of the labour market to their graduates. The quest for recognition has opened up another important area of negotiation over what constitutes Islamic knowledge.

A perhaps unintended consequence of the proliferation of seminaries and other imam training initiatives is the emergence of a class of young men and women who combine a European education with immersion in various disciplines of Islamic learning. Although probably only a minority of them find (or aspire to fulfil) a formal position as imam, chaplain or teacher, they do interact with other young Muslims and contribute significantly to discussions on religious subjects. Discussion groups of young educated Muslims, in mosques, student associations, or informal neighbourhood groups are among the most significant loci of production of Islamic knowledge. It is often the students or former students of these various institutes and courses (along with those of their highly motivated peers who are self-taught) who connect the discussion of contemporary concerns with the scriptural tradition.

Developments in mosques specific to the European setting

Many of the minor mosques in Europe only distinguish themselves from the average neighbourhood mosque in the countries of origin by the absence of any distinctive architectural features, not by the nature of activities in and around it. Some of the larger mosques, however, have become the hearts of Muslim communities in a more pervasive way than is presently the case in the home countries. They serve as primary meeting places for men of all ages, and sometimes for women as well. In some mosques, or adjoining them, there are teashops, barbershops, and stalls or shops that sell books, cassettes, perfume, bric-à-brac, and *halal* food. Youth associations and women's associations affiliated with the mosque may meet here outside prayer time. The former may also organize sports and other activities that have nothing to do with religion.

Research carried out by Kadir Canatan in mosques in Rotterdam showed that around half of the mosques organize social and cultural activities that are not strictly religious, such as language and computer courses, schoolwork assistance, social counselling, and, inevitably, football and other sports.[15] These mosques generally succeed much better in attracting youth than those which refrain from such activities. According to Canatan, it is not the imams who make the difference here but the mosque committees: there is a strong correlation between the ethnic background and age composition of the committees and the willingness to organize non-religious activities. Moroccan mosques in Rotterdam tend to be controlled by committees consisting of first-generation migrants, who reject the idea of organizing any other than strictly religious activities, the daily and weekly prayers and Qurʿan education. Most Turkish mosque committees, on the other hand, are now controlled by second-generation youth of pious family background.[16] Only the Süleymancı mosques restrict themselves to purely religious activities; they are also less transparent than the other Turkish mosques and the entire Süleymancı structure is more hierarchically organized. Not surprisingly, younger men do not play important roles here. The other mosque committees organize a whole range of activities in order to draw the younger generation to the mosque.[17] Pakistani mosques resemble the Turkish mosques in this respect, whereas the mosques of Surinamese and smaller national communities are more like the conservative Moroccan ones.

Similar observations were made in a survey of youth activities in Berlin mosques by Jeanine Elif Dagyeli (2006). She notes a significant increase in the number and the range of activities offered by mosques since the late 1990s – to the extent that public institutions for youth work complain of the competition by mosques and part of public opinion perceives a threat of fundamentalism undermining the integration process and creating 'parallel societies'. The mosque activists themselves, on the other hand, present their activity programmes as an effort to redress early school leaving, massive youth unemployment and the threat of drug addiction. Remedial teaching for youth of school age and counselling young unemployed on the job market constitute, besides sports and other leisure activities in a good Muslim environment, the most conspicuous non-religious activities. For women, there are various types of courses: cooking, sewing, cosmetics, handicrafts, as well as reading circles in which books, mostly religious, are read and discussed.

Efforts by community leaders to improve relations with European authorities and to overcome the negative attitudes of neighbours and suspicions of what goes on in the mosques have led to a number of new practices that have been rapidly adopted by numerous mosques. In the early 1990s, or perhaps as early as the late 1980s, some committees began inviting city officials and neighbours to the mosque for a common meal on the occasion *iftar*, the sunset breaking of the fast during Ramadan.[18] Within a few years, this practice spread to many other mosques, which now at least once during Ramadan invite non-Muslim guests inside to take part in an *iftar* meal. Although it appears a real innovation to invite non-Muslims to the mosque to take part in an activity with religious connotations, it does not appear to have given rise to much protest or religious argument. It was the mosque organizers who took the initiative, and the imams quietly acquiesced.

The chief Milli Görüs mosque in Amsterdam went a step further. In 2001, it organized for the first time a public debate following the *iftar* meal, with prominent Dutch intellectuals debating issues of Islam, integration and multiculturalism; this was repeated in 2002. Both the *iftar* and the panel discussion took place – unlike the practice in other mosques – in the main prayer hall, into which rows of tables and chairs had been placed. The carpet had been covered with plastic foil, so that the guests could keep their shoes on. Again, these activities could be initiated without much debate; it was just the then director of the Milli Görüs Federation of the Northern Netherlands who pushed this through at his own initiative, supported by young mosque committee members. There was some protest from the women's wing, which thought that the Dutch guests should at least take off their shoes when entering the mosque, but they were overruled. None of the Milli Görüs imams protested or showed signs of disaffection; the *mufti* (who is the most highly educated of the imams and also acts as a co-ordinator among them) was present in the deliberations but did not consider it as a serious issue that needed an explicit *fatwa* (opinion).[19] He and other imams showed their consent by being present at the *iftar* and discussion, as did some board members of the European Milli Görüs federation.

Whereas the Milli Görüs *iftar* debates were occasions in which the Dutch public sphere and its concerns temporarily invaded a Turkish mosque and most of the usual mosque congregation were at best present as passive listeners, a different format of panel discussion, inviting more interaction between Muslims and their non-Muslim environment, has become the hallmark of the Parisian mosque in the rue d'Alger. Here the remarkable Larbi Kechat (see Valérie Amiraux' contribution to this volume) organizes encounters between Muslim scholars approaching a problem from the point of view of Islamic legal thought and European scholars with a more sociological approach. These discussions take place in a seminar room separate from the prayer hall, and they are more clearly separate from the everyday activities in the mosque. The audience is mixed but largely Muslim, consisting of a more varied and more highly educated audience than the mosque's regular congregation. To what extent the discussions have an impact on the life-world of the Muslims who consider the mosque theirs remains unclear, but like the Milli Görüs panels, Kechat's initiative makes the important statement that debates about Islam and the Muslim presence in Europe can and should be carried out with Muslims, and that the mosque can be a site of intellectual exchange.

****

An interesting example of an Islamic practice that has changed its form, at least in part in response to pressures from the non-Muslim environment, is the organization of slaughter for the Feast of Sacrifice. The issue of *halal* slaughter has been one of the more difficult problems of accommodation of Muslims in all European countries. My concern here is not with *halal* slaughter as such (on which see Bergeaud-Blackler 2007), but with the animal sacrifice of Kurban Bayrami/ʿId al-Adha. Traditional practice in the rural parts of the Mediterranean region was for families to keep the sacrificial animal in or near the house for some time and to embellish it with paint and ribbons, to cherish it and develop an attachment to it, so that slaughter would result in a feeling of loss. It was important for the paterfamilias to slaughter the animal himself. These were obviously practices that in this form were not acceptable to European society – 'cultural' practices, some might say, that were only accidental local forms in which a religious obligation was carried out; but to many Muslims, the very form was part of the obligation. The questions of whether, how, and where Muslims should be allowed to slaughter their own animals were hotly debated, and ultimately various compromises between traditional practices, Islamic rules and European practices were found. In most cases this resulted in a practice where Muslims delegated the buying and slaughtering of the animals to the mosque organization and received the meat after slaughter in the slaughterhouse (Shadid and van Koningsveld 1992).

In more recent years it has become common to add one or two chains to the delegation process: money for sacrificial animals is collected among Muslims in Europe and sent to Muslim countries, preferably to disaster-stricken areas, where animals are bought and ritually slaughtered at the appointed time, after which the meat is distributed among the poor. The cost of an animal (sheep or cow) is precisely calculated; one pays the exact sum it costs to buy one animal, or more than one, but never sees it nor tastes its meat. Charitable giving had always been part of the sacrifice – the meat was usually divided between relatives, friends and poor neighbours – but charity has now become its main form. One (Dutch-educated) mosque activist explained the practice to me as a form of 'development aid'.

Among the Turks in the Netherlands, the new practice allegedly began with a mosque chairman collecting *kurban* money from the congregation and taking it personally to Eastern Turkey. This practice has meanwhile become so widely adopted that it appears to be completely replacing the original way of celebrating the feast. Presently the central organization of Milli Görüs in Germany coordinates the collection of *kurban* contributions among its followers all over Europe and organizes slaughter and distribution of meat in dozens of countries in Asia, Africa and Latin America, preferably among victims of wars and natural disasters. The campaign to raise contributions explicitly plays on the dual meanings of *kurban* as 'victim' and 'sacrificial animal', and effectively says 'make a sacrifice, help a victim!'[20]

This gradual transformation of sacrifice came about without a great deal of debate or controversy and apparently did not need a *fatwa* from respected ulama. It was practically minded managers of the Milli Görüs organization who simply went ahead, following a trend towards rationalization of sacrifice that was in evidence in the Muslim majority world as well but giving it a new twist. In several countries, foundations emerged that took care of the entire process of slaughter if one paid a set price for an animal before the Day of Sacrifice and that either delivered the meat or promised to distribute it to the poor afterwards.[21] The idea of distributing sacrificial meat among poor Muslims elsewhere in the world instead of one's direct environment had its precedent in discussions in the Muslim World League, as early as the 1960s, on what to do with the millions of animals slaughtered near Mecca during the hajj. The Day of Sacrifice is the culminating moment of the pilgrimage, and every pilgrim family has an animal slaughtered, which used to cause enormous logistical problems and waste. Excess meat is now processed, packed in pastic foil, and sent to poor Muslim countries for free distribution. Outsourcing the sacrifice itself to the regions most in need, as Milli Görüs does, was perhaps the logical next step in rationalizing the process.

****

The two examples in this section concern forms of practical Islamic knowledge that developed quite naturally out of interaction with the environment. The surprising thing about the new practices is how little controversy they generated, although they are directly related to core values of Islam, sacred space and sacrifice. Imams or higher religious authorities did not play a conspicuous role (although their silent endorsement may have been critical). Where decision-makers can be identified, these were the managers and organizers of the mosque associations. In religious practices concerning the congregation (as opposed to individual beliefs and private acts), associations and movements are important sites of production of Islamic knowledge.[22] There is yet another area of knowledge production in which at least some associations and movements play a major role, i.e. in shaping the habits and dispositions that constitute the Muslim subject. The next section will deal with that aspect.

Muslim movements as disciplining institutions

Qurʿan courses and mosque-based discussion groups convey more than discursive knowledge alone: they are also meant to impart certain attitudes and dispositions that make up the Muslim personality. More pervasive forms of disciplining are offered by various Muslim associations and movements. In this section, I shall briefly discuss some forms of disciplining specific to the Süleymanci movement and the Fethullah Gülen movement, both primarily active among Turkish Muslims, and the Tablighi Jamaʿat, which is of Indian origin but has in Western Europe found followers of diverse ethnic origins.

The Süleymanci movement has a number of boarding schools, in Turkey as well as various European countries, where the students are protected from the seductions of modern Western consumer society and live under a regime of affectionate but strict social control. The formal religious teaching there is only a minor part of the total disciplining process, which includes not only the scrupulous performance of all religious obligations and strict avoidance of all that is forbidden or disapproved, but also the active participation in the devotions of the Naqshbandi Sufi order. The adaptation to European cultural norms is minimal; the movement prides itself in producing young people who can function productively in secular society without being tainted by its culture. In many parts of Western Europe, the Süleymanci were the first Turkish Muslims to establish mosques and present themselves as Turkish Muslim counterparts in contacts with churches and other European institutions, which has long enabled them to maintain a large degree of autonomy in internal affairs, while limiting contacts with European society to the leadership level. They have, however, come under increasing pressure to open up and accommodate Western values in their education.[23]

****

Unlike the Süleymanci, the various branches of the Nurcu movement have not established mosques nor do they organize Qurʿan courses, but they have nonetheless their own distinctive method of disciplining. The Nurcu movements takes its name from the *Risale-i Nur*, the collected writings of the Turkish-Kurdish Muslim thinker Saʿid-i Nursi (d. 1960), and the communal reading of parts of this complex and difficult text constitutes the main form of textual education within the movement. The readings, by groups of peers under the guidance of a more knowledgeable 'elder brother' (*abi*), can take place at private homes or semi-public places; in Western Europe as well as in Turkey, student dormitories constitute a major site for such readings.

Various wings of the Nurcu movement are active in Western Europe, but in the past decade it has been especially the wing led by Fethullah Gülen that surged into public prominence, publishing newspapers and magazines, establishing schools, organizing Muslim businessmen in associations and appealing for dialogue through its own foundations. The Gülen movement is a fascinating example of a piety movement that appears to concentrate on secular activities as an expression of a deeply religious attitude to life. It has established an extensive network of modern schools in numerous countries around the world, but the schools offer an entirely secular curriculum. Similarly, the newspaper *Zaman*, which appears in many different languages, does not appear to support any specifically Islamic agenda (though it is largely supportive of the AKP government in Turkey), and many of its contributors are secular intellectuals. If any overt ideology can be discerned in the movement's public activities, this is Turkish nationalism rather than Islamism (the schools do not teach religion but almost everywhere they do teach Turkish as a foreign language).[24]

Religious values and religious dispositions are inculcated by more informal disciplining processes. The movement not only has schools but also, much less visible and even more effective, a vast network of student homes, pensions, and dormitories that support students' scholarly performance and provide moral and spiritual guidance. For secondary school students (not only in Gülen schools but for Turkish students in any school), there is regular homework assistance by older students, and some of them may actually live in pensions (*yurt*) where they receive 24-hour supervision and support. The 'elder brother' (*abi*) who supervises the *yurt* may also help in placing the student in the most appropriate school and maintaining contact with the school authorities. Students in higher education may stay in smaller student homes (ordinary houses, adapted for four to five students), in which one older student acts as the *abi*. Much of the after-school time is spent on school work, and the students are really pushed to be successful. This is only one part of the discipline, however. Regular performance of prayer and reading of sections of the *Risale-i Nur* or listening to audio or video recordings of the simpler *sohbet* (religious talks) by Fethullah Gülen constitute another part. There is no coercion; some students initially do not pray regularly, but the example of the others usually leads to imitation. The students do get time for sports, especially in the weekends, but there is no time for frivolous activities such as watching television, listening to music on the radio or reading anything apart from school textbooks and the works of Nursi and Gülen. Political discussions are strictly forbidden, and socializing outside the circle of the Gülen community is strongly discouraged.

It may be argued (and it is argued, in fact, by other Muslim groups) that the Gülen movement appears to transmit very little Islamic knowledge to the people it disciplines. The works of Nursi are often obscure to the point of unintelligibility, and Gülen's *sohbet*s, though capable of moving the listeners to tears, are essentially simple homilies with little information content. Little of the rich learned tradition of Islam, none of the various Islamic sciences, is systematically studied and transmitted in the movement. Significantly, very few leading figures of the movement apart from Fethullah Gülen himself have a thorough theological education. The Islamic knowledge produced and transmitted in the movement is one of habits and dispositions: modesty and industriousness, a strong work ethos, trust in God, obedience to the elders (there are *abi* at every level, who supervise and guide those placed under them) and willingness to serve. The last-named aspect, serving (*hizmet*), understood as the desire to serve God by being of service to the movement and to society at large, is so central to the self-understanding of the movement that members commonly refer to the Gülen movement as *Hizmet*. When the movement calls upon them and assigns them a task, most will obey without questioning, even if it means they will have to move to another city or even another country.

The Gülen movement has been highly successful in producing, both in Turkey and abroad, a new, educated Turkish elite with a pious attitude, capable of competing with and eventually replacing the earlier, Kemalist secular elite.[25] Many young men and women of poor and culturally deprived backgrounds have been able to get a good education thanks to the cheap lodging and permanent stimulation provided in the student pensions and homes. Some left the movement after completing their education or even earlier because they found the degree of social control and lack of intellectual freedom stifling; others had to leave because they violated moral rules, e.g. in dating a person of the opposite sex. Even such persons, however, tend to maintain a certain loyalty towards the movements and appreciate its positive contribution in their lives, though they may claim to feel liberated having left behind the permanent surveillance of behaviour and control of ideas.[26]

****

Even more than the two movements just discussed, the Tablighi Jama⁣ᶜat endorses the principle of learning by doing. Although the movement has established madrasas in South Asia and also can boast one in Britain (in Dewsbury, see Birt and Philips in this volume), most of the members never follow any formal Islamic education but simply absorb basic knowledge and acquire appropriate behaviour through intimate association with a community of Tablighis. The Jamaᶜat is a revivalist movement of lay preachers, who attempt to emulate the Prophet in minute details of everyday behaviour, including sartorial style and ways of eating, sleeping and especially praying.[27] Performing the five daily prayers in congregation, preferably dressed as supposedly the Prophet used to be, and inviting other Muslims to join them in prayer, constitutes the primary form of disciplining. The movement has its own basic teaching literature, notably the *Fazaᶜil-i Aᶜmal* ('Virtuous Deeds'), a simple annotated compilation of hadith and Qurᵓanic verses, arranged by themes such as Lives of the Prophet's Companions, the Qurᵓan, prayer, *dhikr* (remembering, i.e. reciting, God's names), and *tabligh* (predication).[28] Tablighis may further deepen their knowledge by studying such hadith collections as *Riyad al-Salihin*,[29] but there is no systematic instruction.

The most intensive disciplining takes place during the missionary tours (*gasht, khuruj*) in which every Tablighi is expected to take part. On tour, they are taken out of their daily environment and spend twenty-four hours per day in the company of other Tablighis, speaking about nothing but prayer, *dhikr* and *tabligh*, and presenting their style of imitation of the Prophet as a model for other Muslims to follow but highly aware of suspicious looks and mocking comments from the environment. The tours provide strong bonding and a sense of intensification of religious experience due to the group dynamic.

The Tablighi Jamaᶜat is even less politically oriented than the Süleymanci and Gülen movements, and although many of its recruits are from underprivileged groups it shows no interest in ideas of social justice or political struggle. It aims at shaping Muslim subjects who embody the Prophetic example in simple, everyday behaviour and rejects calls to join the struggle for a better society. This is one criticism often directed against them by more politically minded Muslim groups, and it is one of the reasons why many leave the movement after some time, either for more overtly politically oriented movements or for movements that offer more of an intellectual challenge. In many individual life histories of young European Muslims, the encounter with the Tablighi Jamaᶜat constitutes a turning point. It was the Tabligh that brought many marginalized youngsters from the ganglands of the *banlieues* to Islam, giving them self-respect and self-discipline. Many young men who later joined various other movements or associations, from the activist to the quietist, Salafi or Sufi, were at one stage of their lives turned into more self-conscious Muslims by the Tabligh movement.

As just one example of such a life history, take the autobiography of the French rapper Abd al-Malik (2004), *Qu'Allah bénisse la France* ('Allah Bless France'). Born of Catholic Congolese parents and growing up among marginalized immigrant youth in the city of Strasbourg, the young black man decided to become a Muslim after reading the autobiography of Malcolm X. An encounter with a small group of Tablighis aroused his admiration for these people, who took the commands of their religion seriously and did not appear to mind what others thought about them. He joined them and took pride in the new discipline of rising early and walking to their small garage mosque to perform the dawn prayers in their congregation. Meanwhile, he continued playing music with friends, as well as voraciously reading all sorts of books. Intellectual curiosity drew him to student circles that were listening to cassettes of Tariq Ramadan and discussing his ideas on how to live as a modern Muslim in secular Europe, and gradually he left the Tabligh movement behind. A visit to the Festival of Sacred Music in Fès, which is organized annually by the Moroccan anthropologist and Sufi Faouzi Skali, became another turning point, because he became acquainted there with the Boutchichiyya Sufi order and decided that the Sufi way was the right style of Islam for him.[30] With the help of Skali, he found a Sufi master in France – ironically a white middle-class convert to Islam – who made him find peace within himself and with society.

Young Muslims in Europe, the quest for true Islam, and the alleged fragmentation of religious authority

Abd al-Malik may not be the average young European Muslim, but his life story highlights experiences that are shared by numerous others. Many others have passed through a period of devotional self-disciplining with the Tablighi Jamaᶜat or another piety movement and then moved on to more intellectually challenging or spiritually rewarding movements, to a more individual conception of Islamic beliefs and values, or to a more politicized reading of the Islamic tradition. Malcolm X is not usually thought of as a religious authority, but his autobiography has been a formative influence on many young Muslims in Europe, from Dyab Abou Jahjah, the founder of the Arab European League, to British Asian Muslim activists (Saeed 2007) and a range of Muslim artists of diverse ethnicity.[31] As long as Muslims experience discrimination in Europe, Malcolm X will remain a powerful icon, representing Islam as a political identity of resistance and as an ideal of justice and equality. The different phases of his life, before and after conversion and his later turn towards 'orthodox' Islam, provide ample opportunity for identification. Followers of quite diverse social and political movements are inspired by him.

For understandable reasons, the participation of young Muslims in Islamic political movements, and notably in the more radical ones, has received disproportionate attention, especially from the press but also from academics. However, Sufism in its various manifestations has, in terms of the number of followers, even among the young, probably become of far greater significance, and in that respect Abd al-Malik's trajectory is not exceptional. The number of those who actually join a Sufi order may be limited, but there is a widespread and still increasing interest in Sufi ideas and in Sufism as a more irenic alternative to Islamism and Salafism, and preachers with a Sufi message enjoy great popularity.[32] The generally positive appreciation of Sufism and great Sufi authors such as Rumi among Western intellectuals – quite different from the general disdain for 'funda-mentalist' Islam – may add to the attraction and prestige of this style of Islam.

Sadek Hamid, writing on the appeal of Salafism among British Asian Muslim youth, notes that a few charismatic Sufi preachers and writers have made a significant dent in the popularity of Salafism (Hamid 2009). Perhaps it is signifi-cant that the three Sufis he mentions are Western converts in their late forties or fifties and highly educated scholars.[33] But Sufism does not even need charismatic teachers to exert its attraction, as the autobiography of the former Hizb ut-Tahrir activist Ed Husain (2007) suggests. This book is of considerable interest for its lively description of discussions and leadership struggles in Muslim students' unions in Britain and the way in which Husain and his friends succeeded in setting the terms of debate and marginalizing opponents. But it also makes an attempt to show why, after a few years of self-righteous Islamist activism, Husain almost inevitably returned to the Sufism-inflected Islam of his parents with which he had earlier broken.[34]

The young men discussed so far appeared to commit themselves strongly to the particular style of Islam that they embraced, and their choices had the force of full conversions, involving a radical change of orientation in life at each turn. Specific social-religious movements that demand a deep commitment loomed large in the narratives: Tablighi Jama‛at, Hizb ut-Tahrir, Salafism, Sufi orders; and charis-matic preachers, persuasive student activists, or the example of uncompromising adherence to simple principles (as in the case of Tablighi Jama‛at) were instru-mental in the conversions. It is, however, only a small minority who make such strong commitments. Many others are content to stick to the Islam of their parents or have little or no interest in religion – although the increasing Islamophobia in European societies makes it hard for youth of Muslim family background to remain indifferent towards Islam. The future of European Islam will probably be largely determined by the important proportion who are neither active members of the major social-religious movements nor passive followers of their parents' tradition but actively seek Islamic knowledge that is meaningful to them in the context of their life in Europe.

In France, Leïla Babès (1997, 2000) and Farhad Khosrokhavar (1997) have written on the emergence of a young generation of Muslims who take their Islam seriously but demand an autonomous space for themselves, outside the sphere of the mosque as well as that of the state. Most of them have little or no formal education in Islamic knowledge but they absorb some from their peers. Students from Arab countries have often helped the locally born young Muslims in setting up associations and acted as mediators of Islamic knowledge; Babès believes that this explains the influence of reformist and Salafi interpretations of Islam among this generation. Further elaborating on the theme of the independent quest for appropriate Islamic knowledge, two other French authors, Olivier Roy (1999, 2000) and Jocelyne Cesari (1998, 2004), have emphasized the selective adoption of elements of Islamic teaching by the current generation of young Muslims and the eclectic and individualized nature of their Islamic belief and practice. Roy has noted that many young people reject much of their parents' (and their imams') understanding of Islam as irrelevant local culture, and that the search for a pure Islam without culture almost inevitably draws them towards Salafism.

These views have been quite influential in the first decade of the twenty-first century, but in retrospect their authors may have been overstating their case. Peer-learning no doubt is an important part of the acquisition of Islamic knowledge, but this has not replaced the various forms of established religious authority. Authority may have become fragmented in the sense that any individual may have access to a wider range of authorities than one or two generations before and thereby theoretically can choose the opinion that is most convincing (or convenient) on any specific issue, but the status of these authorities has not declined. Even the much-maligned imams continue to play a part in the background.

Other authors have emphasized the role of the new media, notably digital databases and the Internet, in democratizing Islamic knowledge by breaking the monopoly of the ulama on accessing and interpreting the sources (Qur'an and hadith as well as the major fiqh works and fatwa collections). Some of the early publications (Anderson 1999, Bunt 2000 and 2003, Mandaville 2000) were very upbeat about the revolutionary potential of the new media; a decade later, more sober assessments have come to prevail. It is true that the unprecedented availability of digitalized and searchable sources, on CD-ROM and online, has given every computer-literate person with sufficient linguistic competence the possibility rapidly to find references to just any issue, in the Qur'an, hadith collections or any other corpus he or she considers authoritative. This has enabled many more people than ever before to scrutinize, and occasionally to challenge, the fatwas and counsels of religious authorities, but it has not led to any attempt to replace these authorities. The same IT technologies after all can also be used by the ulama to strengthen their positions, and they have in fact lent some of them – the obvious example being Yusuf Qaradawi – an unprecedented influence (Gräf 2007; see also Mariani in this volume).

The volume and variety of Internet usage in Islamic communication have rapidly multiplied, as Bunt's most recent work (2009) amply illustrates. However, it seems to be especially in Salafi circles that a pattern of knowledge production through Internet-based communications has emerged. The Salafi style of reasoning, in which every opinion has to be supported by evidence (*dalil*) in the form of one or more 'authentic' hadith, appears to be highly compatible with communication in Internet forums. Carmen Becker, who has studied Salafi online forums extensively, notes that much of the communication aims at improving the forum members' command of the relevant sources. However, rather than formulating their own opinion on a specific issue they commonly adopt the ruling of an established scholar – but they consider it their duty to make sure this ruling is based on valid *dalil* (Becker 2009).

Similarly, peer learning in face-to-face situations, such as in student and youth associations, which constitute major sites of production and transmission of discursive Islamic knowledge, does not replace the more traditional forms of authority, but rather is one of the media through which the latter exert themselves. The discussions may be between (more or less) equals, who exchange information that they have culled from diverse sources – books, journals, television or Internet, or knowledgeable individuals – but there is little evidence that 'cut-and-paste Islam', the eclectic hybrid patchwork some have expected to emerge, is becoming a dominant mode of Islamic knowledge. Ultimately most opinions are justified by the authority of specific ulama or Muslim intellectuals. Moreover, in practice peer learning is rarely a negotiation between equals but usually involves deliberate teaching by some peers who are more knowledgeable than the others and act as guides or teachers. These may have some formal training in the Islamic sciences or be largely self-taught – but the latter too need to establish their credentials through a demonstration of their mastery of the scriptural sources or reference to a recognized, established religious authority.

Conclusion

Islamic knowledge takes many forms, and it is produced and disseminated in many different settings, some of them formal, others informal. The classical, madrasa-style mode of transmission continues in Europe in the forms of the Qurʿan courses and various colleges of higher Islamic learning, but it has been complemented by various other modes of production and reproduction of knowledge. The sources to which reference is made are the standard Islamic references: Qurʿan and hadith, and the various Islamic sciences that have developed over the ages, from *tafsir, fiqh* and *kalam* to Sufi treatises. Besides these standard authoritative references, sources of a very different type have entered into Muslim discourses: Western converts to Islam, but also Western non-Muslim authors and even politicians. These Western references have increasingly contributed to framing contemporary Muslim discourse, if only because of the search for Islamic answers to questions they raised. Moreover, Western authorities, from Malcolm X to John Rawls and Jürgen Habermas, are occasionally invoked in Muslim debates to add persuasive force to an argument, and they have definitely contributed to shaping Islamic knowledge in Europe in the early twenty-first century. This does not mean, however, that they are in any sense recognized as authorities in their own right, on a par with conventional Islamic authorities. Iconic figures like Malcolm X and intellectual challengers like the liberal philosophers have inspired the attitudes and convictions of many Muslims; but most of the latter strive to find scriptural foundations for these attitudes and convictions, and in this quest often follow the guidance, mediated or personal, of persons they recognize as religious authorities.

Not all Islamic knowledge is discursive; bodily practices, attitudes and dispositions constitute an important part of what it is to be a Muslim. Much of early training, by parents or in Qurʿan courses, concerns these embodied forms of Islamic knowledge. Several of the most prominent Muslim movements active in Western Europe (and elsewhere) place a special emphasis on these non-discursive forms of Islamic knowledge and the disciplining practices through which they are imparted. There is little room for eclecticism in these disciplines; they expect of their followers a high degree of commitment and obedience to authority.

However, since these movements cannot exert full control over their followers, it is not uncommon for many of them to leave the movement after some time and either remain aloof or join another movement, with a distinctly different discipline. The eclecticism that some observers have noticed is in many cases the result of successive commitments to different movements, each with their strict discipline.

Notes

1 For an insightful survey of this literature, see Peter 2006. It was especially Olivier Roy who has suggested that increasing numbers of young Muslims everywhere nowadays construct their own 'cut-and-paste' version of Islam, selecting from heterogeneous sources (Roy 1999, 2004), and some of the early writings on the effects of new digital media on Islamic discourses have endorsed that perception.

2 Jonker 2002: 184, 189n. Jonker cites Berlin census data according to which only 18 per cent of Turkish parents state that their children visit a Qurʿan course (perhaps this figure is lower than those reported elsewhere because Berlin has a relatively large Alevi population) and calculates that most of these children, approximately 3,500 out of 4,000, visit Süleymanci courses. On other Qurʿan courses in Berlin mosques, see Mohr 2006.

3 One particular subgroup of such 'internal conversions', those of inmates in prisons, has recently received some attention: Khosrokhavar 2004, Beckford, Joly and Khosrokhavar 2005. There is some earlier work on the turn to Islam in the context of popular youth culture: Khosrokhavar 1997, Khedimellah 2002.

4 This is what Bowen calls the *diacritic* attribution of meaning to the ritual. Another level of meaning that he briefly discusses is the *iconic* signification, in which the form of prayer is taken as a model of (or for) features of society (1989: 612–13).

5 The reference is to the PKK-affiliated Union of Pious Persons of Kurdistan (Kürdistan Dindarlar Birligi) or Union of Patriotic Imams (Kürdistan Yurtsever Imamlar Birligi) established by Abdurrahman Durre. It controls a mosque in Berlin and claims a number of others elsewhere in Germany, France and the Netherlands. In a similar development in the (non-political) Nurcu movement in Turkey, some Kurds have become alienated from the Turkish mainstream and several separate Kurdish Nurcu groups have emerged (see Atacan 2001); I do not know to what extent this split has been reproduced in Western Europe.

6 I use the term 'Salafi' here for the movements that currently claim this name for themselves and that are ideologically close to the leading ulama of Saudi Arabia and Kuwait. The term has been applied to various groups who claim to model themselves on the first three or four generations of Muslims (*al-salaf al-salih*, 'the pious predecessors'), and who reject the classical Islamic sciences in favour of exclusive reliance on Qurʿan and hadith. A century ago, the term 'Salafi' was used to refer to such modernist thinkers as Muhammad ʿAbduh, who combined their return to the Qurʿan and sunna with a rational interpretation of those sources. Current Salafis reject such rationalism and insist on the unquestioning, literal reading of the sources. More tradition-minded Muslims object not only to the purist urge but to the very appropriation of the term 'Salafi' by these groups (because the *salaf salih* are venerated by all Muslims) and often refer to them as 'Wahhabi' – a term that is used with even less precision for all critics of traditional practices.

7 Nasir al-Din al-Albani, who was born in Albania, spent his formative years in Syria, taught in Saudi Arabia and died in Jordan in 1999, was one of the most influential Salafi scholars of the twentieth century. He was a largely self-taught expert on *hadith* and has distinguished himself by his uncompromising rejection of much established Muslim practice that he found lacking in solid *hadith* support. He was one of the most strictly

non-political Salafi scholars, a staunch opponent of all forms of political activity (see Lacroix 2009). For a sample of his writings, see the website dedicated to him, <http://www.albani.co.uk>, or a collection of his answers to questions from Muslim students in America at <http://www.uh.edu/campus/msa/articles/tape_.html>. The English translation of the book on the Prophet's prayer is online at: <http://www.qss.org/articles/salah/toc.html>. Understandably, al-Albani has been a source of many controversies and the object of equally fierce criticism, for which see e.g. <http://www.sunnah.org/history/Innovators/al_albani.htm>. The book on prayer is fiercely attacked at: <http://www.ummah.net/Al_adaab/alfiqh.html> (all websites mentioned were last accessed in November 2009).

8 Turkey's *imam-hatip* schools were originally established by the state to educate personnel to serve as imams and preachers (*khatib, hatip*) in the official mosques, but they recruit many more students than could ever find a paid position as mosque personnel. Rather, these schools came to function as channels of social mobility for children of the pious rural families that were not accommodated in the secular schools, and the vast majority of graduates of these schools went on to other professions.

9 There was a more fundamental reason for the failure of the experiment; the school's founders had taken it for granted that the Diyanet bureaucracy would employ its graduates preferentially to send them back to the Netherlands as imams, but there was no guarantee that this would actually happen.

10 Research carried out by Kadir Canatan and others in 2002 on behalf of the city council of Rotterdam; personal communication from Canatan; see also Canatan et al. 2003.

11 See Reeber 2000, 2004; Frégosi 2004; Kroissenbrunner 2002; Battiui & Kanmaz 2004; Kamp 2006; Birt 2006; Boender 2007; Oubrou 2009.

12 Several cases of such conflicts are mentioned in Landman 1992, and one is extensively described in de Koning 2008.

13 Eric Roose's dissertation on mosque design in the Netherlands (Roose 2009) gives fascinating examples of the interaction and negotiations between various actors (mosque committees, architects, local government and neighbourhood committees) and types of knowledge (Islamic, legal, architectural) in the process of designing and building new mosques.

14 South Asian Deobandis established several seminaries in Britain from the 1970s onwards; in 1987 the Azhari scholar Zaki Badawi established, with Libyan support, the Muslim College of London; the Muslim Brotherhood-affiliated UOIF established the European Institute of Human Sciences in Château Chinon, France, in 1992; Turkish Muslims established the Islamic University of Rotterdam in 1997 and the Islamic Academy of Religious Pedagogy in Vienna in 1998; and the Süleymancı movement has been training its imams in Germany in a more informal setting since the mid-1980s. See Gilliat-Ray 2006; Birt and Lewis (in this volume); Frégosi 1998; Peter 2003; Boender 2006; Jonker 2002.

15 Canatan et al. 2003 and personal communications from Canatan. Earlier observations on the importance of non-religious activities around the Milli Görüş and Diyanet mosques in Rotterdam are made in Sunier 1996.

16 More correctly perhaps not second generation in the strict sense but the in-between generation, who received (part of) their secondary education still in Turkey, in many cases in an *imam-hatip* school, and who came to the Netherlands to join parents already working there.

17 Similar observations in Sunier 1996: 178–90, where a comparison between the three major streams of Turkish Sunni Islam (Milli Görüs, Diyanet and Süleymancı) is made.

18 Sunier mentions such *iftar* meals in Rotterdam for the early nineties and suggests they had been started a few years before (1996: 120). Haci Karacaer, former director of Milli Görüs – Northern Netherlands, claimed that the Milli Görüs mosque in Amsterdam was

in the Netherlands the pioneer of this new practice (personal communication). The same practice became established in other European countries. Most mosque committees hold these *iftar*s in a space beside the mosque's prayer hall or, if that is not available, in a nearby restaurant.

19 Haci Karacaer, personal communication.

20 See the slick film about the 2009 *kurban* campaign on the Milli Görüs website: <http://www.igmg.de/tr/teskilat/kurban-kampanyasi.html>. The organization claims to have co-ordinated the slaughter and distribution of an average 25,000 to 30,000 animals in the past few years (at a price of EUR 100 per animal).

21 In Turkey, this is done by the Türk Hava Kurumu (Turkish Aviation Society), a semi-governmental body. One of the foundation's major sources of income had long been its government-granted monopoly on collecting the skins of sacrificial animals. From there it was a small step to organizing the entire process of sacrifice. Strong government support no doubt smoothed the introduction of this new development. The Turkish Red Crescent also collects *kurban* contributions, and it keeps the processed meat for distribution in poor regions of the country and among victims of natural disasters.

22 I do not wish to imply that the practices that have emerged are in any sense definitive. They may at any time be challenged by members of the congregation, or by outsiders, either because new adaptations are felt to be necessary or because they are believed to be in conflict with authoritative interpretations of scripture. The simplest and perhaps most effective way to challenge an existing practice is by requesting a fatwa from a recognized authority.

23 Jonker's sympathetic study of the Süleymanci movement in Germany (2002) clearly shows up the strains in its relationship with Western society.

24 The tension between piety and secularity in the Gülen movement is commented upon by Özdalga (2000) and Agai (2002, 2007). There is a rapidly growing literature on the movement, some of it hostile and denouncing it as a threat to Turkey's secular order, but much of it presenting the movement as 'moderate' or 'liberal' and compatible with the secular state (Yavuz and Esposito 2003). Surprisingly, none of the literature discusses the disciplining practices in the after-school support groups and student dormitories, which constitute the core of the movement's programme of shaping the pious Muslim subject.

25 This trend was recognized more than a decade ago by the prominent left intellectual Ömer Laçiner (1995). Laçiner is one of few on Turkey's left who have been sympathetic observers of the movement.

26 These few paragraphs on the Gülen movement are mostly based on my own interviews with members and former members and an ongoing research project carried out by Mehmet Sahin.

27 The standard work on the Tablighi Jamaᶜat is Masud 2000; the first study to draw attention to the Jamaᶜat's successful proselytization among North African Muslims in France was Kepel 1987. Insightful observations on the Jamaᶜat and French Muslim youth culture are to be found in Khedimellah 2002 and 2006.

28 The *Fazaᶜil-i Aᶜmal* was composed by a scholar associated with the movement, Mawlana Muhammad Zakariya Kandhalawi. Several English translations can be consulted online, e.g. at <http://www.fazaileamaal.com>.

29 *Riyad al-Salihin* ('Gardens of the Pious') is a classical collection of hadith, compiled by the thirteenth-century scholar Yahya al-Nawawi, which is popular in traditionalist circles but also highly valued by Salafis.

30 On the Boutchichiyya and Faouzi Skali, see also Sedgwick's chapter in this volume.

31 See the videoclips titled 'I am Malcolm X' on the website of The Radical Middle Way, <http://radicalmiddleway.co.uk/videos?id=58&art=58&vid=224> (accessed November 2009). Nikola Tietze found a similar admiration for Malcolm X among her Turkish informants in Germany (2001: 57).

32 The growing popularity of Sufism among young European Muslims is reflected in a rapidly growing number of academic studies, see for instance Geaves 2000, Werbner 2003, and the studies in Westerlund (ed.) 2004, Malik and Hinnells (eds) 2006.
33 He mentions the Americans Hamza Yusuf Hanson and Nuh Ha Mim Keller and the British academic Abdal Hakim Murad (alias Tim Winter). All three command respect for their learning in traditional Islamic sciences. On the impact that the former two have had in spreading an intellectually sophisticated Sufism, see also Roald 2004: 221–9.
34 The book reads here and there like the confessions of a repentant sinner, but is interesting as one of very few detailed accounts from within a radical movement. Since publishing this autobiography, Husain has joined the Quilliam Foundation (<http://www.quilliam foundation.org>), which describes itself as 'the world's first counter-extremism think tank,' and which received a considerable amount of British government funding for its work to counter Muslim radicalism.

Bibliography

Abd al-Malik (2004) *Qu'Allah bénisse la France*, Paris: Albin Michel.

Agai, Bekim (2002) 'Fethullah Gülen and his Movement's Islamic Ethic of Education', *Critique: Critical Middle Eastern Studies*, 11(1), 27–47.

Agai, Bekim (2007) *Zwischen Netzwerk und Diskurs. Das Bildungsnetzwerk um Fethullah Gülen (geb. 1938): Die flexible Umsetzung modernen islamischen Gedankengutes*, Berlin: EB-Verlag.

Anderson, Jon W. (1999) 'The Internet and Islam's New Interpreters', in Dale F. Eickelman and Jon W. Anderson (eds.), *New Media in the Muslim World: The Emerging Public Sphere*, Bloomington and Indianapolis: Indiana University Press, pp. 41–56.

Asad, Talal (1986) *The Idea of an Anthropology of Islam*, Washington D.C.: Center for Contemporary Arab Studies, Georgetown University. Occasional paper.

Atacan, Fulya (2001) 'A Kurdish Islamist Group in Modern Turkey: Shifting Identities', *Middle Eastern Studies*, 37, 111–44.

Babès, Leïla (1997) *L'islam positif, la religion des jeunes musulmans de France*, Editions de l'Atelier/Débattre.

Babès, Leïla (2000) *L'islam intérieur: passion et désenchantement*, Paris: Al Bouraq.

Battiui, Mohamed El and Kanmaz, Meryem (2004) 'Mosquées, imams et professeurs de religion islamique en Belgique. État de la question et enjeux', Bruxelles: Fondation Roi Baudouin.

Becker, Carmen (2009) '"Gaining Knowledge": Salafi Activism in German and Dutch Online Forums', *Masaryk University Journal of Law and Technology*, 3(1), 79–98.

Beckford, James A., Joly, Danièle and Khosrokhavar, Farhad (2005) *Muslims in Prison: Challenge and Change in Britain and France*, London and New York: Palgrave Macmillan.

Bergeaud-Blackler, Florence (2007) 'New Challenges for Islamic Ritual Slaughter: A European Perspective', *Journal of Ethnic and Migration Studies*, 33(6), 965–80.

Birt, Jonathan (2006) 'Good Imam, Bad Imam: Civic Religion and National Integration in Britain post-9/11', *The Muslim World*, 96, 687–705.

Boender, Welmoet (2006) 'From Migrant to Citizen: The Role of the Islamic University of Rotterdam in the Formulation of Dutch Citizenship', in Gerdien Jonker and Valérie Amiraux (eds), *Politics of Visibility: Young Muslims in European Public Spaces*, Bielefeld: Transcript-Verlag, pp. 103–22.

Boender, Welmoet (2007) Imam in Nederland: opvattingen over zijn religieuze rol in de samenleving, Amsterdam: Bert Bakker.

Boender, Welmoet and Kanmaz, Meryem (2002) 'Imams in the Netherlands and Islam Teachers in Flanders', in W.A.R. Shadid and P.S. van Koningsveld (eds), *Intercultural Relations and Religious Authorities: Muslims in the European Union*, Leuven: Peeters, pp. 169–80.

Bowen, John R. (1989) 'Salat in Indonesia: The Social Meanings of an Islamic Ritual', *Man*, 24, 600–19.

Buffin, Frédéric (1998) 'Les imams et la sécurité nationale: état des lieux et perspectives', in Franck Frégosi (ed.), *La formation des cadres religieux musulmans en France. Approches socio-juridiques*, Paris: L'Harmattan, pp. 83–9.

Bunt, Gary R. (2000) *Virtually Islamic: Computer-Mediated Communication and Cyber-Islamic Environments*, Cardiff: University of Wales Press.

Bunt, Gary R. (2003) *Islam in the Digital Age: e-jihad, Online Fatwas And Cyber Islamic Environments*, London: Pluto Press.

Bunt, Gary R. (2009) *iMuslims: Rewiring the House of Islam*, University of North Carolina Press.

Canatan, Kadir (2001) 'Turkse islam: perspectieven op organisatievorming en leiderschap in Nederland', Ph.D. thesis, Rotterdam: Erasmus Universiteit.

Canatan, Kadir, Oudijk, C.H. and Ljamai, Abdelilah (2003) *De maatschappelijke rol van de Rotterdamse moskeeën* [The social role of mosques in Rotterdam], Rotterdam: Centrum voor Onderzoek en Statistiek.

Cesari, Jocelyne (1998) *Musulmans et républicains: les jeunes, l'islam et la France*, Bruxelles: Éditions Complexe.

Cesari, Jocelyne (2004) *L'islam à l'épreuve de l'occident*, Paris: La Découverte.

Dagyeli, Jeanine Elif (2006) 'Jugendarbeit – Perspektiven islamischer Vereine auf ein umstrittenes Feld', in Riem Spielhaus and Alexa Färber (eds), *Islamisches Gemeindeleben in Berlin*, Berlin: Der Beauftragte des Senats von Berlin für Integration und Migration, pp. 52–7.

Frégosi, Franck (1998) 'Les filières nationales de formation des imams en France: L'Institut Européen des Sciences Humaines (Château-Chinon) et l'Institut d'Etudes Islamiques de Paris (Paris)', in Franck Frégosi (ed.), *La formation des cadres religieux musulmans en France. Approches socio-juridiques*, Paris: L'Harmattan, pp. 101–39.

Frégosi, Franck (2004) 'L'imam, le conférencier et le jurisconsulte: retour sur trois figures contemporaines du champs religieux islamique en France', *Archives de Sciences Sociales des Religions*, 49 no. 125, 131–46.

Geaves, Ron (2000) The Sufis of Britain: An Exploration of Muslim Identity, Cardiff: Cardiff Academic Press.

Gerholm, Tomas and Lithman, Yngve Georg (eds) (1988) *The New Islamic Presence in Western Europe*, London: Mansell.

Gilliat-Ray, Sophie (2006) 'Educating the ᶜulama: Centres of Islamic Religious Training in Britain', *Islam & Christian Muslim Relations*, 17, 55–76.

Gräf, Bettina (2007) 'Sheikh Yusuf al-Qaradawi in Cyberspace', *Die Welt des Islams*, 47, 403–21.

Hamid, Sadek (2009) 'The Attraction of "Authentic Islam": Salafism and British Muslim Youth', in Roel Meijer (ed.), *Global Salafism: Islam's New Religious Movement*, London: Hurst & Company, pp. 384–403.

Husain, Ed (2007) *The Islamist. Why I Joined Radical Islam in Britain, What I saw Inside and Why I Left*, London: Penguin Books.

Jonker, Gerdien (2002) Eine Wellenlänge zu Gott: der Verband der islamischen Kulturzentren in Europa, Bielefeld: Transcript Verlag.

Kamp, Melanie (2006) 'Mehr als Vorbeter: Zur Herkunft und Rolle von Imamen in Moscheevereinen', in Riem Spielhaus and Alexa Färber (eds), *Islamisches Gemeindeleben in Berlin*, Berlin: Der Beauftragte des Senats von Berlin für Integration und Migration, pp. 40–4.

Kepel, Gilles (1987) *Les banlieues de l'islam*, Paris: Editions du Seuil.

Khedimellah, Moussa (2002) 'Aesthetics and Poetics of Apostolic Islam in France', *ISIM Newsletter*, 11, 20–1.

Khedimellah, Moussa (2006) 'Young Preachers of the Tabligh Movement in France', in Nilüfer Göle and Ludwig Ammann (eds), *Islam in Public: Turkey, Iran, and Europe*, Istanbul: Istanbul Bilgi University Press, pp. 369–94.

Khosrokhavar, Farhad (1997) *L'islam des jeunes*, Paris: Flammarion.

Khosrokhavar, Farhad (2004) *L'islam dans les prisons*, Paris: Balland.

Koning, Martijn de (2008) Zoeken naar een 'zuivere' islam: Geloofsbeleving en identiteitsvorming van jonge Marokkaans-Nederlandse moslims [In search of a 'pure' Islam: religious experience and identity formation of young Dutch-Moroccan Muslims], Amsterdam: Bert Bakker.

Kroissenbrunner, Sabine (2002) 'Turkish Imams in Vienna', in W.A.R. Shadid and P.S. van Koningsveld (eds), *Intercultural Relations and Religious Authorities: Muslims in the European Union*, Leuven: Peeters, pp. 181–207.

Laçiner, Ömer (1995) 'Seçkinci bir gelenegin temsilcisi olarak Fethullah Hoca cemaati' [The Fethullah Hoca congregation as the representative of an elitist tradition], *Birikim*, 77, 3–11.

Lacroix, Stéphane (2009) 'Between Revolution and Apoliticism: Nasir al-Din al-Albani and his Impact on the Shaping of Contemporary Salafism', in Roel Meijer (ed.), *Global Salafism: Islam's New Religious Movement*, London: Hurst & Company, pp. 58–80.

Landman, Nico (1992) 'Van mat tot minaret: de institutionalisering van de islam in Nederland' [From Prayer Mat to Minaret: The Institutionalization of Islam in the Netherlands], Ph.D. thesis, Utrecht: Rijksuniversiteit Utrecht.

Malik, Jamal and Hinnells, John (eds) (2006) *Sufism in the West*, London: Routledge.

Mandaville, Peter (2000) 'Information Technology and the Changing Boundaries of European Islam', in Felice Dassetto (ed.), *Paroles d'islam; Individus, sociétés et discours dans l'islam européen contemporain*, Paris: Maisonneuve-Larose, pp. 281–97.

Masud, Muhammad Khalid (ed.) (2000) *Travellers in Faith. Studies of the Tablighi Jama'at as a Transnational Islamic Movement for Faith Renewal*, Leiden: Brill.

Mohr, Irka-Christin (2006) 'Koranunterricht in Berliner Moscheen', in Riem Spielhaus and Alexa Färber (eds), *Islamisches Gemeindeleben in Berlin*, Berlin: Der Beauftragte des Senats von Berlin für Integration und Migration, pp. 46–51.

Oubrou, Tareq (2009) *Profession imâm. Entretiens avec Michaël Privot et Cédric Baylocq*, Paris: Albin Michel.

Özdalga, Elisabeth (2000) 'Worldly Asceticism in Islamic Casting: Fethullah Gülen's Inspired Piety and Activism', *Critique: Critical Middle Eastern Studies*, 17, 83–104.

Peter, Frank (2003) 'Training Imams and the Future of Islam in France', *ISIM Newsletter*, 13, 20–1.

Peter, Frank (2006) 'Individualization and Religious Authority in Western European Islam', *Islam & Christian Muslim Relations*, 17, 105–18.

Reeber, Michel (2000) 'Les khutbas de la diaspora: enquête sur les tendances de la prédication islamique dans les mosquées en France et dans plusieurs pays d'Europe occidentale', in Felice Dassetto (ed.), *Paroles d'islam; Individus, sociétés et discours dans l'islam européen contemporain*, Paris: Maisonneuve-Larose, pp. 185–203.

Reeber, Michel (2004) 'La prédication (khutba) dans les mosquées en France et en Europe: en quête d'une nouvelle légitimité?', in Martine Cohen, Jean Joncheray and Pierre-Jean Luizard (ed.), *Les transformations de l'autorité religieuse*, Paris: L'Harmattan, pp. 187–98.

Roald, Anne Sofie (2004) *New Muslims in the European Context. The Experience of Scandinavian Converts*, Leiden: Brill.

Roose, Eric (2009) *The Architectural Representation of Islam: Muslim-commissioned Mosque Design in the Netherlands*, Amsterdam: Amsterdam University Press.

Roy, Olivier (1999) *Vers un islam européen*, Paris: Éditions Esprit.

Roy, Olivier (2000) 'L'individualisation dans l'islam européen contemporain', in Felice Dassetto (ed.), *Paroles d'islam; Individus, sociétés et discours dans l'islam européen contemporain*, Paris: Maisonneuve-Larose, pp. 69–83.

Roy, Olivier (2004) *Globalised Islam: The Search for the New Ummah*, London: Hurst and Company.

Saeed, Amir (2007) 'Malcolm X and British Muslims: A Personal Reflection', *Journal of Religion and Popular Culture*, 16, online at: www.usask.ca/relst/jrpc/art16-malcomxbrits-print.html.

Shadid, W.A.R. and Koningsveld, P.S. van (1992) 'Legal Adjustments for Religious Minorities: The Case of Ritual Slaughtering', in W.A.R. Shadid and P.S. van Koningsveld (eds), *Islam in Dutch Society: Current Developments and Future Prospects*, Kampen: Kok Pharos, pp. 2–25.

Sunier, Thijl (1996) *Islam in beweging: Turkse jongeren en islamitische organisaties*, Amsterdam: Het Spinhuis.

Tietze, Nikola (2001) *Islamische Identitäten: Formen muslimischer Religiosität junger Männer in Deutschland und Frankreich*, Hamburg: Hamburger Edition (HIS Verlagsges.).

Werbner, Pnina (2003) *Pilgrims of Love: The Anthropology of a Global Sufi Cult*, Bloomington: Indiana University Press.

Westerlund, David (ed.) (2004) *Sufism in Europe and North America*, London: RoutledgeCurzon.

Yalçin-Heckmann, Lale (1998) 'Growing up as a Muslim in Germany: Religious Socialization among Turkish Migrant Families', in Steven Vertovec and Alisdair Rogers (eds), *Muslim European Youth: Reproducing Ethnicity, Religion, Culture*, Aldershot: Ashgate, pp. 167–92.

Yavuz, M. Hakan and Esposito, John L. (eds) (2003) *Turkish Islam and the Secular State: The Gülen Movement*, New York: Syracuse University Press.

2 Muslim voices, European ears

Exploring the gap between the production of Islamic knowledge and its perception

Stefano Allievi

Introduction: speaking of Islam or Muslims?

Islam has, in the last decade, burst in upon the European public scene, as a topic of debate and especially as a hot issue on the political, cultural, social, religious, and academic agenda. This has happened for quite obvious reasons: the emergence of Islamic terrorism and security agendas connected to Islam at a global level, specifically affecting the West on the one hand, and various problems connected with the presence of Islamic populations in Europe on the other. What is less obvious, however, is that Islam, especially where it concerns the latter, is quite naturally considered as an object rather than a subject, an abstraction rather than an empirically analyzable phenomenon, a set of unvarying definitions rather than a group of living (and changing) populations. There exists an almost natural tendency to reify Islam, as we see occurring in most debates in the public sphere. And we tend to forget that the real issue is not Islam as such but rather Muslims, and in particular Muslims in Europe. The problems are about persons, not concepts or abstractions.

This is more than just a minor difference, even if most of the time it passes unobserved, and it has serious scientific and ethical implications. In the classical Orientalist approach, the objectification or reification of Muslims used not to be considered a problem at all: on the contrary, this was part of the accepted way of studying Islam, the dominant method, style, and definition of the subject. It was the prominent Italian Orientalist Francesco Gabrieli who stated once that he studied Muslims like an entomologist studies insects – the starting point being the obvious superiority of Western civilization and (white, Christian, secular) European culture. Since the debate over Edward Said's *Orientalism* (1978), this approach has lost part (but not all) of its attraction in academic circles, but it has acquired new importance, and growing success, in the public debate. In perceptions – which are not exactly the same as experience – the default mode is often reification.

In this essay I attempt to shift the level of discussion from Islam to Muslims, for a reason that might sound simple and even naïve, but which is decisive: Islam cannot answer questions but Muslims can, and in fact do – we can talk to 'them' and 'they' to us. So, it is possible to de-objectify the discourses. The opposite attitude, which seems to be a feature of many current debates on Islam and

Muslims in Europe, is problematic, from the point of view of a correct knowledge and interpretation: a form of essentialism, which proceeds from a basically prede- fined image of what Islam is, in which it tries to place real Muslims bodily in a process of 'over-Islamisation of Muslims' (Al-Azmeh 2004). And if they do not fit that image, too bad for them. This approach is widespread and not limited to Orientalism. We find, for instance, among authors in many disciplines – theologians, political experts, journalists, sociologists – the same tendency to make sweeping statements on Islam in Europe on the basis of an often indirect if not second-hand knowledge of the Islam of Muslim countries. Assuming that generalities about Islam in a majority situation will also hold where Muslims are in a minority posi- tion, without even taking into account these fundamentally different contexts, is precisely the sort of essentialism of which we should be aware.

Islam in the abstract is static, Muslims are dynamic; Islam is rigid, Muslims are flexible; Islam is (can be interpreted as) univocal, Muslims constitute a cacoph- ony of dissident voices. This implies that the use of this category of Islam, when given an excessively essentialist stress, creates more problems than it solves for the common view of Muslim communities and populations, especially when they are used not only to study and comprehend the dynamics and changes of Islam (of Muslims) in Europe but also to understand what happens more evidently through the so-called second generations (and following) – which in fact repre- sent the *first* generations (and following) of European Muslims, i.e. of Muslims of a different context. And we know how, in social sciences, the context is impor- tant in determining the text, how the frame not only contextualizes, but also redefines what it includes.

In studying the processes of production and dissemination of Islamic knowl- edge, two crucial factors that are often neglected should be kept in mind. First of all, Muslim voices do not speak to Muslim ears only. And second, there are forms of knowledge about Islam and about Muslims in Western Europe that are not produced by Muslims themselves, but that play a significant role in creating an image of them, as well as in shaping Muslims' discourse on Islam. What Europeans think, say, and write about Islam and Muslims influences the way in which Muslims themselves construct their own idea of what is a correct Islamic belief and practice, and has an impact on the way in which Islamic knowledge is produced. We have therefore, to put it briefly, to question the idea that the production of Islamic knowledge in Western Europe is a simple and obvious process internal to Muslim communities alone.

This is why two different subjects are referred to here, Muslim voices and European ears, which are nevertheless sometimes inverted in their roles: European voices about Islam and Muslim ears in Europe – the feedback processes are reciprocal and rich with consequences.

Islam in Europe, European Islam

In the sociological analysis of Islam in Europe a few approaches have predominated. One is that of comparing the situations in the various countries by juxtaposing different national cases (France, Great Britain, and Germany, sometimes the Netherlands and Belgium, less frequently the Mediterranean countries of Southern Europe and the Scandinavian countries). In most cases these studies are not really comparisons, because they are not the product of the work of a single researcher or team of researchers: they consist of collections of papers or essays by various authors, rarely with a common structure and common aims, and often they are the outcomes of a seminar.[1]

Another frequent approach has been to study the presence of Muslim populations in a particular local environment, or in a specific country.[2] A third type of studies focuses on specific ethnic or national groups, such as the Senegalese in Italy or the Turks in Germany; in some cases research in Europe is combined with part of the fieldwork conducted in the countries of origin.

Other studies deal with specific subgroups, such as second- and third-generation Muslims or European converts to Islam, the legal and juridical matters related to the Muslim presence, specific issues like Islam in schools and Islamic education, imams and mosques, inter-religious dialogue, the place of Islam in prisons, and many others, including various conflict situations, with a national or transnational character, from the headscarf to fundamentalism and terrorism.

A more general synthesis of the different processes at work has only rarely been attempted by specialists describing some of the various implications of the Islamic presence in Europe.[3] A proper and coordinated synthesis, which would require the interdisciplinary collaboration of scholars with expertise in a broad range of European countries and ethno-national Muslim groups, being difficult to organize, expensive, and time-consuming, has been extremely rarely attempted thus far.[4] In sum, there is no lack of literature, but studies on the Muslim populations in Europe have tended to be very descriptive and poor in theoretical analysis. It is an important and useful body of studies, constituting the basis for most of the publicly available information, but it is not enough to fully understand all implications of the Islamic presence in Europe.

Questions concerning the production of Islamic knowledge, in particular, are almost absent from the existing literature or, at best, only constitute a minor argument in it. In this entire body of scholarship, little attention has been paid to cultural production by the Muslims in Europe and intra- and inter-generational cultural transmission in general, of which the production of religious knowledge is a major aspect. Even less attention has been paid to the interrelation between religious production and its perception, and the influence of this perception on the production of knowledge itself.

To understand how Muslims in Europe produce their image of their own religious role is important in itself, in order to understand which role they attribute to themselves in European societies and their plural religious landscape. Given the hot debates on Islam and Muslims in Europe, which sometimes tend to become explicitly anti-Muslim, it is important to understand how European Muslims are developing the ideas they have of themselves and of the role they play in European societies, the connections they have and maintain with their multiple countries of origin, and also their projects and perspectives – including cultural and religious ones – in the European context become a relevant factor. In other words, it is crucial to take into account the knowledge they have and the interpretations they give of themselves, and of the contexts they live in, for social and political reasons as well – the implications of which have grown considerably after the events of September 11 in the United States, and their consequences elsewhere, including in Europe.

It is also important to arrive at a better understanding of the views that public opinion in various European societies has of the Muslim presence in their midst, and how these views are changing (also in connection with events relating to Islam outside Europe). The perception of the Islamic presence in Europe, and specifically the attention paid to its intellectualization (i.e. the production of Islamic knowledge and its visibility) play in fact an important role in the global perception of this Muslim presence, as well as in the perception of Islam in general. Therefore it is important to understand the role and the effects – also on Muslim themselves – of debates *on* Islam in the public space, which include, among others, what is discussed in the media, in the political arena, and in the intellectual production.

In fact, we are now facing a dynamic phase of transition. In the recent past, the transition was from the existence of two cultural worlds (Islam *and* Europe), self-represented as distinct and often incompatible, to a situation in which, owing to and through international migratory flows, Islam has become part of the European religious and social landscape (Islam *in* Europe). Now, with the passage from one generation to another, we are increasingly facing a shift from the previous situation (Islam *in* Europe) to a third phase, which we might call the phase and process of indigenization of Islam (in which an Islam *of* Europe may be emerging). As a subcategory of the latter, both social behaviour and a new intellectualization produced by Muslims are showing the growth of a newer process: the construction of a *European* Islam.

The intellectual instruments we need to use to understand these new phenomena cannot be the same as those we used in the past to study an essentialized Islam, Islam in (so-called) Muslim countries, or even the first waves of migrations into Europe. The scientific community also has to change substantially its theoretical frameworks and the methodological tools used to understand these processes (Allievi 2005a). This innovation of the interpretative categories is only in its initial stages, especially in the everyday media coverage of Islam, where the use of tools possibly pertinent only to the first phase of comprehension, that of the (debatable) confrontation of civilizations in themselves, is still the norm, with very little awareness of the processes actually taking place in the field. One of the main problems for a correct interpretation of the production of Islamic knowledge and of its perception is that it is located in this complex wider process of change, in different ways in phases two, three, and four.

Islam(s) and Muslims in the European public space

Islam in Europe has very different characteristics from its appearance in countries where Islam is the majority religion. Specifically, the position of Islam in the public space in Europe is that of a minority in a pluralistic and secularized context: an aspect which is obvious in many ways, but the consequences of which are rarely understood in all their dimensions. This is not unique to Europe and the United States, or at least not entirely. Islam is and has been a minority elsewhere: in India, in South Africa, and several other African countries, in Russia, in China, and many other places. But the process of secularization of Europe and the US, their progressive self-definition as plural societies (which has been historically the case for the US, though much less so for most countries in Europe), their free and democratic political systems, in which individual and group rights (including, though with limitations, those of Muslims and immigrants in general) are recognized and protected, make the West very different.

From the theological point of view, the situation of Muslims in Europe could be compared to the situation of Muslims in the city of Mecca at the inception of Islam (Allievi 2005b). During this period, the prophet Muhammad still had a small following and the Muslims were a minority group that had no major influence, being excluded from positions of power and dominance. Only in Yathrib/Medina did Islam become the dominant, ruling world-view and there it did, among other things, produce common law. It was *din wa dunya wa dawla*, as Medinan Islam is often defined and self-defined in Islamic politico-religious terms – i.e. religion, everyday life (literally, low temporal existence, earthly life) and organized living, in other words, institutions, government, and in its modern form the state, and hence politics. On the other hand, this image, which is often used to interpret majority Islam, is probably a mere intellectual construct. It is interesting to note that the Arabic root of the word *dawla*, which is used to indicate a reign or dynasty, and by extension a power, also means alternation, change, and instability, almost as if to underline the inevitable transient dimension of any political and institutional structure. Incidentally, this also applies to the religious structure, in that no legitimizing centre exists that is able to issue licences of orthodoxy or heterodoxy, and this dimension is therefore substantially subject to the logic of *de facto* powers of contractualization and contestation, but also of permanent regeneration. The imbalance is experienced in a very modern way as largely structural. And if this is true for majority, and hence hegemonic, Islam, it is all the more true for minority Islam.

The conceptual problem is that, even though the present situation of Muslims in Europe resembles, from some points of view, that of Mecca before the *hijra*, the conception of Islam held by most non-Muslims, as well as many individual and collective Muslim actors, is often much more that of Medina. Much of the cultural production *about* Islam and much of what comes to us *from* Muslim countries implicitly refers to situations where Islam is hegemonic.

This lends urgency to projects of constructing a form of Islamic religious thought that takes the minority situation as its point of departure. There are several such projects, with different emphases, one being the effort to produce a minority *fiqh*, in which many jurists in Muslim countries, as well as the European Council for Fatwa and Research, are involved. Another project aims at elaborating a theology of Islam in a situation of religious plurality as part of a new and different society; this appears to be the direction in which authors such as Tariq Ramadan and others have been developing their ideas.[5]

Not only is European Islam 'Meccan' (in the sense of being a minority); it is also, in this respect, internally pluralistic, as it reproduces in itself different cultural, national, theological and juridical interpretations of Islam, to a degree that is hardly observable elsewhere. This characteristic of internal plurality is in fact far more accentuated in present-day Europe and in other Western countries than in the Muslim-majority world. The origins are multiple, and even in those countries where there is (or there was) one identifiable dominant ethnic group or a dominant geographical provenance among Muslim immigrants or where most of them are from a single region of origin (as is the case in, e.g. Germany, the United Kingdom, and France), the Muslim communities are by no means homogeneous and do not relate to an easily identifiable single centre of authority. Instead, the observable panorama shows us not only a plurality of presences and contributions in terms of law schools (all coexisting, which makes them lose much of their traditional meaning) and mystical brotherhoods (a far greater diversity of which can be encountered more easily in the West than elsewhere, and whose boundaries are easier to cross in Europe), but also a plurality of ethnic groups and of religious denominations and sects (Sunnis of all persuasions, Shi‘is, Isma‘ilis, and the like). Finally, it also shows us a plurality of languages, both those of the countries of origin, which are numerous (Arabic, itself often a plurality of dialects and registers, Turkish, Persian, Urdu, Wolof, and many others), and the various European languages, the dominant languages spoken in the respective host countries. The latter are often the only languages in which all immigrants of Muslim origin can communicate among themselves. This becomes more true the further removed they are from the moment of immigration and is increasingly the case as the first generation of immigrants is replaced by the second, the third, and so on.

In many ways, the concept of the *umma* as uniting believers of all skin colours and languages corresponds more closely to what can be perceived in Europe and America than in most countries of origin, where believers will primarily find others like themselves, of the same nationality, language, belief, and interpretation of these beliefs (within a specific law school). Moreover, in European countries, Muslim immigrants who activate their religious belief (and even those who don't, owing to a certain number of 'push factors' coming from the non-Muslim surrounding society) may experience a need to define themselves as Muslims, which in their countries of origin would have been simply obvious and pleonastic. The internal diversity among Muslims is then, ordinarily, more evident in Europe, the US, and in other host countries than elsewhere, and certainly more than in most countries of origin of the Muslim immigrants. The *umma*, in this sense, becomes a unifying concept (as a desire, as an emotion, and even as a rhetorical tool much more than as a reality) precisely because it is internally divided – and Muslims know that.

This internal diversity has important consequences. A particularly relevant example is provided by the law schools, which are so crucial for the self-interpretation of Islam in Muslim countries. All of the *madhhab*s are present in Europe; but the major difference from the situation in the countries of origin is that they mix much more easily, and individuals can find their way *through* them even more than *in* one of them. To use the words of one of my interviewees, born in Africa but of Yemeni origin and living in London:

> I am a Shafi'i, but I have to follow the most common *madhhab* here, which is the Hanafi one. Personally, as far as the *hajj* is concerned I am a Hanafi, for *jihad* I am a Maliki, for the conception of minority I am a Hanbali ...

Thus it is no wonder that European Muslims are beginning to speak of the European school – sometimes the Western and minority one (including the United States) – as the 'fifth law school' in progress. The internal plurality brings traditional beliefs and practices into question and produces self-reflexivity, which in turn accelerates the process of pluralization. (Allievi 2005b)

Theological definitions of Europe: towards a European Muslim theology?

A good test for measuring, or at least underlining, the process of Europeanization of the production of Islamic knowledge, also from the theological point of view, can be clearly seen in the evolution of the concepts used. To take but one example, we may quote the process that is currently leading to the modification of what is often considered a key concept in the self-interpretation of Islam: the classical *dar al-islam/dar al-harb* dichotomy.

It was not unusual, in the first decades of the Muslim presence in Europe, to hear Muslims referring to this dichotomy as a way of making sense of their presence in Europe, sometimes in order to justify a lukewarm commitment to religious duties, more rarely to justify a combative or missionary attitude. In the following period it was mostly Europeans speaking about Muslims who referred to these terms, as a way of explaining how Muslims were supposed to see the world, whereas they seemed to have lost their relevance for most Muslim representatives or simple believers, who rarely, if ever, referred to that classical dichotomy. Nowadays Muslim leaders in Europe, particularly those of the younger generation, are also openly questioning and frequently rejecting this traditional dichotomy, even though it has become a standard ingredient of the public debate about Islam, particularly in anti-Islamic circles (as part of a broader 'Muslims consider us the enemy' argument; a way to justify the fact of considering 'them' the enemy).

It is interesting to note that according to traditional terms Europe should actually be considered *dar al-harb*.[6] We can choose a position that was interestingly developed in Europe, before the *reconquista*, by Ibn Rushd, the *qadi* and *imam* of the Grand mosque in Cordoba and the grandfather of the more renowned philosopher bearing the same name. He established that *hijra* (emigration) was obligatory for Muslims in the case of domination by the infidels: the believers could only return to their homeland (in his case *al-Andalus*) once the Islamic order had been re-established, as did the Prophet's followers, who followed him to Medina, and returned to Mecca only after its conquest and Islamization. Similar positions were established after the end of Islamic dominion in Sicily. A Moroccan jurist, Ahmad al-Wansharisi, went so far as to say that a Muslim could not even live under the rule of just and tolerant Christians, because the risk of apostasy was in this case even higher (Lewis 1996).

In more recent times the problem of living under infidel rule posed itself when Muslim territories came under colonial domination, and particularly brutally in the 1920s, with French laws offering individuals French citizenship if they agreed to be subjected to French civil law instead of Islamic law – a proposal that led the seminaries of Zaytuna and al-Azhar to consider the acceptance of French citizenship as apostasy.[7] Similar problems were posed in Palestine after 1948, where the ulama declared that *dar al-islam* had been transformed into *dar al-kufr*, the land of unbelief, as they had done in other Muslim lands that were colonized. The traditional dichotomy was undermined even further in the radical Islamist thought of Sayyid Qutb and his followers, who consider contemporary Muslim states no longer to be *dar al-islam*, because they are not ruled on the basis of real Islamic principles. And if there is no *dar al-islam* any longer, how can we speak of *dar al-harb* or *dar al-kufr*?

This may explain other developments. We can follow what is happening in the European country with the highest percentage of Muslims, France. Here Marseille's mufti, the progressive Soheib Bencheikh (1998), considers the traditional dichotomy 'archaic and dangerous', and the rector of the mosque of the Rue du Tanger, Larbi Kechat, proposes, if from a different position, 'to delete this notion from our terminology' (1998). But even an authority whose orthodoxy is beyond suspicion, Yusuf al-Qaradawi, rejects it; as did in the past no less a person than the great thinker admired by many later radicals, Ibn Taymiyya, who held that a Muslim may sojourn wherever he wishes, as long as he is able to fulfil his religious practices, remain a Muslim, and live in safety.

Faysal Mawlawi, currently a member of the European Council for Fatwa and Research, has, together with others, started to speak of non-Muslim countries in which Muslim populations have settled in terms of *dar al-ᶜahd*, land of covenant, and then of *dar al-daᶜwa*, land of predication or mission. Many migrants call it *dar al-hijra*, which is true in a literal sense only for the first generations of migrants. The next step was taken by the likes of Rachid Ghannouchi, who referred (at a UOIF conference in 1989) to Europe simply as *dar al-islam*, for the reason that Muslims can live freely there, and even spoke of Muslims' burial in Europe as their definitive '*dar*'. And then there was Tariq Ramadan (1999), who introduced the term of *dar al-shahada*, 'land of giving witness', arguing that Europe no longer is a land of mission against the infidels, but a land of giving witness of one's own religious principles in practice and in action, not *against* someone else but *for* a common goal, *together* with the people with whom one shares a common destiny.

So, from being *dar al-harb*, land of conflict, and *dar al-kufr*, land of unbelief, Europe has become *dar al-hijra*, land of migration, then *dar al-ᶜahd*, land of the covenant, then *dar al-daʿwa*, land of the mission, then *dar al-shahada*, land of the witnessing, and finally simply *dar al-islam* in a full and proper sense: nothing more and nothing less than the European part of the *umma* – but in the sense of land *also* of Islam, and of Islam *among* others.

As in the case of the *dar al-islam/dar al-harb* dichotomy, many other concepts are undergoing profound changes, and are shaping the intellectual representation of Islam in Europe: *umma*, *jihad*, the various concepts related to the *halal/haram* distinction – which constitute such a large part of the self-definition of Islam, and of its consequences in terms of orthopraxis in the daily life of Muslims – and many others, including the idea of minority as *dhimmi*, sometimes applied by Muslims to themselves. As a consequence of these processes, even the legitimacy of the idea of *ijtihad*, and the social actors that can legitimately produce it (through *fatwas*, new *fiqh*, and so on), is profoundly challenging the traditional categories of interpretation of Islam. Often it is non-Muslim observers, such as Orientalists, theologians, political experts, but also anthropologists and sociologists, who seem to remain attached to the traditional meanings of these words, while Muslims seem to be more innovative, at least in practice. Quite surprisingly in fact, on the Muslim side all these innovations often seem to find no great obstacles and opposition, and do not arouse very much controversy; at least not as much as observers might expect, particularly if they are reading these processes with the static lenses offered by much of the traditional intellectual and common media production on Islam. As one of my Muslim interlocutors once commented, while talking about the fact that in Yusuf al-Qaradawi's popular tours, which I witnessed, hundreds of people were always asking him the same, sometimes trivial, questions: 'do you know why they always ask the same questions? Because they keep hoping for different answers.' And sometimes they do hear them, and if they do not, they search for them elsewhere, and if they do not find them elsewhere, they supply them themselves, through a personal *ijtihad*, even if it is not really considered as such; sometimes even before new actors, like those analysed in this book, start doing it explicitly. There does not seem to be the need for an official reopening of the gate of *ijtihad*, in a sort of 'Vatican Council' producing the necessary *aggiornamento*, as happened for the Catholic Church, and as sometimes is asked for by opinion leaders. Things are simply happening, in a more ordinary way, but with no lesser consequences.

Seeking knowledge about Islam: different demands

Not every Muslim born in Europe is in search of knowledge about Islam. We can divide the Muslim populations in Europe roughly into three parts. They represent different tendencies that will continue to be present: no single one will cancel out or dominate the other.

A substantial part of the Muslim populations is simply being (or wants to be) progressively integrated, or, to put it differently, is and will more and more be progressively similar to the autochthonous populations of which it is becoming part: this happens also in matters that concern religious belief and practice.

This means that among Muslims one can observe the same tendencies observable in every other religious milieu in Europe, where beliefs are passing through important transformations, and practice, of the traditional kind, is diminishing. A recent report written on behalf of the European Parliament (Dassetto, Ferrari, and Maréchal 2007) estimates that probably only one third of the Muslim populations of Europe actively practice their religion in some way: this means that two thirds do not, that the majority do not seek (new, different) religious knowledge – they may have a vague secondary interest in it and be happy if they find it, possibly to use it for their sons and daughters (they are a possible open market), but they are apparently not involved in the active search for, and production and transmission of, religious knowledge. This is a rough and inevitably contestable estimate, but the numbers in this case are less important than the argument.

Another segment of the Muslim populations is, for the opposite reason, not interested in the quest for (new) Islamic knowledge: because it believes that its traditional beliefs and practices constitute the perfect Islam, or in any case the kind of Islam with which it identifies. Its members are a segment that often lock themselves up in their religious and ethnic ghettos, and the Islamic knowledge they cultivate is that of their countries of origin, of their language of origin, with their imams and codes of behaviour *à dénomination d'origine controlée*, with their books and TV programmes with certificates of origin, and so on. This segment of the Muslim populations is primarily of the first generation of migrants: destined to become smaller; even each new wave of immigration results in a new 'first generation'. Due to the force of inertia their attitude remains present also among the following generations.[8]

These 'traditional' Muslims often constitute the most conspicuous segment of the Muslim population, or at any rate the most visible segment, and it receives disproportionate media attention. It is particularly this segment that is relatively often involved in clashes of cultural values and has caused incomprehension among the European public. Typically these are the people who keep speaking in their original languages (thus showing their extraneousness to European eyes), who dress, eat, and marry differently, who educate their children differently, who do not like at least some common Western values and practices, who more often produce incidents of miscommunication, and so on. This does not mean that the dimension of change is absent: it is an illusion, even if people believe in it, to hope that a tree transplanted in a completely different ground and climate will grow in the same way. In this sense this is not just cultural reproduction, but it is in any case transformation, at least in its consequences: but this is more an unexpected secondary effect than a desire and a goal voluntarily constructed.

These 'traditional' attitudes, or this brand of Islamic knowledge, are widespread, not only among the first generation, and they are strengthened by new forms of transnational communication, including the new electronic media (satellite TV, Internet), and by transnational organizations. Transnationalism, in fact, does not only have innovative or progressive effects – it can simply be a new channel through which traditional views can be spread (as in the very un-innovative content of most Islamic websites, and literature in bookshops). But many of these traditional points of views are ineffective, and fail to offer explanations appropriate to the situation of Muslims in Europe, for the precise reason that they come from very different situations and contexts, in which Muslims are by definition, by default, a majority, the main if not the only admitted religious reference in the public space – Medinan situations, not Meccan ones.

There is however another part of the Muslim populations that is desperately searching for new interpretative tools, thus demanding new religious knowledge and actively promoting and producing it. This third segment does not constitute the majority, nor can it be considered in any sense more representative of newer trends. The quest for new interpretations is, most of the time, related to efforts to integrate into the societies in which they live, and not to remain separated. In any case, it is their way to find their place in European societies, constructing their religious identities in different forms, which need elaboration and, in many ways, a creative attitude. In their case, the production of Islamic knowledge is or can also often be a way of positioning themselves in the European or national public sphere, a means of expressing cultural diversity so as not to be like others but be together with others, playing the same games. Not by chance do they normally do this through the language of the country they live in (which for the second and later generations is anyway the language they know best). In this respect they have the same interests, the same demands, and the same need for answers as converts, together with whom, contrary to their fathers, they are working in the same line (see Allievi 1998). There is considerable originality in the contribution of the European situation, and of European Muslim social actors and intellectuals, to the production of autochthonous European knowledge and new discourses about Islam (Dassetto 2000). This can be noticed in books, cassettes, magazines, radio, and TV programmes, but also in *khutbas*, and in the discourses that can be heard in the associative networks. It is possible to observe in these various media how new contents that are specifically Islamic *and* European are emerging.

It is important to note that there is another important aspect of these processes: their transnationalization.[9] These social phenomena cannot be studied, observed, or measured by using the traditional approach of national-level case studies, marked by the borders of the different countries. Processes involving communication flows, including the production and dissemination of Islamic knowledge, can only be properly understood if we adopt a transnational perspective. The links between Muslim communities and their countries of origin, as well as among Muslim communities within Europe, seem to be important elements in the current development of discourses concerning the social and political role of Muslim communities. They are also crucial to their theological status as minorities not living in Muslim countries, not exposed to an accepted common religious authority, and with no possibility of referring to a shared religious law. In this sense, plurality (which is not only internal to Europe, representing diversities transplanted into the new context, but also external, transnational) constitutes an opportunity rather than an obstacle for the production of Islamic knowledge and its dissemination. It represents a source of different solutions for the problems encountered, rather than a problem in itself, even if religious representatives, whose starting point is often an implicit idea of internal homogeneity, do not always like to interpret it as such.[10]

What seems important to underline here is that these transnational dynamics do not only go from a 'there' identified with Muslim countries to a 'here' identifying Muslim minorities (or simply Muslim groups and individuals) coming from their countries of origin but settled in Europe. They also go in the opposite direction, and there is an important role played by these cultural and religious feedback effects that has not yet been sufficiently analyzed by scholars and researchers. And this element is also – I have the impression – profoundly related to the production of Islamic knowledge in Europe, how it happens, and the effects it has: 'here' and 'there'.

Islamic voices: many media, little knowledge?

The production and transmission of Islamic knowledge take place through various media. The most important of these, the least studied but the most widespread, and still probably the most effective, is that of oral transmission. Orality is not only typical of most forms of daily transmission of knowledge, including religious knowledge, within the family and peer groups. Much of the transmission of Islamic knowledge, including the processes of production of Islamic knowledge in Europe, is also primarily oral, be it in the form of personal counselling given by imams and other ulama, Friday sermons, communications at religious meetings and festivals, in social, political, and religious networks, and through various modern media such as television, radio, video, and audio cassettes. Many Orientalists and other scholars have commented on the intensely oral and aural character of Islamic civilization. It is therefore perhaps surprising that there has been so little study of these oral communications among Muslims in Europe. We may speculate about the reasons for this neglect: an academic tradition that values written over oral records, insufficiently developed research tools, and the relative difficulty of observing and recording these oral communications.

Other media play important roles: Muslim media in Europe, including transnational ones, which play a significant and underestimated role as a means of building Muslim communities, as a way of maintaining links with the countries of origin, and globally as a way of building delocalized (or newly localized) Islamic knowledge (Muslim voices); and the news on Muslims conveyed by the general and specialized media, as an instrument for reading and interpreting these cultures (European voices on Islam and Muslims; on both see Maréchal, Allievi, Dassetto, and Nielsen 2003). These media are a sounding box for problems and the construction of criteria to interpret them, and are a powerful tool to construct a collective imaginary. In a certain sense, even more than on the reality of the social processes under way, it is on their perception that much of the direction that they take and their success depends. This aspect is also of fundamental importance when we come to policies on Islam: which, more than influencing the imaginary, to a great extent *depend* on it.

What effect do the media – particularly those produced by Muslims – have on the production of Islamic knowledge? Is there a relationship, suggested by McLuhan's famous slogan, between the medium and the message? Are there any changes in the latter? The answer apparently is not univocal. On the one hand we have new leaders who are using the old media (such as books) and derive their legitimacy from them, and on the other hand there are traditional leaders using the new media (satellite television and the Internet). But apart from the means, can we say that new, specifically European Islamic contents are appearing through European Muslim media or European media in general? The answer is probably yes, but it needs a more careful analysis and more empirical research for this to be demonstrated. The signs are in fact contradictory.

European ears: selective views on Islam and Muslims, and their feedbacks on Muslim populations

Muslims have settled in Europe. But the image we have of them is for the greater part not made by them. Is not even *based* on them. This process is so much in contrast with the idea we have of our sources of information that it deserves some reflection.

Discourses about Islam are not only, and not even mainly, the product of Muslim interlocutors and social actors. There is an overwhelming production of discourses about Islam that are becoming discourses about Muslims, and particularly Muslims in Europe, that are produced by non-Muslims, but are having important effects on the (often problematic) view of the settlement and the presence of Islam that European public opinions do have. These discourses are having important effects also on Muslims, and on the production of Islamic knowledge.

Another surprising observation is the often complete lack of any empirical basis for statements concerning Islam. In this way of thinking (or absence of thought) a single event is enough to indicate a tendency, through 'a common process of fabrication of stereotypes, in which an ethnographic fragment is perceived as an ethnologic type'.[11] When a husband beats his wife or a father forces his daughter into marriage, the first inclination is to explain this behaviour as essentially inherent in Islam, and therefore inherent in Muslims, and therefore inherent in Muslims settled in Europe, and therefore in their children, and so on, from one therefore to another, in a concatenation of causalities that, instead of needing to be proved, is considered its own proof.

Where Islam is concerned, it appears not necessary to have a personal empirical knowledge of the facts in order to take part in the public debate – it is the opinion that counts; and not, as is an important journalistic principle, opinions rigorously separated from the facts, but opinions *instead* of facts. Thus it has been possible for certain so-called experts to contribute to shaping public opinion about Islam by pontificating about what goes on in the mosques of Europe without ever having set foot in any of them.[12]

The common lack of a socio-historical perspective and of a diachronic dimension (examples of which are the implicit assumption that nothing relevant has changed in the countries of origin, the common neglect of the rupture between the first and second generation in the host country, and so on), as well as the fact that links with the country and culture of origin are considered obvious, unidirectional, and not subject to reinterpretation, are but a few illustrations of this way of thinking.

Obviously theoretical perspectives and systems, and the need for abstraction, are legitimate and implicit in the process of understanding all phenomena, social phenomena included. But we must be aware that this way of seeing things is not only a part, and *only* a part, of the complexity of the social phenomena concerned (in this case, there is a simple solution: do the other part, and then add them together). There is also a *cognitive* problem that needs to be taken into account.

Muslims, like anyone else, learn about their situation in Europe through experience. Even when they are dealing with their own systems of belief, and starting to understand their situation from them, they are obliged to study and apply them differently, given the different context. On the contrary, when we deal with Muslims' systems of belief, we often start from the system, and we tend to deduce the situation of Muslims from these systems. But systems have not at all a systematic effect in men and women's lives, in their experience, and even in their comprehension and self-comprehension, and they do not systematize them. Systems are often incomplete, contradictory; in any case the use men and women make of them is incomplete, contradictory, ambiguous, partial, and instrumental, as is the way they belong to them, and the feelings they have towards their beliefs. Orthopraxis comes before orthodoxy. This means that we cannot simply deduce persons from systems. The problem is that this is a mistake we often make where Islam is concerned, especially in the case of controversial issues (to quote randomly: the *hijab*, polygamy, female circumcision, gender roles and relations, separation between politics and religion, probably also the whole issue of fundamentalism and terrorism), to such a degree that this attitude should be an object of interest and a field of study in itself. Only from this could we learn a lot about the way our societies deal with certain cultural and religious issues, and with the persons belonging to these different cultures and religions.

The view we have is selective, in the sense that it chooses certain characteristics of the actor, or of his/her image, more or less well understood, and forgets or misunderstands others. The role of this selective perception in shaping the image of a social, cultural, and religious actor in a wider context is decisive also because there is an important feedback effect to the actor himself, who is obliged to deal with this image, which becomes part of his/her construction, and take it into account: he or she will always be obliged to respond to it, and to have an attitude in respect to it. The underestimation of this element is the source of many hermeneutical incidents and cultural misunderstandings regarding Islam. We can observe these effects, and not only in a relatively abstract cultural-religious framework. They are very concrete and immediate, and can be seen and measured at an everyday level.

Perception and self-perception therefore influence the construction and reproduction of European knowledge about Islam. An interesting paradox is that this does not necessarily mean that it helps in Europeanizing Islamic knowledge produced in Europe. As a not completely exceptional case, we might say that the socio-cultural (and even academic) perception of Islam as an external reality, imported but not really integrated (or even incompatible, as in some cultural, political, and religious theorizations), taken for granted despite the social and cultural processes which might be observable (if they were observed), can even push in the opposite direction. In this sense, the role of European ears is decisive in determining the internal changes of Muslim social actors, pushing them in one direction or another: to put it bluntly, that of integration or that of separation and opposition or even rejection.

Nevertheless, the push factor of the European interpretation can also go in the direction of endogenization. Muslim social and religious actors and producers of Islamic knowledge, in order to be understood, also need to use cognitive categories that can easily be understood by society at large: this too leads to a certain degree of Europeanization of knowledge about Islam in the categories used (including philosophical and theological language and references, but also internal organization, ways of institutionalization, and so on)[13] and in the end, in terms of the final results and the image of it.

Selective perception also has another effect. Not only can it *choose* between different aspects of Islam, and push in one direction or another. It simply does not *see* certain aspects of it. This can happen in particular with aspects of Islamic knowledge that are less visible in the public space (popular religious practices, for instance): these do exist, but they are not seen in the same percentage. In this case probably the gap between production of Islamic knowledge and its interpretation can lead to a sort of double standard, or a double image, or even a double discourse: one internal, and one possibly addressed to the public space, the media, political actors, and the like.

The issues concerning reality and perception, of course, do not relate only to Muslims and the production of Islamic knowledge in Europe. They are common phenomena in our society, more common and more visible (but, paradoxically, not often *seen* and stressed) the more the (post-)modern society in which we live is a mediated, if not virtual, reality. The phenomenon, then, is not entirely new, but its dimensions are. And, as we have learned, especially through the severe lessons of ecology – often too late, after some environmental disaster – quantitative limits, if exceeded, can imply qualitative problems and changes.

In the case of Islam in Europe it is a whole cultural and religious history that is implied, which has very much to do with the whole idea of the identity of Europe (in cultural, religious, historical, political terms). This is what makes this issue more sensitive and delicate than others, in terms of the possible consequences of misunderstandings (Allievi 2007).

Conclusions

Having referred to numerous problems of misperception and misunderstanding between Muslims of Europe and majority ('host') societies, we have to take into account that, owing to the time factor, many things are changing, and we should be aware of the dynamic of developments among and inside Muslim populations in Europe.

The degree of integration of Muslim groups and communities into wider society, as well as of the individuals which constitute them, and the level of their self-organization and mobilization, is making rapid strides with the passing of time. Significant processes of recognition and institutionalization are taking place, especially at the local (in any case at the sub-national) level, more often than at the state level. And the level of awareness and knowledge of society at large, despite the still prevalently negative attitude of the media (which is also subject to change, incidentally) towards this new presence in the social landscape, is also increasing. In the medium term this may mean that a process of normalization of the Islamic presence (in the sense of considering it normal – and becoming norm, maybe) should take place in Europe. From the perception of pathology that frequently surrounds it, we might shift to one of physiology: no more than an element, even if more significant than others, of the process of accelerated cultural pluralization that the Old Continent is at present undergoing.

Obviously this does not mean – as it does sometimes in some excessively optimistic presentations – that the process is or will be peaceful, without social and cultural conflict. We have already experienced that it is not so. But it could mean that these conflicts might progressively be understood as conflicts we can deal with, as many others (society *is* conflictual, after all): not necessarily the Huntingtonian clash of civilizations, and the final (deadly) combat between the Western hero and the global Muslim terrorist (in theological terms dear to an incredibly widespread Protestant literature on Islam, the Armageddon), even though sometimes this runs the risk of being a particularly effective example of a self-fulfilling prophecy.

Notes

1 Typical examples are Gerholm and Lithman 1988, Shadid and van Koningsveld 1991 and 2002, Lewis and Schnapper 1992, Waardenburg et al. 1994, Nonneman, Niblock, and Szajkowski 1996, Vertovec and Peach 1997, Haddad 2002, Haddad and Smith 2002, Hunter 2002, Cesari and McLoughlin 2005, Al-Azmeh and Fokas 2007.

2 Local studies are too numerous to quote. They constitute an important literature worth consulting when in search of empirical data; too often, however, they are lacking in theoretical profundity. Influential studies on national situations, which from different point of views have opened the debate on the Islamic presence in their respective countries, include Dassetto and Bastenier 1984 for Belgium, Kepel 1987 for France, Landman 1992 for Holland, Allievi and Dassetto 1993 for Italy (with a revision after ten years in Allievi 2003), and Lewis 1994 for Britain.

3 Among others Dassetto and Bastenier 1988, Nielsen 1992, Shadid and van Koningsveld 1995, Dassetto 1996, Allievi 2002, Cesari 2004, and the state of the art in Maussen 2007.

4 One of the few such attempts at synthesis is the study by Maréchal, Allievi, Dassetto and Nielsen 2003. This study also provided part of the data for a more recent report for the European Parliament Dassetto, Ferrari, and Maréchal 2007. A new Eurislam project funded by the European Commission was recently started (in 2008): limited to six countries only, its results are expected by 2011.

5 This is the thrust of the argument in many of his texts, from Ramadan 1999 up to his increasingly more lucid recent publications, notably Ramadan 2004.

6   More details concerning this part in Allievi 2002.
7   I follow here van Koningsveld 1996. See also Fierro 1995.
8   Inertia and imitation do not mean immobility and absence of change. But they can have a great power in motivating people or justifying their behaviours: an attitude more than a consequence.
9   On which see Allievi and Nielsen 2003; see also Mandaville 2001.
10 This presumption of homogeneity, and the perception of internal and external diversity as matters of pathology rather than physiology, incidentally, is not peculiar to Islam, and not even to religions only. It is a more general epistemological problem: we tend to start our understanding of cultural and social phenomena from a presumption of homogeneity, interpreting plurality as a sort of addition to an initial 'one'. But plurality as a starting point brings – and needs – a different logic, and using it as a starting point might presuppose a different way of reasoning.
11 Al-Azmeh 2004, in which the polemic is addressed both against Gellner-type academic essentialism and the common mediatization of Islam.
12 As an example we can quote the case of a well known anti-Islamic personality in Italy who, after having presented his opinions about (against) Islam in a television debate, was asked by the anchorman if he had ever actually met a Muslim, and simply answered: 'No, but it is not important ...' The implicit message was that, because Islam is 'like that', Muslims inevitably will also be that way. The rest (life, reality) does not matter.
13 For instance: the creation of umbrella organizations at a national level similar to other minorities (Jews, for instance), the 'Christianization' of the figure of the imam, and the 'churchization' of mosques in terms of roles and functions (celebration of marriages, which is extraneous to Islamic traditions in countries of origin, etc.), presence and visibility of women, etc. On mosques and mosque conflicts see Allievi 2009.

Bibliography

Al-Azmeh Aziz (2004) *L'obscurantisme postmoderne et la question musulmane*, Paris: Sindbad-Actes Sud.
Al-Azmeh, Aziz and Fokas, Effie (eds) (2007) *Islam in Europe: Diversity, Identity and Influence*, Cambridge: Cambridge University Press.
Allievi, Stefano (1998) *Les convertis à l'islam: les nouveaux musulmans d'Europe*, Paris: L'Harmattan.
Allievi Stefano (2002) *Musulmani d'occidente: tendenze dell'islam europeo*, Roma: Carocci.
Allievi, Stefano (2003) *Islam italiano*, Torino: Einaudi.
Allievi, Stefano (2005a) 'How the Immigrant has Become Muslim: Public Debates on Islam in Europe', *Revue Européenne des Migrations Internationales*, 21: 135–63.
Allievi, Stefano (2005b) 'Conflicts, Cultures and Religions: Islam in Europe as a Sign and Symbol of Change in European Societies', *Yearbook of Sociology of Islam*, 6: 18–27.
Allievi, Stefano (2007) Le trappole dell'immaginario: Islam e occidente, Udine: Forum.
Allievi, Stefano (2009) *Controversies on Mosques in Europe: Policy Issues And Trends*, London: Alliance Publishing Trust/Network of European Foundations.
Allievi, Stefano and Dassetto, Felice (1993) *Il ritorno dell'islam: I musulmani in Italia*, Roma: Edizioni Lavoro.
Allievi, Stefano and Nielsen, Jorgen (eds) (2003) *Muslim Networks and Transnational Communities in and across Europe*, Leiden: Brill.
Bencheikh, Soheib (1998) *Marianne et le Prophète: l'Islam dans la France laïque*, Paris: Grasset.

Cesari, Jocelyne (2004) *When Islam and Democracy Meet: Muslims in Europe and in the United States*, Palgrave: Macmillan.

Cesari, Jocelyne and McLoughlin, Sean (2005) *European Muslims and the Secular State*, Aldershot: Ashgate.

Dassetto, Felice (1996) *La construction de l'islam européen: approche socio-anthropologique*, Paris: L'Harmattan.

Dassetto, Felice (ed.) (2000) *Paroles d'islam: Individus, sociétés et discourses dans l'islam européen contemporain/Islamic Words: Individuals, Societies and Discourses in Contemporary European Islam*, Paris: Maisonneuve & Larose.

Dassetto, Felice and Bastenier, Albert (1984) *L'islam transplanté: vie et organisation des minorities musulmanes de Belgique*, Antwerp: Epo.

Dassetto, Felice and Bastenier, Albert (1988) *Europa: nuova frontiera dell'Islam*, Roma: Edizioni Lavoro.

Dassetto, Felice, Ferrari, Silvio and Maréchal, Brigitte (2007) *Islam in the European Union: What's at Stake in the Future?*, Strasbourg: European Parliament.

Fierro, Maribel (1995) 'La emigración en el islam. Conceptos antiguos, nuevos problemas', in M. Abumalham (ed.) *Comunidades islámicas en Europa,* Madrid: Trotta.

Gerholm, Thomas and Lithman, Yngve G. (eds) (1988) *The New Islamic Presence in Western Europe*, London and New York: Mansell.

Haddad, Yvonne (ed.) (2002) *Muslims in the West: From Sojourners to Citizens*, Oxford: Oxford University Press.

Haddad, Yvonne and Smith, Jane I. (2002) Muslim Minorities in the West: Visible and Invisible, Walnut Creek: Altamira.

Hunter, Shireen (ed.) (2002) *Islam, Europe's Second Religion: The New Social, Cultural and Political Landscape*, Westport: Praeger.

Kechat, Larbi (1998) 'Pour un islam humaniste', *Esprit*, no. 1.

Kepel, Gilles (1987) *Les banlieues de l'Islam: naissance d'une religion en France*, Paris: Seuil.

Landman, Nico (1992) *Van Mat tot Minaret: De Institutionalisering van de Islam in Nederland*, Amsterdam: VU Uitgeverij.

Lewis, Bernard (1996) *Cultures in Conflict: Christians, Muslims and Jews in the Age of Discovery*, Oxford: Oxford University Press.

Lewis, Bernard and Schnapper, Dominique (eds) (1992) *Musulmans en Europe*, Poitiers: Actes Sud.

Lewis, Philip (1994) *Islamic Britain: Religion, Politics and Identity among British Muslims*, London: I.B. Tauris.

Mandaville, Peter (2001) *Transnational Muslim Politics: Reimagining the Umma*, London: Routledge.

Maréchal, Brigitte, Allievi, Stefano, Dassetto, Felice and Nielsen, Jorgen (2003) *Muslims in the Enlarged Europe*, Leiden: Brill.

Maussen, Marcel (2007) *The Governance of Islam in Western Europe: A State of the Art Report*, IMISCOE Working Paper, no. 16.

Nielsen, Jorgen (1992) *Muslims in Western Europe*, Edinburgh: Edinburgh University Press.

Nonneman, Gerd, Niblock, Tim and Szajkowski, Bronislaw (eds) (1996) *Muslim Communities in the New Europe*, Reading: Ithaca Press.

Ramadan, Tariq (1999) *To be a European Muslim*, Leicester: Islamic Foundation.

Ramadan, Tariq (2004) *Western Muslims and the Future of Islam*, Oxford: Oxford University Press.

Said, Edward (1978) *Orientalism*, New York: Vintage Books.

Shadid, Wasif and van Koningsveld, Sjoerd (1995) *Religious Freedom and the Position of Islam in the European Union*, Kampen: KokPharos.

Shadid, Wasif and van Koningsveld, Sjoerd (eds) (1991) *The Integration of Islam and Hinduism in Western Europe*, Kampen: KokPharos.

Shadid, Wasif and van Koningsveld, Sjoerd (eds) (2002) *Religious Freedom and the Neutrality of the State: The Position of Islam in the European Union*, Kampen: KokPharos.

van Koningsveld, Sjoerd (1996) 'Loyalty to a Non-Muslim Government: An Analysis of Islamic Normative Discussions and of the Views of Some Contemporary Islamicists', in W. Shadid and S. van Koningsveld (eds) *Political Participation and Identities of Muslims in Non-Muslim states*, Kampen: KokPharos.

Vertovec, Steven and Peach, Ceri (eds) (1997) *Islam in Europe: The Politics of Religion and Community*, London and New York: Macmillan and St. Martin's Press.

Waardenburg, Jacques et al. (1994) *I musulmani nella società europea*, Torino: Edizioni della Fondazione Agnelli.

3 An emerging European Islam
The case of the Minhajul Qur'an in the Netherlands

M. Amer Morgahi

Introduction

The Minhajul Qur'an (Path of the Qur'an) is a traditionalist Islamic movement of Pakistani origin that in the Netherlands has succeeded better than most other movements in reaching out across ethnic and national boundaries, and appears to have an especially strong appeal for young Muslims of various backgrounds. The Minhajul Qur'an (henceforth: MQ) is not a numerically large movement – it controls only three mosques and one simple prayer room in the Netherlands – but deserves attention because of its flexibility and the emergence of localized cultural forms in its public activities.

Let me begin this narrative of the MQ in the Netherlands with two vignettes that describe two different settings within which this movement operates. They not only depict two different generations of the MQ, but also tell us something about the location, expectations, and aspirations of these two generations. In the course of my fieldwork I participated in various religious gatherings of the MQ that were targeting a broader public. One such occasion was the annual *'urs* or death anniversary of Data Gunj Bukhsh, a twelfth-century Sufi saint buried in Lahore. The all-male gathering, mostly first-generation Pakistani migrants, resembled similar gatherings that can be observed in any South Asian Barelwi mosque. However, there was one notable difference: all the invited speakers, with the exception of one, were lay scholars who had no traditional madrasa education. Their speeches, although in Urdu, showed their familiarity with Dutch society. However, their speeches were interspersed with stories of inter-Barelwi rivalries and anti-Deobandi rhetoric.

In the same time period I attended a meeting of the Minhaj Youth League (MYL) that was held in the Muslim prayer room of the Erasmus University Medical Faculty. It was a preparatory meeting for the *Milad* Festival that the MYL was planning to hold on the birthday of the Prophet Mohammad. This was a 'mixed' gathering as it included female as well as male students; moreover, not all of the female students wore a headscarf. Further, the meeting was conducted entirely in Dutch. The participants were ethnically mixed, including, besides Pakistanis, students of Moroccan and ethnic Dutch Muslim backgrounds. The chairman of the MYL, who was presiding over the meeting, had informed the participants in advance on the various issues that were to be discussed. These issues were discussed freely and (as he later proudly explained to me) democratically, without anyone imposing views upon the others. On some of the issues a decision was taken, while others were postponed for consideration in a future meeting. One of the decisions taken was to place the *Milad* Festival in the context of a broader programme of cultural festivities taking place in Rotterdam – a clear effort to locate the event in the broader multicultural life of the city.

The two vignettes illustrate the contrasting ways in which two different generations of followers of the same movement express their religious identity in a European context. The difference is due to the contrasting experiences of these two generations in the Dutch setting. The religious activities of the first generation are mostly limited to the mosque, where religious discourse is still predominantly expressed in the language and idiom of that first generation of immigrants. The younger generation has recourse to a more diverse range of localities, and while its gatherings are structured differently, it, most importantly, appears to have adopted a more self-conscious religious identity that it relates explicitly to the social and cultural environment. Its members exemplify, in their negotiations with inherited tradition and cultural environment, the shift towards what some have called 'European Islam' (e.g. Nielsen 1992: 39). This phenomenon entails a process of accommodating religious identity in the European context in order to ease social participation in European societies. Other observers have analysed such developments as part of a broader on-going process of 'internal reforms' within 'Muslim traditions', and have emphasized that this internal dynamic of traditions was not interrupted, but in fact continued with the migration process and emerging influence of religious movements in the Western context (Amir-Moazami and Salvatore 2003).

These processes of accommodation and internal reform, sometimes also called 'localization of Islam' in Europe, became salient in the case of the MQ, when the organization established its first mosques (and even more so with the establishment of a Sufi lodge in Nuneaton in the UK). The argument that I wish to put forward is that religious movements rooted in 'folk Islam' with its Sufi inflections appear to find it easier to adapt their message to new environments, and to adopt cultural forms that enhance this process of accommodation more so than the more scripturalist movements. During such processes the local idioms of social and religious integration are used to localize the message; however, in this very process of localization also lie the germs of a public manifestation of religion that challenges the supposed private–public dichotomy in the role of religion in European societies.

Studying these processes of localization, I focus on the movement of the Minhajul Qur'an, which has its networks in almost all of the West-European states, with a relatively strong presence among youth and women. In this chapter I examine the way the MQ performs in the Netherlands. I shall also deal with the implications this could have for perceptions of Islam in Europe. I first present a brief description of the Pakistani and Surinamese community in Holland where the MQ operates. Thereafter, I will provide an introduction to the MQ in the Netherlands, followed by a brief description of the MQ discourse, and the nature of its leadership patterns in both generations. Finally, the transnational character of the movement is discussed.

Pakistani and Surinamese communities in the Netherlands

An unofficial estimate puts the size of the Pakistani community in the Netherlands at about 18,500 (Centraal Bureau voor de Statistiek 2006). The majority of these people are originally from the smaller cities of Eastern Punjab and the adjoining areas of Kashmir in Pakistan. Mostly of low educational background, the community grew through a process of chain migration. The Pakistani organizations in the Netherlands are either mosque-based or social welfare organizations. Revolving around financially affluent figures, these mosque bodies are further a conglomerate of family networks, which are linked to other families belonging to the same cities or areas of origin.

The size of the Muslim–Hindustani community in the Netherlands is roughly 35,000. The Hindustanis are migrants from the former Dutch colony of Surinam. The Hindustanis were actually brought over from northern India to Surinam in the nineteenth century as contract labourers to work on sugar-cane plantations. On the eve of independence of Surinam in 1975, many of them migrated to the Netherlands. Most Hindustanis in the Netherlands are Hindus, but there is a sizeable Muslim minority. Due to the missionary activities of Barelwi ulama in Surinam, many Muslim Hindustanis came under Barelwi influence. A small minority among them are Ahmadiya (both the Lahore and the Qadian Ahmadiya are represented).

The majority of the Pakistani and Muslim–Hindustani organizations are affiliated with the Barelwi stream of Sunni Islam, which is associated with Sufism and the popular practices related to shrines. This stream owes its name to the ulama in South Asia who follow the school of Ahmed Raza Khan Barelwi (1854–1921), and who call themselves *ahl-i sunnat wa 'l jama‘at*. The Barelwi ulama profess belief in miracles, the intercessionary powers of saints, and the dispensing of amulets and charms (Alavi 1987: 84). Usha Sanyal, the author of an important study of the Barelwi movement, makes a distinction between the shrine-visitors and the Barelwi ulama, and argues that not every visitor to Sufi shrines is a Barelwi and vice versa (Sanyal 1996: 11).

The belief in the intercession by saints, and in the various magical and devotional practices associated with Sufi shrines, which are allowed and even endorsed by the Barelwi ulama, are criticized as un-Islamic by the ulama associated with the reformist Deobandi movement, named after the reformist madrasa in Deoband, established in 1867 (Metcalf 1982). One of the most important religious events of the year for Barelwis is the *Milad*, or the commemoration of the birth of the Prophet Muhammad. Deobandis strongly object to the Barelwis' belief that the Prophet is spiritually present at *Milad* celebrations, and moreover, that he will personally intercede on behalf of his devotees on the Day of Judgement. The Ahl-i Hadith, an even more radically puritan reformist movement in South Asia, are more fiercely critical of traditional practices and reject all that smacks of

local culture. These debates have been carried to the Netherlands, although reformists are a minority among the Pakistani community. Ulama preaching in the one
Deobandi mosque, and the small congregation of Ahl-i Hadith followers in The
Hague, can be heard to inveigh against the devotional practices of the Barelwi
majority.

The MQ emerged within the Barelwi stream of Islam and accepts all Barelwi
premises. The early intellectual life of Allama Tahirul Qadri, the founder of the
MQ, shows his intensive participation in debates between the two main streams
of Pakistani Islam, in which he defended the Barelwi positions against the
Deobandis (Rafiq 1996: 231–3). He was not in full agreement with all his Barelwi
colleagues, however, and soon after Qadri founded the MQ, in Lahore in October
1980, differences between the MQ and other Barelwi ulama came to the surface.
Qadri started criticizing these ulama for their continuous sectarian rhetoric and
castigating their madrasas for spreading archaic religious knowledge that cannot
cope with the problems of modern society.

Through an institute that he founded, Qadri started publishing lectures and
books, and producing audio and video recordings of his lectures. These materials
covered different aspects of daily life, and through them Qadri tried to answer
everyday problems according to the teachings of the Qur'an and *sunnah* (sayings
and doings of the Prophet). These publications, along with his regular appearance
on television, helped him create a network of religious teaching at the informal
level. Later, Qadri established the Minhajul Qur'an University in Lahore in 1986. In
this university, modern subjects are also taught alongside the traditional *dars-i-nizami*
syllabus, and its graduates not only receive the informal title of *fazil* (pl. *fuzla*; a
common South Asian term for scholar), but also an MA degree in Islamic studies.
A selected number of these *fuzla* is sent to the MQ centres abroad.[1] These MQ *fuzla*
differ from traditional Barelwi ulama in having received an education in modern
subjects besides the traditional Islamic disciplines; moreover, many of them are
well-trained public speakers, with good rhetorical skills.

The MQ also developed a much more elaborate organizational structure than
is common among the Barelwis. The mosques it controlled became more than
just houses of worship but also centres for holding various social and cultural
activities, notably those for and by youth and women – two categories that hardly
find a place in traditional Barelwi mosques. The intention to turn the mosques
into centres with multiple functions is also indicated by the term that the MQ uses
to refer to them: *idara*, which can be translated as 'office' or 'centre'. Traditional
Barelwi ulama looked upon these changes, especially the greater participation of
women, with suspicion. In their view even women's participation in congregational prayer is not advisable because it may lead to a degeneration of morals.

In the diaspora context, the MQ has, if anything, given even more priority to
involve youth and especially women in its activities. This was particularly important for women, because of the non-availability in Europe of traditional venues of
veneration and ritual performance associated with popular Islam, which make up
most of women's public participation in religion. Thus writing on the Pakistanis in
Norway, among whom she distinguishes followers of both 'popular' and 'normative'

Islam, Ahlberg speaks of a process of 'masculinization' of religious performance, which is especially conspicuous among the former, since their women are totally excluded from public religious life such as they had in Pakistan. (This was before the emergence of the MQ.) The adherents of 'normative' Islam, on the other hand, adopted a highly defensive attitude towards the host society (Ahlberg 1990: 247–9). Other observers have explained the relative success of Islamists and reform-ists, compared to traditionalists and popular Islam in the context of the diaspora, through their attention to institution-building and their deliberate outreach to youth (Geaves 2000: 220). In its insistence on women's activities, the MQ resembles more the reformists than the other Barelwis. However, recently, more traditional ulama have become increasingly aware of the importance of women's participa-tion in the mosque, and accordingly are opening it up for them in the European context.

Behind the mistrust of the MQ's activities among the traditional ulama and their followers, a broader spectrum of anxieties of the elder generation of Pakistanis can be detected. The nature of these anxieties is related to what Werbner calls the dilemma of the older generation. In the alien context of modern urban living and the 'magnetizing attractions of Western popular culture', the older generation faces the task to 'preserve and recreate community not merely as a domain of religious observance but also as a site of fun, leisure, and celebration where young Pakistani men and women can be socialized' (Werbner 2002: 223). It is a quest for a controlled socialization, through which the older generation seeks to maintain the initiative for socialization in its control. In her description, however, Werbner does not attribute an appropriate place to religion and family in this process of socialization. The family is a domain where the established norms are further developed, leading, in the words of Werbner, to a socially encapsulated culture.

The family is of central importance in the MQ's approach to the Pakistani community. It tries to involve the whole family in its *daʿwa* or missionary activ-ities. A crucial element in this is the consumption of audio-visual and other aesthetic religious material produced by the MQ. Through this material, rever-ence for the founder of the movement, and, through him, love for the Prophet is created. Furthermore, the religious aesthetics are enhanced through the use of devotional music like *qawwali* in homes and in MQ functions. More devoted members also have portraits of the founder in their homes in order to 'educate the children about the personality of our leader', as they put it. The birth of the Prophet (*Milad*) is celebrated in the homes of some families. Homes are specially decorated for the occasion while food is prepared for the guests, most of whom are families of the members of the MQ.

The importance of the family sphere is also evident in the organizational struc-ture of the MQ. A local body of the MQ consists of elders of the families of its most active members while their women are represented in the local chapter of the Minhaj Women's League. Many issues are decided at the broader 'family of the MQ' level.[2] MQ mosques provide space for the activities of women and youth. Although the MQ claims that 'women and youth are autonomous with reference to organizing their activities', its organizing body makes sure that the gender boundaries are maintained during such programmes. Behind the rhetoric of its independence, the Minhaj Women's League (MYL) only organizes programmes specifically for women. In addition, despite the presence of some competent women in the movement, the MQ organizing body is still male-dominated. Similarly, as I will explain later, the Minhaj Youth League (MYL) has its own conflicts with the older generation.

Message and activities

The activities of the MQ movement in the Netherlands include:

a)   the provision of knowledge of the Qur'an and basic Islamic teachings to Muslim children.
b)   activities for youth such as weekly sessions of *dhikr*; separate *dhikr* sessions for women; some professional programmes like basic courses in journalism, public speaking, and computer use.
c)   the organization of various religious and secular functions and activities, such as commemorating *Milad* or the birthday of the Prophet, *Ashura* or the martyrdom of Imam Hussain, the *ʿurs* or death anniversaries of some Sufi saints, *hajj* trips, *ziarat*-trips to Baghdad (to the shrine of the Sufi saint ʿAbd al-Qadir Jilani), and *mina*-bazaars or crafts exhibits for women.
d)   political activities: the MQ movement in Pakistan has a political wing called Pakistan Awami Tehreek (PAT), which is in fact a political party that had participated in the 2002 and 2007 elections. In the Netherlands, the PAT mostly organizes activities like celebrations on Pakistan Day, etc. At the same time it also networks among the diaspora Pakistanis to give financial support to its sister organizations in Pakistan. In this way it provides new spaces for the deeply politicized Pakistani community in the Netherlands. The MQ's activities in this regard target first-generation Pakistani migrants, who are otherwise marginalized in the Dutch political sphere.
e)   welfare activities, through the collection of donations such as the annual *zakat* and relief funds, to finance different educational and health projects in Pakistan run by its head-office.

In the wide range of the MQ's activities one can discern numerous elements of the traditional Barelwi tradition: *dhikr*-sessions and functions to commemorate *Milad*, *Ashura* and *ʿurs*. How, then, does the MQ distinguish itself from the Barelwi tradition? The difference lies in the new breed of ulama that the movement is producing, and the transformation of religious discourse in the Barelwi tradition that these *fuzla* are enabling.

Almost all *fuzla* of the MQ mosques are graduates of the Minhajul Qur'an University. One of the purposes of establishing the Minhaj University in Lahore is to prepare ulama who would actively work for the movement in Pakistan and abroad. The *fuzla* act as the *amir*s or directors of newly created or already established centres or *idara*s. Organizationally, the *fuzla* are subordinated to the *idara* committee. They lead Friday prayers, although for the daily prayers the MQ sometimes recruits imams from other Barelwi denominations. I found these imams in different Minhaj centres in the Netherlands, as well as in the United Kingdom.

The MQ *fuzla* differ from traditional ulama with regard to the educational activities that they organize for women and youth, and also as concerns some aspects of their behaviour and interaction with others. They organize for these groups separate classes that meet two hours a week. Most of the participants are members of the MWL and the MYL. The themes discussed in these classes range from basic items of beliefs, to various social and religious issues. The language used in these classes is Urdu, since not all *fuzla* can easily understand Dutch.

It is the direct access to the ulama and the somewhat informal atmosphere during class sessions that make them attractive for most of the youth and women, many of whom appreciate this attitude of 'understanding and not that of rejection' in contrast to that of the majority of traditional ulama. Women can openly ask questions related to any religious and marital issue. Generally, the *fuzla* do not display an authority-conscious behaviour during these classes. Being young imams they also make an effort to maintain an informal atmosphere during these classes.

The discourse of traditional Barelwi ulama often contains strong anti-Shiᶜa invocations. The MQ *fuzla*, however, try to downplay the traditional anti-Shiᶜa polemics and seek accommodation with the Shiᶜa. The MQ founder declared the Sunni-Shiᶜa difference a mere matter of *furuᶜ* (practical rules), rather than *usul* (principles), implying that the difference was similar to that between the four Sunni legal schools, all of which are considered equally legitimate. He was, for this reason, accused by other traditionalists of creating 'a new *fitna* (dissension among the believers)'; nevertheless he continued reaching out to the Shiᶜa. The MQ movement regularly observes the day of the martyrdom of Husain, the grandson of the Prophet, who occupies a particularly revered place in Shiᶜa piety. Husain is upheld as a model for Muslims to emulate because of his readiness to sacrifice his life for the sake of the faith. The MQ has adopted the symbolism of Husain's martyrdom as valuable to all Muslims, not just the Shiᶜis, and it seeks in other ways to decrease the distance between Sunni and Shiᶜi. On the occasion of a *Milad* gathering, the director of the MQ in The Hague, Raza, who is a Minhaj University graduate, said that 'if you would eradicate the idea of the *imamat* (hereditary charismatic leadership) such as it exists in Shiᶜism, then there would be no difference left between Sunni Islam and Shiᶜism'. The MQ as a matter of principle usually invites the local Shiᶜa community to its celebrations.

The anti-sectarian message of the movement goes a step further, thus further challenging the traditional positions of the ulama both in Pakistan as well as in the diaspora. The well-known *hadith* of the Prophet that provides a basis for the traditionalists to justify their sectarianism has it that '[the Prophet said,] Christianity has been divided into 72 sects, and my *umma* will be divided into 73 sects, and only one of them will be *naji* (saved)'. Various sects have later claimed that they alone were that single saved group (*firqa najiya*), implying that all other sects would be eternally damned. The MQ has adopted a less exclusivist discourse, and gives a different interpretation of the same hadith. At a gathering in The Hague, one of the MQ ulama, Imtiaz Ahmed, challenged the common view that the Prophet had predicted that most Muslims would be led astray, and asserted that 'the number of 73 sects simply denoted *kasrat* (a multitude)', and that there are no grounds to consider all Muslims outside one's own group as doomed to perdition.

As on the issue of sectarianism, the MQ ulama in the Netherlands often adopt more accommodating positions on various other contentious issues. Thus, for instance, several MQ ulama do not consider it compulsory for men to cover their heads during prayer.[3] They justify their argument on the basis of the concept of *ʿurf* (custom): if a certain trend is adopted by a group of Muslims, and it is not harmful and does not violate the shariah, then there is no objection to adopting it. It is significant that positions such as these are unacceptable to many traditional Barelwi ulama.

The ulama and youth

It is interesting to look at the ways the second generation is confronted with the issues discussed above. How far do they reflect the teachings of the MQ ulama in their perception of Islam? What is the nature of this relationship? What kind of view of Islam or Islamic knowledge can we get through the different sources used by the youth in the MQ? What is the nature of Muslim leadership that the youth seeks to promote? In this section of the chapter I shall try to answer these and related questions on the basis of my discussions with different members of the MYL, and my observations on religious sessions organized by the movement.

Before attempting an ethnographic answer to these questions I want to place the predicament of the MQ youth within the broader studies about the Muslim youth in Europe. In this regard I specifically deal with the issues of individualization and authority-debate. Among the studies of the second generation of Muslims in Europe a major theme deals with the individualization of religious practices (Roy 1999, 2004; Cesari 2003), thus emphasizing a 'break' as a result of the migration process. Cesari, for example, observes a 'fundamental rupture' between Muslim practices in Europe and in the country of origin as a result of 'transformations in Islamic identity under way among the generations born or educated in the West'. These changes involve a 'secularization process', thereby repositioning 'Islam into the private sphere'. Thus, as a consequence of their participation in the democratic societies in the West, the process of social adaptation of Muslim minority groups has led to a decline in the 'classical religious patterns' – i.e. orientation to the mosque, the imam, etc. – among the younger generation of migrants (Cesari 2003: 260).

Studies on individualization of Muslim practices in the European context rightly distinguish a transformation of religious practices; however, to interpret this transformation as a development towards 'secularization' seems an overstatement. Some observers have commented on the constant tension between the individuality promoted by Western society and on the collectivity rooted in extended families (Cressey 2002: 48). Studies about the 'individualization of the Muslim subject' have been further criticized by scholars who have adopted the framework of 'Islam as a discursive tradition' (Asad 1986). They see the alleged 'fragmentation', of which these studies speak, as part of a historical process of 'reform of tradition', as these 'traditions' are under 'permanent internal interventions, […] since their inception' (Amir-Moazami and Salvatore 2003: 55).

I believe it is useful to examine the inter-generational debates within the MQ and vis-à-vis the larger Barelwi tradition, as part of an 'internal reform' within Barelwi Islam. Rather than postulating a break with traditional Islam as it exists in Pakistan, I try to focus on the internal dynamic of the tradition in its encounter with new social and political circumstances. With this in mind, I look at the process of adaptation on the part of the MQ within the new context. In the coming pages I will examine the discussions among the MQ youth so as to see how they have come to differ from their elders, what new questions and demands they express towards their religious authorities, and how the religious leadership of the MQ responds to these expectations.

One of my key informants is the young man I shall call Syed, who was elected president of the Minhaj Youth League in Rotterdam. Syed was born in the Netherlands; his father had come from India and become the imam of a local Surinamese mosque. Syed commented on the traditional ulama of his father's generation,

> if you went to a [traditional] mosque, then you would find yourself at such a big distance from the ulama there that you could not speak on many things that were important to you, about how you should relate to the society in which you live.

Regarding the nature of the themes that were discussed in most of the traditional mosques he said,

> you went there to get lessons in the mosque, and there was a stress [only] on ritual aspects of the religion, not on the social aspects. You learned about fasting, *salat* (prayer), and about what is allowed or not allowed in Islam, but much less attention was given to how one should treat other people, to Islamic norms, and value patterns. But there is much discussion of these issues in MQ mosques.[4]

In the beginning Syed had reservations about the *fuzla* of the MQ mosques, fearing they would be no different from the 'traditional' ulama. 'When I first went to the MQ mosque in Rotterdam for a weekly *hadith*-session for the youth, I was sceptical about the imam', he told. 'Perhaps, I thought, he may not know about the problems of the youth. His knowledge of the European society might be minimal.' However, it turned out that the imam not only had a good grounding in the Islamic sciences, but was also aware of the problems of the youth in Dutch society.

Because of this, Syed found that youth listened to him. As an example of the things that could be discussed with the imam, he cited:

> Last week someone raised the issue of chatting on the Internet, and whether you can chat with girls on issues of their interest before your marriage, and whether you can meet women before marriage. The parents of the youth would, by and large, disallow this, but the perspective of Islam, the imam told us, is that 'it is permissible for you to talk to a girl whom you are going to marry and you can also chat with her on the Internet, provided it remains within certain limits'.

It is important to note here that what mostly inspires the youth about the 'Islamic' nature of the MQ youth gatherings, is the atmosphere in which they can openly discuss different issues. In the words of Syed, '[In these gatherings] you can talk on every issue, it is very open, and you do not need to hide anything. It is what the youth mostly like: in a sense you give value to them. Islam gives this freedom of discussion, but the parents and the imams of the traditional mosques disallow it'.

The MQ imams understand the merits of dealing with youth differently in this society. As the imam of the MQ mosque in Rotterdam says:

> What we do is to provide a *pak* (pure) atmosphere; for you know that here the youth finds *burai* (immorality) all around them. ... Those things are stuck to their minds; so one must have some place where one can become *pak* (purified) of all this.[5]

Another significant point about the MQ youth gatherings is that during the discussions the frame of reference is always Dutch society. Syed is very positive about this. As he puts it:

> Our religious leader tells us how one should live in Dutch society, not from a Pakistani or Indian perspective, but from the perspective of the reality of Dutch society: the West or the Netherlands has certain values that also exist in Islam. Thus he tells us that we should take Dutch society as an example and not as an enemy. This is inspiring for the youth.[6]

The significance of such observations is that the traditional ulama are responding to the social issues that their followers, mostly youth, confront in new contexts. The need for such responses within new contexts should be seen in view of new challenges to the traditional Muslim authority in Europe. Instead of the disappearance of traditional patterns of authority, these observations point to their persistence, notwithstanding their readjusting in new settings (cf. van Bruinessen, in this volume).

New Muslim intellectuals

The discussions among the Minhaj youth reflect new perspectives on what it means to be Muslim and Dutch at the same time. Such discussions also have consequences within the movement, leading to inter-generational differences and conflicts. One such occasion of conflict between the Minhaj youth and the main MQ organization took place when the MQ objected to some gender-mixed gatherings of the Minhaj youth during their hadith-session. This event reveals the dilemma of the elder generation, mentioned earlier, in which the first generation of the MQ wanted all youth activities to take place under its gaze. It is not only a question of control, however. In addition to this, there was the question of how the two generations look at Islam and their position in Dutch society. Whereas the first generation may find gender-mixed gatherings during such hadith-sessions 'problematic', the youth do not look at it in this way, seeing no difference between such gatherings and the mixed schools they attend. Obviously one can speak of a culture clash or a generational gap between the two generations within the MQ, but one should be cautious about calling it a 'break' within the religious practices, due to the compulsions of the new context. At the junction of this 'break' I see the emergence of a new intellectual effort by new preachers, described in the literature as the 'new Muslim intellectuals (Eickelman and Piscatori 1996), who redefine Islamic practices in new settings.

These new preachers act as a lynchpin of the 'internal reform' described earlier, and they are also the motor behind the shift in bringing Islamic education outside the mosque arena – a key manifestation of Islam in Europe. Generally, these new self-styled young preachers are educated in the European school system, and are mostly self-educated in religious matters. In case of the Minhaj youth, Tasneem Sadiq, the main figure behind the organization, is a typical example of these 'new Islamic preachers' in European societies. His parents came from Pakistan, but Tasneem Sadiq was born and brought up in the Netherlands. He has for many years been president of the MYL and now acts as a mentor for the MQ youth. He received a private religious education at a Pakistani-Surinamese mosque in The Hague. Later he studied Arabic at Leiden University and Islamic Studies at the Islamic University of Rotterdam. Besides this, the literature and audiovisual material of the MQ are sources of his Islamic knowledge. Last but not least, Sadiq frequently accesses the Internet, which is an unavoidable source of Islamic knowledge for new preachers like him (interview 27 February 2004).

In the past Sadiq organized weekly hadith sessions in The Hague and Rotterdam for the MYL, conducted in Dutch. Now, he organizes these sessions through an Islamic Society in the Technical College of the Hague. He also has a discussion column about *tafsir* or Qurˤanic exegesis on the Dutch-language web-forum of the Minhaj (Minhaj.nl). Outside the mosque, these hadith sessions are a basic source of Islamic information for this group of youths. A majority of the present MYL members came into the movement through participation in these gatherings.

The nature of these Dutch-language gatherings is very democratic and is geared to promote discussion and debate. After a brief presentation of some topic, people are free to discuss all sorts of issues related to this topic and the implications for their daily lives. Describing the nature of the knowledge promoted in these gatherings, Ashraf Ashrafi, the MYL president of The Hague, notes:

> Traditionally, it is said that if you want to lead prayers you should have a beard of one *muthi* [the width of a hand] long, while in the Minhaj I have seen people with short beards leading prayers. And on such issues Tasneem Sadiq gave me satisfactory answers.[7]

The discussions in these gatherings always take Dutch society as the frame of reference. In the words of Syed,

> The emphasis is on how we as youth should follow Islam in this society. How we can accommodate or perhaps fit our Islam in this society. There is less talk about how things are going in Pakistan or India. The time of the Prophet is taken largely as an example, but more stress is paid to how the values that Islam stresses should be applied in the context of the contemporary Netherlands.

The above-mentioned Islamic society in The Hague was established by the MYL after the emergence of differences with the parent organization MQ. It was actually a brain-child of Tasneem Sadiq, and he uses it as a platform to run a fortnightly *tafsir* session. An average gathering at a *tafsir* session consists of about forty students, male and female. In every session a chapter of the Qur'an, or a part of a chapter, is recited and translated, and then its exegesis is presented verse by verse by Sadiq, using a PowerPoint presentation. He uses exegetical works of Barelwi scholars from South Asia for this purpose, including the works of Tahirul Qadri. However, his presentation of the Qur'anic exegesis is contextualized in order to make it intelligible to his audience. Thus, for instance, commenting on the translation of the Qur'anic verse: '*Did He not find you lost and guide you*' (93:07),[8] Sadiq first criticized this translation saying that the correct translation should be '*Did He not find you searching (for his love) and led He not you to your destination?*'. Sadiq then added:

> This verse was revealed when the Prophet was meditating in the cave of Hira. This was when the Prophet was in search, and what was he looking for? What were his wishes? He was in a similar situation like you young people, discovering life and asking questions about its meaning. Islam gave him the answers. And so you too, young people, if you are busy with Islam, if you do your regular prayers, then you find a certain serenity in your life. Youth is a phase of life when you are searching for something; it is always good that you ask about life: what is good and what is bad. Everyone goes through this phase and comes out of it.

Such self-reflective answers seem to be the product of the reflective attitude towards texts taught in the Western education system. However, the necessity of these self-taught new intellectuals becomes more acute when the youth do not get answers to their queries from the traditional ulama. Sadiq's own interaction with these ulama makes such situations obvious. For instance, he cites an incident of querying a traditional *ʿalim* years ago when he was studying medicine. 'I asked him what he thought of AIDS patients. His answer was that such a person is a sinner and hell is the place for him in the hereafter. I ran away and I never asked anything from him again.' Sadiq accuses the traditional ulama of mental rigidity.

The differences between the traditional ulama and the new preachers involve complex questions of legitimacy and authority. Contrasting the traditional ulama with the new preachers associated with groups like the MYL, a traditional *ʿalim* would say: 'These are quacks who consider themselves experts of Islam after reading a few books. You cannot claim to be a doctor if you have not done the full medical course. Similarly, an *ʿalim* spends a specific period of time to acquire Islamic education before he qualifies to be an *ʿalim*. On the other hand, Sadiq's relations with the MQ *fuzla* are also complicated. He cannot challenge their role and authority in the mosque as prayer leaders and spiritual guides of the community. At the same time, however, he has the upper hand when it comes to the religious and practical guidance of the youth. This latter aspect, importantly, provides the new intellectuals with the possibility of using the potential of their youthful following to organize themselves outside traditional places like mosques and madrasas and take part in the broader public arena. It is in this latter field that the new Muslim intellectuals manifest themselves fully.

New religious spheres

In my discussions with different respondents of the MQ, mostly belonging to the MYL, it became clear that the annual organization of the *Milad* festival held on the birthday of the Prophet is their most publicly significant event. Having held the event for more than ten years, the MYL looks for cooperation with other local Dutch Muslim organizations, mostly the Turkish and Moroccan. These organizations have certain elements in common: they are predominantly followers of 'popular' Sufi traditions that stress love and devotion for the person of the Prophet. In most contemporary Muslim countries, the modern celebration of *Milad* has acquired an official status, emulating the Christian celebration of the birth of Jesus. In the diaspora it is typically an event for voluntary associations to engage in; and since reformists frown upon many of the practices associated with these celebrations and claim they are not authentically Islamic, we find mostly the traditionalist associations involved in organizing *Milad* festivals.

In the past years, the MQ youth have organized the *Milad* festival using the name of Al-Hidaya as the organizing committee. Al-Hidaya is the name of the organization in Great Britain that arranges various events for MQ followers, with the explicit blessings of Allama Tahirul Qadri. Although independent from the British MQ organization, the MQ in the Netherlands adopted the name of Al-Hidaya to affirm its ideological affiliation. In 2007, the festival took place in

Rotterdam's Zuidplein Theatre. The influence of the larger British branch of the MQ was not only evident in the name of the organizing committee, but also in the list of speakers and the composition of the programme. However, the relaxed and carnival-like atmosphere was typical for the MQ youth culture in the Netherlands, where girls' participation and the involvement of youths of other ethnic backgrounds are more common than in the UK. The festive atmosphere spread from the hall on to the streets, where members of the MQ offered passers-by flowers with special *Milad* texts. At the entrances to the hall, girls in green and orange dresses were standing to welcome and guide the participants. The occasion seemed especially attractive for children and women, who were present in large numbers in colourful traditional dresses. The sitting arrangement was gender-mixed, in spite of private objections from some of the British-based speakers.[9]

A dominant feature of this gathering was the multi-ethnicity in its organization and participation. A local Moroccan musical group opened the event with a performance of the *Qasida Burda*.[10] This was followed by a brief lecture on the life of the Prophet by Sadiq. There were two guest speakers, invited from the UK: Ramadan Qadri, who acts as the MQ youth co-ordinator in the UK, and Imam Abu Bakir Sudani, who teaches in London at the Islamic school run by Yusuf Islam, the former musician Cat Stevens. Their easy manner of speaking intermixed with light self-criticism and humour, delighted the audience. The speeches alternated with a stand-up comedian of Palestinian origin from the US, and a performance of *nasheed* (devotional songs) by the group Shaam from the UK.

My respondents of the Minhaj Youth League repeatedly mentioned the *Milad* festival as a significant achievement of the MQ in the Netherlands. They stressed the 'atmosphere of love and brotherhood' at the festival, which they found 'truly Islamic'. The visibly multi-ethnic attendance, the informal and mixed-gender character of the gathering, and the easy and open relations between participants of different generations all contributed to a *'leuke sfeer'* (pleasant ambience). For the youth, the celebration is an occasion to come out of the controlled social norms, by providing them with a space to negotiate their cultural identities. The *Milad* festival is a new form of public manifestation of religious identities, feeding on the demand for a public role of Islam in European societies. Its coming out of the traditional place of mosque together with its public form of religiosity challenges the established boundaries of both public and private domain in Western societies. Moreover, although such celebrations remain circumscribed within the cultural and national boundaries of the state, they develop in response to the impact of various transnational Islamic influences (Bowen 2004).

Transnational links

Islam in the diaspora is constantly linked with the 'motherland' through a variety of transnational links, thanks to modern means of communication. In the case of the MQ, the founder of the movement, Tahirul Qadri, annually visits different centres of the movement outside Pakistan. At the same time, the MQ has a constant supply of visiting scholars, *fuzla*, graduates from its university and the recently established Institute of Classical and Islamic Studies (ICIS). Conversely, MQ members from the diaspora usually receive a special welcome at the MQ's head office in Lahore, no doubt partly due to their financial position.

The MQ realized the importance of the religious needs of the diasporic Muslim communities from very early on. It established its first centre outside Pakistan in Denmark in 1984. Tahirul Qadri regularly visits the MQ centres now established in many Western countries. The MQ followers look forward to these visits and consider his presence a big intellectual asset and spiritual blessing for them. In June 2003, an annual European MQ gathering, to which followers from different European countries were invited, was held in Paris. Qadri asked the new entrants in the movement to stand behind him, while photos were made, and he declared them the new 'stars' of the MQ in Europe. After this he delivered a passionate speech and, amidst sobs, narrated the story of Abu Lahab, an uncle of the Prophet who did not accept Islam:

A companion of the Prophet saw Abu Lahab in a dream after latter's death. Abu Lahab told him 'all that the Prophet told us about the hell is true'. Now when I, Qadri, look at my deeds I do not believe that Allah will forgive me on the Day of Judgement. But I have only hope in you, those who are sitting before me. I hope someone from you will recognize me on that day and may become a source of forgiveness for me by Allah.

Listening to these emotive words, the audience broke out in tears. Collective weeping, often loud and uncontrollable, as an expression of grief, fear of the hereafter, and of religious reverence has a strong tradition in Sufism. However, in this case it also served to reinforce the centrality of Qadri himself in the life of his followers, which is noticeable elsewhere too. For the majority of them, he has become a household figure: he is at the same time a *pir* or spiritual guide, a family member, a political leader, and a popular hero, whose portrait has pride of place in the drawing room. At the same time his video-preaching should be watched and followed because it provides guidance for a proper way of life.

For some youth in Western countries Qadri's special religious attraction is related to his function to bridge the gap that arises as a result of their growing up 'between two cultures'. Tasneem Sadiq, who was introduced above, is very explicit about the meaning Qadri holds for him. Speaking of the time when he had already begun taking an interest in religion and had also enrolled in the medical faculty of Erasmus University, Sadiq narrated his feelings:

[T]here was always a big gap between the two worlds. What I learned in one environment was impossible to apply in the other and vice versa. What I learnt in the madrasa, the Qur'an and Hadith, was only a 'dead Islam'. In my house I was a different personality from who I was outside. At home you have this atmosphere of *adab* or respect, while outside you make jokes with friends, etc. It was Allama Qadri who filled that gap for me and made me learn that your home and outside life have much to do with your Islam. He is for me somebody who brought theory into practice, the 'living Islam'.

Some youth called it a 'practical presentation of Islam' – Qadri defined Islamic teachings for them in the way they should be put into practice in Western societies.

Besides spiritual, intellectual, and organizational matters, the European trips of Qadri are occasions for fund-raising of MQ projects in Pakistan. This aspect of the transnational network building may be called a 'reverse link', where the MQ entices diasporic Muslim communities to donate to the religious, educational, and welfare activities of the movement in Pakistan. For this purpose the MQ has a special 'Directorate of Foreign Affairs' that deals with these issues. Some expatriates also helped to formulate the election programme for the political party allied to the MQ, the Pakistan Awami Tehreek, in 2002, and a large number of them went to Pakistan to run its election campaigns.[11] Similarly, the Institute of Classical and Islamic Studies (ICIS), mentioned above, was established especially for the training of Muslim youth coming from European countries to Pakistan for their advanced education. After returning, these youth are expected to organize study circles and to disseminate religious knowledge. One such graduate, originally from the Netherlands, now runs the recently founded MQ centre in Dublin.

Conclusion

I have sought to describe a number of different processes and themes in the understanding and expression of Islam as they occur in the Minhajul Qur'an movement. The movement originated in Pakistan and it belongs to the popular religious tradition in South Asia also known as Barelwi. However, the MQ movement has transformed the Barelwi tradition, making it more inclusive and adaptable by projecting an anti-sectarian image. At the same time its main institute, the Minhajul Qur'an University in Lahore, is creating a new breed of ulama who are enthusiastic about spreading the message of the movement.

The MQ is a transnational movement with a large presence in Western countries, including the Netherlands. Having originated in Pakistan, it has a fairly strong base among the Pakistani diaspora. However, thanks to the inclusive nature of its religious message it is no longer limited to them. However, taking into account the difference in the outlooks of the first- and second-generation diaspora South Asians, it approaches their concerns differently. For this purpose, it has developed separate wings for youth and for women that act autonomously.

The inclusive nature of the MQ religious discourse makes it equally attractive to different generations of migrants, even as it determines the new face of the movement in the European context. The anti-sectarian approach of the movement catches the fancy of the first-generation migrants who had daily observed the menace of sectarianism in their home country, and who are attracted towards the universal message of Islam due to their minority position. At the same time the movement provides them with opportunities to become actively engaged in for religious and community activities, thereby enhancing their prestige.

The charismatic personality of Allama Tahirul Qadri provides different meanings for different followers of the movement. He is a religious guide, a reformer, a spiritual leader, and a hero who could be a member of one's household. He regularly visits the diaspora communities to maintain the spiritual and organizational momentum of the movement.

For the MQ youth, Allama Qadri is a religious guide and reformer. But it is more than the figure of Allama Qadri that attracts many youth towards the MQ. Significant in this regard is the religious atmosphere that the movement provides for the youth. Contrary to ulama of their parent's generation, the *fuzla* of the movement provide religious knowledge in an interactive way, diluting the traditional pattern relationship between ulama and 'ordinary' Muslims. Contrary to the first generation that took the mosque as the focus of its religious activities, for the Muslim European youth events like the *Milad* festival organized by the MYL constitute an important public sphere for expressing their religious commitment. Through events such as these they seek to root religion in the local social context.

Notes

1 The term *fazil*, used by the MQ for the graduates of its university, does not have the same connotations as ‘*alim*. The *fazil* acts as imam and is the main figure in spreading the message of the MQ in a local *idara*; he is not necessarily a man of great learning. The MQ's *fuzla* adopt the sartorial and behavioural style of the Barelwi ulama but do not have a high status in the eyes of the senior traditionalist Barelwi ulama, because of their allegedly flexible relation to tradition.
2 In this connection, it is worth noting that there is a tendency towards endogamy within the MQ community. In the Netherlands, this has taken the form of marriages between children of MQ members already resident there. (In Britain, on the other hand, I noticed a stronger tendency for fathers to look for sons-in-law in Pakistan.)
3 Interview with Ahmad Raza, the MQ imam in The Hague, 6 July 2002.
4 Interview with Syed (pseudonym), 30 November 2002.
5 Interview with Zubair Ahmad, the MQ imam in Rotterdam, 8 October 2003.
6 Interview with Syed (pseudonym), 30 November 2002.
7 Interview with Ashraf Ashrafi, 30 November 2002.
8 This translation is from *The Quran: A New Translation* by M.A.S. Haleem, Oxford: Oxford University Press, 2004.
9 Ramadan Qadri, the co-ordinator of MQ's youth activities in the UK, told me (in an interview 16 October 2006) that he objected to the easy mixing of the sexes at the events in the Netherlands.
10 The *Qasida Burda* ('Ode of the Prophet's Mantle') is a devotional poem written by the thirteenth-century Egyptian Sufi al-Busiri.
11 Pakistani daily *Dawn*, 16 September 2002.

References

Ahlberg, Nora (1990) *New Challenges, Old Strategies: Themes of Variation and Conflict among Pakistani Muslims in Norway*, Helsinki: Finnish Anthropological Society.
Alavi, Hamza and Halliday, Fred (eds) (1987) *State and Ideology in the Middle East and Pakistan*, London: MacMillan.
Amir-Moazami, Schirin and Salvatore, Armando (2003) 'Gender, Generation and the Reform of Tradition: From Muslim Majority Societies to Western Europe', in Stefano Allievi and Jørgen S. Nielsen (eds) *Muslim Networks and Transnational Communities in and across Europe*, Leiden: Brill, pp. 52–77.

Asad, Talal (1986) 'The Idea of an Anthropology of Islam', Occasional paper, Washington D.C.: Center for Contemporary Arab Studies, Georgetown University.

Bowen, John R. (2004) 'Beyond Migration: Islam as a Transnational Public Space', *Journal of Ethnic and Migration Studies*, 30 (5): 879–94.

Centraal Bureau voor de Statistiek (2006) *Allochtonen per Regio naar Herkomstgroepering: Pakistan*, Voorburg/Heerlen: Centraal Bureau voor de Statistiek.

Cesari, Jocelyne (2003) 'Muslim Minorities in Europe: The Silent Revolution', in John L. Esposito and Francois Burgat (eds) *Modernizing Islam: Religion in the Public Sphere in the Middle East and in Europe*, London: Hurst, pp. 251–69.

Cressey, Gill (2002) 'Followers of Tradition, Products of Hybridity, or Bearers of Change: British Pakistani and Kashmiri Young People', *Sociale Wetenschappen*, 45 (2): 44–60.

Eickelman, Dale F. and Piscatori, James (1996) *Muslim politics*, Princeton, NJ: Princeton University Press.

Geaves, Ron (2000) *The Sufis of Britain: An Exploration of Muslim Identity*, Cardiff: Cardiff Academic Press.

Metcalf, Barbara (1982) *Islamic Revival in British India: Deoband, 1860–1900*, Princeton: Princeton University Press.

Nielsen, Jorgen (1992) *Muslims in Western Europe*, Edinburgh: Edinburgh University Press.

Rafiq, Mohammad (1996) *Nabigha-i ʿasr (the sage of our time)*, Lahore: Minhajul Qurʿan Publications.

Roy, Olivier (1999) *Vers un islam européen*, Paris: Éditions Esprit.

Roy, Olivier (2004) *Globalised Islam: the search for the new ummah*, London: Hurst and Company.

Sanyal, Usha (1996) Devotional Islam and Politics in British India: Ahmed Raza Khan Barelwi and his Movement, *1870–1920*, Delhi: Oxford University Press.

Werbner, Pnina (2002) Imagined Diasporas among Manchester Muslims, Oxford: James Curry.

4 Religious authority, social action and political participation

A case study of the *Mosquée de la rue de Tanger* in Paris

Valérie Amiraux

Introduction

Compared with other religious leaders active in France or in Europe, Larbi Kechat is certainly not a celebrity for a non-Muslim audience.[1] Names like those of Tariq Ramadan, the notorious and controversial Muslim intellectual now living in Great Britain, or Dalil Boubakeur, the director of the Great Mosque of Paris (Grande Mosquée de Paris), are much more familiar than Larbi Kechat's. He does not lead a national federation and he did not take part in the highly publicized 2002–3 discussions that led to the creation of the French Council of Muslim Worship (Conseil français du culte musulman, hereafter CFCM).[2] He rarely participates in talk shows and does not make public statements when something happens in the Muslim world. As he once said to me when I asked him to introduce himself at the beginning of a round-table discussion I had organized to discuss a report dealing with the discrimination of Muslims in Europe,[3] 'I can't be classified' ('je suis inclassable'). The man's position, relatively popular among Muslims in Paris and its neighbourhood, but also among journalists, local politicians, researchers, and academics can indeed hardly be located on the *Islam de France* map, which at the time of our exchanges and conversations was in the process of being completely reshaped by the implementation of CFCM.

Born in Algeria, Larbi Kechat is discreet and favours back stages to front stages. He is nevertheless a well-known figure for Muslims living in France, at a national, but in particular, at a local level. He is known as the imam of the mosque that is inside the building hosting the Social and Cultural Centre of the Rue de Tanger, in the 19th arrondissement in the north-eastern part of Paris.[4] Part of his popularity among young Muslims appears to be due to his decision to preach in French instead of only in Arabic. Two major events have also contributed to his larger visibility in the media. First, in 1994, the then Minister of Interior Charles Pasqua had Kechat (along with twenty-five other persons) placed under arrest in Folembray. They were charged with Islamist militancy and accused of incitement to hatred of the West. After three weeks, Kechat was released, in particular thanks to the mobilization of several intellectuals and religious leaders from various communities. Following this episode, 'Monsieur le Recteur', as he is called,[5] decided to launch regular seminars and conferences on Saturday afternoons in his Centre, inviting Muslims and non-Muslims, and religious and non-religious scholars to discuss social problems and political questions. The second event that attracted journalistic attention to the Rue de Tanger was an attack on the mosque in March 1997 that ended in one person being injured. In the course of investigations by the police, a large amount of cash was discovered in the private residence of some members of the association, apparently to be sent to Islamic organizations abroad. The most recent accusation against Kechat's mosque concerned the presence of young activists involved in radical movements, who were allegedly recruiting young French Muslim volunteers to be sent to Iraq.[6] To sum up, during the past fifteen years, Kechat and his Centre (including the mosque) have been quite systematically presented as ambiguous in their political and religious acquaintances. Both logically became targets of active police surveillance.

My focus in this chapter will be on the Centre itself, located in the same building as the mosque, on the Centre's local significance, and on the way Larbi Kechat managed to become such a popular local religious leader, with an appeal far beyond his strict religious domain of competence, and far beyond the community of Muslim believers. I met with him on numerous occasions between 2000 and 2004, had discussions with some of his collaborators, mostly women, and attended some of the Saturday conferences, observing the settings. However, I did not conduct systematic interviews with the visitors (Muslims or non-Muslims) of the mosque, and I cannot provide the reader with an assessment of the profile of the mosque's regular audience.[7] In the first part of this chapter, I focus less on the individual life history of Kechat than on the Centre's trajectory, roughly since the 1970s. This will provide the background, first, for an analysis of the transformation of religious authority in secular contexts and, second, a broader exposition of the different paths to civic participation for religious associations.

The setting

Without pretending to provide an accurate and exhaustive biographical picture of Kechat, I open this chapter with some pertinent information on the life trajectory of the Rue de Tanger's leader. My intention is not to present a life history type of analysis, but it will be difficult to speak of the institution without some background on the rector and on the circumstances that caused him to have such an impact on the Centre. Indeed, the dynamism of the place is intimately linked with the personality of Larbi Kechat and both stories merge and overlap.

Larbi's itinerary: from Constantine to the Rue de Tanger

Larbi Kechat was born in Algeria near Constantine before the end of the 1940s.[8] He came to France to study in 1972.

> I was studying general linguistics at Paris III and sociology at Paris IV, following the courses taught by Georges Balandier. I was so young at that time!

I met Bani Sadr (the Iranian revolutionary and future president) there too! He was a PhD student of Balandier.

Kechat was, with other Muslim students whom he met at the Sorbonne, involved in the activities of the first Muslim students' association (the Association des Étudiants Islamiques de France, hereafter AEIF),[9] which was established in 1963. He came under the influence of Mohammed Hamidullah, who later on gave regular Sunday lectures in the mosque of the Rue de Tanger.[10]

Larbi was the first of his family to migrate to France: 'And I am the first in the family who has access to Western culture'. He likes to tell the story of his father who put him in contact with the oral culture of migrants, Algerians coming back from France for the holidays.

> My father was famous in the region of Constantine. At that time, workers used to migrate without their family. I forgot to tell you that I discovered Paris thanks to the addresses on the letters sent by migrants to their families! People brought those letters to my father, perhaps a hundred letters each week; because most women could not read or write, the mothers and wives were queuing in front of our house. And I heard my father reading these letters. ... The same happened with boxes that were sent and then distributed, also every two weeks; my father distributed money that was sent from France. During the holidays, all immigrants came to visit us. ... When I came to France, I had several questions, in particular why were these women unable to read? Then, how come all those people trusted my father so much?

Kechat does not hold a degree in traditional Islamic studies delivered by one of the renowned Islamic universities. His religious training was mostly 'home-made'. By that I mean first that he received some religious teaching locally, in Algeria, before his departure for Paris. Second, this religious education was mostly provided in private by his father and grandfathers who were all local religious figures.

> When I was a kid, I learned the Quran. I went through a double training then: I went both to the French school and to the Quranic school. Then I received a higher level of religious education under a sheikh who had a good local reputation. It was obvious that the teaching of Islam and Arabic in official institutions in Algeria was worthless. I had the chance to have a sheikh who was both extremely good in Islamic knowledge and a spiritual father at the same time. He had a double authority, spiritual and intellectual, Sheikh Omar Abu Hafez, in the region of Constantine. ... I never followed a curriculum in the biggest Islamic institutions. And I don't regret it. ... When I happen to speak with Egyptian, Syrian, Middle Eastern ulama such as [the Egyptian Muslim Brother] Sheikh Muhammad Al-Ghazali ... or [the Syrian scholar] Sheikh Sa'id Ramadan al-Buti, they ask me where I studied. I say: in Algeria. 'Where in Algeria?' Everybody knows there is no university there for that.

In spite of not having a formal degree from a recognized institution, Kechat clearly enjoys legitimacy as a person of religious learning, besides being widely seen as a wise, independent (regarding the French 'Muslim politics'), and responsive leader (morally speaking) – qualities that need to be analysed.

Kechat does not want to speak much about his own itinerary. 'The particulars of my life do not bring much to the understanding of the world'. It is hard to disentangle the impact of external mentorship and personal efforts at self-education in Kechat's training. His reputation as a leader and a man of wisdom as well as his profound personal commitment to the survival of the community goes back, at least, to the 1970s, when he was involved in the precursor of the current mosque, then located in the Rue de Belleville. Through the years, Kechat has assigned himself a particularly difficult task consisting of encouraging the Muslim audience to an active and committed citizenship, with no tolerance for ignorance and passivity. His ability to articulate scriptural religious knowledge with incentives for commitment in civic life is particularly salient in the final statements with which he concludes the Saturday conferences. Certainly, Kechat's lyricism plays a role in his capacity to move (in both senses) Muslims attending the conferences. For the occasional visitor, his lyricism and flowery style may at times appear excessive or even ridiculous. But regular visitors appreciate that Kechat's style as a speaker stands in the service of his mission of the conciliation of spiritual and social needs ('*la verticalité et l'horizontalité*') towards the implementation of a peaceful social cohesion.

When concluding the Saturday conferences, his particular attention to the linguistic form and his poetic enthusiasm never stop him from correcting the most radical attendants, to reaffirm his commitment to 'an enlightened and active citizenship' ('*une citoyenneté active et éclairée*'). Most of the topics of the Saturday conferences are related to issues of social exclusion and marginalization (AIDS, drugs, prisons), violence (war and political violence in particular in Muslim contexts), and equality (gender, poverty, secularism). On these arguments, Kechat seeks harmony and active interaction between faith and citizenship. Social action and spirituality can, in his view, go very well together: 'I encourage people not to forget the "how" while thinking of the "why"'. Expressions that recur frequently in his sermons and speeches concern the complementarities of verticality (the relation to God) and horizontality (social integration), of love and solidarity (one of his favourite metaphors is that of joining hands in order to reach 'the True, the Good, and the Beautiful'). He therefore appeals to solidarity and consolation ('*une solidarité réconfortante*'), to intellectual curiosity and understanding ('*exploration*', '*connaissance stimulante*'), and to love of God and one's neighbours ('*adoration de Dieu, amour des siens et des autres*'). We find him oscillating all the time between the position of a moral counsellor, mobilizing a religious repertoire of responsibility ('God has enabled us to do so many things'), and the position of a political mediator, referring to the Republican framework of equality with pompous metaphors.

As mentioned above, Kechat has been involved in the mosque of the Rue de Tanger even before it moved to its current neighbourhood. The beginnings of the mosque and its congregation were in the Rue de Belleville, about two kilometres south-east. Abd el Kader Ben Ahmad, the Algerian owner of a small hotel in this neighbourhood, opened a prayer room there for the migrant workers and students of the neighbourhood. This early mosque was not under the control of any single group or association; there was for instance also a Tablighi group that used to congregate here.[11] Leading personalities in the mosque were mostly Algerian and Egyptian (the imam, for most of the 1960s, was an Egyptian). The room was soon too small to accommodate all the believers – especially students – who wished to perform their daily prayers there. Towards the end of the 1960s, renovations of the neighbourhood began and, as a temporary replacement, the nearby church of Menilmontant offered the Muslims the use of part of this Catholic house of worship as a prayer hall. They stayed there until the end of the 1970s, when the mosque moved to its current location in the Rue de Tanger.

> We had an immense space in this church. ... We arranged for a door and a wall to separate the two spaces for worship. We had hidden the images, the icons, very quickly. This place was available every day, for the five daily prayers. A lot of believers came and joined our congregation. Gradually, the Great Mosque of Paris was abandoned by Muslims who came to us.

And so the mosque of the Rue de Tanger emerged as the second important mosque of Paris, in terms both of size and of number of worshippers, especially on Fridays and during festivities. The project of implementing a decent Islamic place for worship started in this context, and the support of Christian communities in Paris.[12]

The place: the ad-Da'wa mosque and the Social and Cultural Centre of the Rue de Tanger

> The mosque in the Rue de Tanger is in a sense the largest popular mosque in Paris. (It is) less intimidating than the mosque on the Place du Puits de l'Ermite in the 5th arrondissement (the Great Mosque of Paris). ... It is commonly called the 'Stalingrad mosque', after the name of the nearest metro station. Its real name is ad-Da'wa, 'the predication'. Since 1985, it has been based in the old textile warehouse Bouchara.
>
> (Ternisien 2002: 17)

Seen from outside, the building looked old but impressive, huge, high, and dark. It certainly does not possess the external characteristics expected of a mosque: there is no dome, no minaret, and no oriental design to distinguish it from the rest of the urban landscape. Moreover, there is nothing to attract the attention of passers-by in this neighbourhood, and, as is the case with most other French mosques, daily attendance is rather low. In her work on the perceptions and representations of the Rue de Tanger mosque in the local neighbourhood, Marie Lejeune notices precisely the extent to which the visibility of the place is related to specific practices and precise moments, in particular during the Friday prayer. On Friday mornings, the crowded pavements suddenly make the existence of the mosque more explicit to non-Muslim neighbours (Lejeune 2000).

Almost next to the mosque there is a state school, and it faces a church (the Église Notre Dame des Forges) across the street. An Islamic bookshop and a shop selling various Islamic goods (clothes, food) have recently opened. Further in the street, bakeries offer oriental pastries and sell Arab bread. In this specific area of Paris, people are of mixed background, Muslims constituting only a part of this diversity (not the majority), and the clientele visiting the Centre for religious motivations is not exclusively local. The rector comments on the new, 'Oriental' urban aesthetics of the street as 'ridiculous': how come a mosque attracts such an ethnic business? Is that necessary for the life of Muslims? 'Does it mean that we should stay among ourselves and continue to live here, in France, as we would be supposed to do it in the country of our parents?', wonders Kechat. The 'orientalization' of the immediate neighbourhood contrasts with the absolute invisibility of any external signs enabling the identification of the Centre.[13]

This notion of visibility of Islam and identification as Muslims from outside by outsiders relates to a key motif of Islam in Europe in the 1980s when 'Muslims sought room, figuratively and literally for the practice of Islam and Islamic practices' (Grillo 2004: 868). In the French context, Kechat underlines the necessity to adopt the local rules and adapt to an environment by confirming to the Republican principles, i.e. those requiring one 'to be discreet and polite' ('*de la discrétion et de la politesse*'). By living as a Muslim in France, Kechat invites the believers to integrate into the fabric of French society, not only to be in France passively (Grillo 2004). Kechat enacts in his Centre the reconciliation of usually opposing structures of justification. The first is based on French positive laws and the French conception of the Republic. The second stems from a religious interpretation of Islamic norms and texts. In doing so, Kechat draws limits and boundaries (what is absolute is Islam, what is pragmatic and concrete is the French context) but performs his personal authority in organizing the dialogue and articulated cooperation between the two repertoires. As expressed by Bowen, 'Muslims participating in these debates may take account of norms, laws and conditions prevailing in France, as elements that are normatively external but pragmatically internal to the debates' (Bowen 2004: 890). Islamic norms and principles have a value of their own, *per se*. However, they should not be considered, says Kechat, as contradictory to French politics and Republican principles (freedom, equality, fraternity). In this respect, Kechat's Centre may be the unique Muslim site where these two repertoires coexist and share a common territory – although this does not mean that interactions are numerous.

Inside the building, social and cultural activities (conferences, mediation, Arabic classes, literacy courses) are strictly separated from the religious and liturgical ones. The space dedicated to worship is completely isolated from the more cultural and social activities, the prayer rooms being on the ground floor (a large one on the left for men, a smaller one on the right for women). A door opens to the stairs that take the visitor to the conference room, the administrative offices, and a small library. The classrooms are upstairs and the Centre also has a restaurant with a kitchen on the top floor where lunches are served during the conferences, and *iftar*s (meals to break the fast) during Ramadan.[14] The mosque (which moved here from Belleville in 1985) and the social and cultural centre (which started its activities in 1994–5) are two separated entities sharing a common territory and a unique legal identification as an association. Both do not attract the same audience but the circulation from one space to the other remains possible. Since 1996, requests for permission to renovate, extend and even reconstruct the entire building were being unsuccessfully submitted to the Paris municipality. Following the Socialist Party victory in the municipal elections of 2001, under the new mayor, Bertrand Delanoë, full permission for the demolition (in July 2001) and the construction of a new building (September 2002) has finally been approved.[15] The project is ambitious and includes the erection of a dome and a minaret, an open garden through which the believer can reach the prayer hall, and a front building dedicated to the social and cultural activities of the place.[16] The main motivation for Kechat is the salubrity of the place and its 'normalization' in the local urban landscape.

In France, questions about the building of mosques usually involve an unanswered dilemma: should a mosque be a place of worship or a cultural centre?[17] Going back to the most important projects of construction of mosques (Strasbourg, Lille, Marseille, Paris), this unanswered question seems to be common to all local political debates that took place in relation with the perspective of having an Islamic place of worship in urban settings (see Frégosi and Willaime 2001; Césari 2005; Lejeune 2000). Besides, mosques have also become a systematic target of police inspection and surveillance, imams and religious leaders being also classical figures of potential threat to the national territory and to the Republican values (Amiraux 2009). Since 9/11, their control became more intense and the eventual deportation to their country of origin has become more systematic, not only in France. In this respect, Kechat was a precursor as his problems with justice and police started long before 9/11.

As mentioned earlier, he was arrested on 10 August 1994, at a period of greater visibility of political movements linked to Islam in the Middle East, but also in Europe. During the different discussions we had, he confessed to not having yet fully understood why he was arrested on that day.

> I was leaving the Centre. It was really extremely hot. I crossed the street and when I came to the Church on the other side of the street, a car stopped. Two persons came out, like in a movie. They surrounded me: 'Mister Kechat ?' I said yes. 'Come with us.' I said: 'Where?' … I wondered: were they robbers or cops? I had never been an activist in France. So, me being arrested by the police, why?

In telling me the story of his arrest, Kechat insisted on the dramatic and incoherent part of it: more people came and at the end they were six; he had neither money, nor ID documents with him; he was very polite to them while they were rude in pushing him into the police car, threatening him with handcuffs. Once in the car, in violation of normal procedures, Kechat signed a declaration based on a report issued by the Ministry of the Interior administration stating that he was a threat to the Republic and an adversary of Western culture.[18] Consistent with his statements on the necessity to respect French norms and rules when address-ing a Muslim audience, Kechat signed despite the fact that he disagreed with the content, 'saying to them that I was doing it in respect of the law of this country. I knew that all that they were doing was against the law'. Kechat was first kept under surveillance for a few hours on the fifth floor of the Paris police headquar-ters on the Quai des Orfèvres, being interrogated about his alleged links to the GIA (Armed Islamic Group) network that was accused of acts of terrorism. He confessed to me that he was impressed by the huge police record on him. He was then sent to Folembray, a military station transformed for this occasion into a provisional prison with place for twenty-six persons.[19]

> I spent one month in Folembray. Then they transferred me here, to the Centre in the Rue de Tanger, changing the detention into house arrest. They consid-ered this my place of residence. I stayed here night and day, sleeping here too, reading, working. ... During the first months, I was not authorized to leave the 19th arrondissement. ... Once, you know I was going to the hair-dresser, I was convinced it was in the 19th arrondissement. And all of a sudden, I raised my head and saw that I was in the 10th! Oops! I immediately made a turn because I went off the limits.

Kechat's arrest had many effects on the local representation of the Centre. First, since this episode, the rector and the mosque have been under close surveillance by the police and secret services, whose officers usually attend the Saturday conferences. It has become one of the usual targets for police services working on Islamist networks and profiling specific leaders and places. Second, following the mobilization of a 'non-Muslim community' of 'intellectuals, academics, cler-gymen'[20] that prevented his expulsion from French territory, Kechat decided to integrate this non-Muslim presence more explicitly in the activities organized by the Centre.[21] The series of Saturday conferences started shortly after his dismissal from prison, as a testimony of his gratitude towards non-Muslim French citizens, who signed a public protest against his arrest.[22] One of the Catholic leaders active in the defence of Kechat stated in 2004 how stupid some of the documents drafted by the police services were, and how dangerous was the impact these writings have on uninformed public authorities (prefects or mayors for instance).[23] *Ex post*, this initiative taken by Kechat on the basis of his personal experience of unfair-ness and in order publicly to thank the group of his defenders, ended up as a way of confirming Kechat's religious legitimacy amongst Muslims and of achieving a civic legitimacy for non-Muslims. The next section of this chapter explores Kechat's continuous work of mediation and dialogue between Muslim and non-Muslim citizens, in the name of Islam but also for the sake of larger French society.

Activities and publics: an ethic of responsibility

Larbi Kechat's mosque is 'not only a space for prayer but also a "community centre", where pre-existing networks of solidarity come together and where various rituals that mark Islamic family life – marriage, circumcision, death – take place' (Césari 2005: 1018). The demographic and sociological changes among Muslim populations living in non-Muslim Europe have had a direct impact on the way people 'use' mosques. To a certain extent, their significance for believers settled in European secular contexts has gained importance, helping the developments of intense networks of activities and socialization beside the sole praying activities. The Muslim population living in France is younger in the 2000s than in the 1980s, and the individualization of the tie to the community of belief is a common denominator. For the younger generation, self-identification as a Muslim and actually practising the religious obligations are not self-evidently connected, as they were for their elders; many of the young have distanced themselves from the daily rituals even as they insist on being Muslims.[24]

With the move to non-Muslim territories, the role of the mosques in the life of the community of practising believers inevitably changed. They gained a renewed centrality in the life of the communities at large, just as the position of the imams became central for migrants (and later for intelligence services), who would have looked down upon them in their countries of origin. Mosques became places to meet, to get advice on daily concerns, to organize celebrations, but also – as in the case of the Centre of the Rue de Tanger – to deliberate about politics and society, to compare one's individual experiences with those of others. The invention of some of these new functions of the mosque went together with the specific needs of Muslims living in non-Muslim societies.[25] In the case of the Rue de Tanger, Kechat's arrest provided the occasion for opening up mosques to activities that were not strictly religious, and to invite non-Muslims to take part in discussions in the Cultural Centre. At least that is the way Kechat justifies his decision to launch this new set of activities in the 1990s. The Social and Cultural Centre was created in 1994, the year he was arrested. He was already travelling and giving conferences in the AEIF network of mosques in France and Europe. 'At that time it was very discreet work, with no media attention. It was work on the ground, with social workers, with students, etc.'

Kechat's pedagogic project of the teaching of religious and civic values is promoted through activities other than those connected solely with worship or rituals. Listening to people, welcoming them, helping them, developing solidarity networks across various communities and in various matters (health, education, civic initiatives), and mixing Muslim with non-Muslim audiences, are the channels through which Kechat's Centre is locally active.[26] The local settlement goes far beyond Muslims, and the initiatives launched by Kechat and his colleagues do not address exclusively Muslims, 'spiralling out' from the restricted community of belief (Lichterman 2005). In his study of nine liberal and conservative Protestant-based volunteering projects, Lichterman points out the different ways that people bring religion into civic life: people do other things with religion than just using religious discourses (or private beliefs) to define goals for action. Beyond limited readings of religion as 'resource' or justification for action, the commitment of a religious community to civic activities does create settings that allow people to 'think and talk about spiralling outward without threatening the group's own togetherness' (ibid. 18). Kechat illustrates for example how groups publicly articulate goals in religious terms with civic participation, mostly by means of a language of solidarity, responsibility and active citizenship, a language of justice and the public good referring to all sorts of moral vocabularies, which at the end also encompass societal values.[27] A good person, in Kechat's religious terms, overlaps with a good French citizen and helps the implementation of a good society. Religion is here to support the implementation of a good and just citizenry, to understand the civic roles of active citizens with the ambitious horizon of 'producing history together' says Kechat.[28] The religious language therefore sustains a sense of connection to society as a whole, which more secular languages would probably be unable to transmit, being based on individualism (Bellah et al. 1985).

The Saturday conferences: debating religious and secular topics

The Rue de Tanger Centre has more than one activity to offer to its visitors. These activities can be classified into three clusters: cultural (teaching activities, mostly the Quran and Arabic), social (Saturday conferences), and religious (prayer in the mosques, and also religious seminars in the Centre). The conferences organized once a month on Saturday afternoons are the core activity, besides the more traditional initiatives like teaching Arabic and Islam.[29] Undoubtedly, the conferences are the most well-known and visible activities of the Centre. Starting in October–November and going on until June, and the final conference which lasts an entire day, they give the visitors of the Centre the opportunity to listen to ulamas, academics, activists, politicians, journalists, and opinion-makers discussing a common topic.[30] The participants include people not residing in Paris, and also not always French-speaking.[31] In that case, the simultaneous translation (quite regularly from Arabic and English) is organized by the Centre. The translator, who may be a woman as well as a man, sits among the speakers and also translates the question-and-answer session following the lectures. From 14:30 until 20:00 with a break for the prayer,[32] presentations by the invited speakers are followed by a question-and-answer session with the audience. Everything is video-recorded. No question is forbidden, no subject taboo. People can choose to ask it directly or to write it down. In that case, once the questions are written and given to the speakers anonymously, one is free to read it or not. Kechat does not provide the participants with rules to follow but the organization of the afternoon obeys an intangible protocol: presentations are made one after the other, following an order pre-decided by Kechat (but it can be changed for matters of convenience and some people need to leave earlier). Usually, the highest religious authority speaks at the end. It is both a matter of having people attend the entire session, and also, implicitly, of establishing a hierarchy between discourses. The most welcome moment of the Saturday after-noon conference is certainly the final speech, invariably given by Kechat. Depending upon his feeling about the afternoon, and depending upon the attitude of the audience (passive, patient, provocative or disrespectful of the speakers), the concluding speech by Kechat will be more or less vehement but always passionate and lyrical.

The themes of the Saturday conferences are often said by people from the audi-ence to be 'hot issues' or 'sensitive topics'. Moreover, non-Muslims are very often surprised that such issues like drugs or HIV (indirectly touching upon moral issues, gender and sexual aspects of social interaction) can be considered issues to be legitimately discussed inside an Islamic Centre. Relying on Lichterman's study of how religion is made quietly public by the Protestant volunteer groups he studied, Kechat's Saturday conferences correspond to the definition of an arena for 'agreeing to disagree' in a respectful coexistence (Lichterman 2005: 68). In Kechat's case this means that a very heterogeneous audience listens quietly to a contrasted bunch of speakers talking about controversial issues such as bio-ethics and cloning. *De facto*, Muslim liberals and Muslim conservatives sit together in public and among the speakers in the Rue de Tanger. The same thing can be said about non-Muslims. All sorts of voices can be heard at Kechat's place on these Saturday afternoons. What makes them sit together and tolerate each other so quietly during the Saturday conference routine? Part of the answer lies in Kechat's personality. The atmosphere remains secular in the sense that reli-gious convictions are not at stake or checked to let people attend the meetings. During the course of the conferences, no activities are conducted that would attest a religious proselytizing project from the Muslim side. The speakers are usually a mixture of local actors, politicians, experts, intellectuals, academics, journalists, and theologians; and they include women as well as men, converts and non-Muslims as well as born Muslims. Kechat remains, however, conservative in his selection of the religious authorities he invites to speak: these are often conservative religious figures (such as Hani Ramadan, or Sa'id Ramadan al-Buti) or imams of the AEIF (for instance M. Daffé from Bordeaux). He also invites Muslim figures that, in a way, could be said to be his own competitors in terms of leadership (Mohammed Arkoun, Tariq Ramadan among others). Kechat takes care that no controversial voice from the Muslim side can be heard,[33] preferring to leave it to non-Muslim speakers, in particular women, to voice subversive and original discourses.[34] For instance, Kechat is very cautious when inviting people to the conference dedicated to the national women's day: he avoids the men-talking-about-women type of round-table,[35] pays attention to the complexity of the debate and its non-religious impact, and shows respect for the diversity of Muslim women when dealing with the issue.

The audience is very heterogeneous. Muslims from all over the world come here. People of different ethnic origins and belonging to different generations mingle and listen together to the speakers. Women and men are not requested to sit in separate parts of the room, but 'naturally' Muslim women tend to sit together on one side and men on the other. However, as the non-Muslims attending take their seats freely, Muslim women end up sitting next to men and the audience is not strictly gender segregated.

Whereas it was initially probably conceived as an element of a network serving the interests of the AEIF, the Rue de Tanger mosque has ended up being an autonomous site for meetings and exchanges, open, and without any attempt to control the audience: there is no need to say your name, questions can be posed, and comments given in writing and anonymously. The Muslim audience attending the Saturday conferences reflects the diversity of the Muslim population in France. This can also be said for the worshippers coming especially for the Friday khutbas: as unusual as it may seem in the European context, the mosque of the Rue de Tanger is a multi-ethnic one. People come from the vast Parisian suburban districts, from far beyond the local neighbourhood. One of the workers of the Centre explains that, for instance, every Friday morning, people call before coming to be sure that Kechat will be conducting the prayer himself.

Non-Arab Muslims and non-French-speaking Muslims attend the conferences. Usually the Centre takes care of a translation from French into Arabic and vice versa. At the time of my research, this was done by a young girl who had recently arrived from Algiers to study American civilization at Jussieu University.[36] The audience's profile is as diverse as the speakers: local imams (preaching in Paris, Evry, Montreuil, Saint-Denis), leaders of Muslim associations, local city hall representatives, social workers, doctors, teachers, students, journalists, housekeepers waiting for their children who are being taught Arabic on the second floor of the Centre, curious neighbours, Muslims and non-Muslims.

Considering the variety of people attending the conferences (and more largely also visiting the mosque), language is not only a minor cosmetic issue in this analysis of the Centre's radiance and Kechat's influence. 'French Islam is a cultural, linguistic, financial, political and theological enterprise' (Caeiro 2006: 71). Historically, French is as central in the republican symbolic apparatus as the flag, the national hymn, or the principle of *laïcité*. Few EU member states make an explicit reference to the national language as the exclusive official language in their Constitution; France is one of them.[37] French is the language of communication in the Centre, even if it provides a translation into Arabic for the programme (sent out at the beginning of the year), on some parts of the website; and Arabic is occasionally used by Kechat to shout at some people in the audience who, he feels, do not get his message if it is expressed only in French. Language became an issue for the Minister of the Interior after an unpublished piece of research on imams in France was conducted on behalf of the Ministry of the Interior in 2004–5, in the framework of a larger reflection on the training of imams. It gave the following results: out of the 1,200 imams working in France, one third does not speak French at all, or with enormous difficulty, one third has an average level, while the final third speaks fluently (Godard 2005: 28). But as pointed out by Godard, one should definitely stop equating bad linguistic skills with low theological training. 'The imams with the worst command of French, the Turkish imams sent by Turkey's official institution for managing religious affairs, Diyanet, are probably the best trained and certainly the imams with the highest number of degrees and diplomas' (ibid.).

The proliferation of activities besides worship:
from spiritual to civic commitment

The opening of places of worship to non-spiritual types of activities is not exclusive to the Rue de Tanger Centre. Various religious associations have made great efforts to reconnect with youngsters, for instance by developing more social activities. The rationale behind the opening up to non-spiritual domains often lies in the need for visibility in the city. Finding out new ways to practise social interaction with youngsters is also a preoccupation of Kechat, who considers the mosque as part of urban life, not as isolated from it because of an untouchable sacred dimension. 'We should not underestimate the social vocation of the mosque to maintain a check on socially deviant behaviour', he says. One of Kechat's internal strategies aims also at reconnecting young Muslim people who are 'alienated from the mosques' (Lewis 2006: 174), thus accepting the risk that some of them may be implicated in radical political networks.[38] The mosque remains the central place for all religious activities, but it also becomes a partner of local initiatives for the management of exclusion and violence for instance. The people visiting the place therefore are of many different backgrounds, without excluding any type of believers. Sacred space enters politics through participation in civic initiatives and various types of voluntary associations. Kechat, however, emphasizes that there is a distinction between both types of actions: praying or commenting upon religious texts cannot be assimilated into political activism.

The presence of women in the Centre, who are in charge of various activities, is not without some problems. The fact that women are visibly active on the front stage in an Islamic Centre has not given rise to controversy among insiders, but the public visibility of women remains problematic for many traditional men, and speaking to unrelated women is even more difficult for them. The mosque and the Centre share certain facilities, such as the telephone switchboard, which is sometimes operated by young female volunteers. These young women told that several callers hung up when they heard a woman's voice. Similarly, men sometimes hesitate to enter the building when they see women at the entrance door welcoming visitors.

The Centre is also involved in various mediating activities implemented by the neighbourhood council, such as actions against violence at school, the rehabilitation of old buildings, and after-school tutoring for children who need it. Kechat is also a partner in a collective anti-crack initiative of the Stalingrad neighbourhood.[39] Addressing educational, health, and civic deficits of various kinds in the local community of citizens appears to be a priority for the Centre's leadership. One of these mediation activities is even based in the Centre. The Social and Health Mediation point (*antenne de médiation sociale et sanitaire*) was opened in 2002 and reaches out to vulnerable groups among the local population (migrants, single mothers, youngsters). By promoting mediation in social and health problems, Kechat intends the Centre to commit itself to the fight against social exclusion, and to provide social assistance in two domains in particular: access to care and health services, and improving the education of people from other cultural backgrounds.[40]

The coordinator of these activities at the time of my regular visits to the Centre was Fatma, a typical representative of how activism may lead to the opening of new professional opportunities and to the 'professionalization' of activism. A mother of three children, she is from Algeria. She studied history but broke off her studies in order to raise her children. She has always been engaged as a volunteer in local associations in her neighbourhood (in the 18th arrondissement). Once the children were a bit older, she was admitted to a course of public health mediation in the Paris hospital designated for training such mediators.[41] Once she had obtained her degree, she started working for the Centre. At the time we met in 2003, she was working as a permanent staff member three days a week, being also the respondent to the mediation phone line (available seven days a week). She defined her mission as one of cultural brokerage (*'je suis un décodeur culturel'*), trying to improve the communication between individuals and institutions (doctors, nurses, but also administrative staff). Through the interaction that she has with the public administration, she notices the lack of competence when dealing with people who are not French citizens, or with French citizens from different cultural and national backgrounds. The administrative staff and the public service are 'culturally too far removed from people's needs. I identify more quickly the needs' (ibid.).

The development of such an activity centred on mediation in health-related matters is in itself not so much of a surprise. In Kechat's view, being a committed citizen goes together with being a good Muslim. The necessity to commit oneself, to be publicly involved as a secular aspiration, to act out a socially useful role on behalf of the religious message, illustrates the social utility of religion in a secular environment, with a corollary conception of beneficiaries not being restricted to the community of believers. Just as the Saturday conferences organize a bridge between a religious association (the Centre) and a larger social group, the mediation activities contextualize the role of a religious group.[42] This connection to a 'wider society' is primarily based on local and immediate surroundings (non-Muslims attending the Saturday conferences are either brought along by somebody or are acquainted with the Centre as local actors) through the identification of sensitive topics that need to be discussed with the right persons (competence and skills) in a 'safe' or protected environment which does not harm the 'cohesive togetherness' of the Centre (Lichterman 2005).

The Mediation point is therefore a natural extension of the Centre, a bridge to the immediate environment and a way to create relationships with the neighbourhood and the immediate environment. As Fatma readily admits, in her role as a mediator she sees herself taking over part of the tasks that traditionally would have belonged to the rector's domain of competence. Kechat delegates to her the part of his activity that is not strictly spiritual, for instance when it comes to mediating between members of a family about mixed marriage. On certain topics, however, Fatma admits that she does not feel competent to answer specific questions and demands. As an example, she mentioned the case of a young Muslim woman who was pregnant and wished to get an abortion. She came to the Mediation point both to receive support in the administrative part of her project, but also to get a religious opinion on her choice. Facing such a request, Fatma says 'I am not qualified', declining any authority in this matter.

Operating at the intersection of spiritual counselling, moral exhortation, and social activism, Kechat's role transcends the traditional boundaries of public and private spheres, and he appeals to civic as well as religious values without appearing to prioritize one over the other. Kechat is not enunciating norms pertaining to worship but instead suggests guidelines for civil commitment. His activities constitute a vivid illustration of Casanova's thesis of the deprivatization of modern religion (Casanova 1994). If one considers that secularization is composed of at least three dimensions (differentiation of the secular spheres from religious institutions and norms, decline of religious beliefs and practices, and marginalization of religion to a privatized sphere), deprivatization, in Casanova's terms, refers to the fact that religious traditions of different kinds are refusing to accept the privatized role which theories of modernity and secularization have reserved for them. Religious beliefs cease to be a matter of purely personal preference and again become the subject of public argument (Amiraux 2006). Concurrently, numerous public matters are re-moralized, and religious authorities intervene in the public sphere of civil society discussions by bringing in ethic notions. The rethinking of the relationship of religion and modernity imposes a reinvention of the way religious associations and other church-based communities relate to the public and behave as civic partners.

> In other words, common norms cannot be presupposed as the premise and foundation of a modern social order but, rather as the potential and always fragile outcome of a process of communicative interaction. ... Through such a process of communicative interaction in the public sphere of modern civil societies, normative traditions can be reflexively reconstructed – that is, rationalized – and the differentiated subsystems of modern societies can be made responsible to a publicly defined 'common good'. By going 'public', religions as well as other normative traditions can, therefore, contribute to the vitality of such a public sphere.
>
> (Casanova 1994: 230–1)

From his lyrical narratives about articulating vertical spirituality and horizontal social solidarity to his management of the internal tensions inside the audience and the speakers, Kechat makes possible a connection between a religious-based group togetherness (Muslims coming to the Centre motivated by religious considerations) and the broader society of non-Muslim French citizens (the non-Muslim speakers and listeners). With specific skills and a recognized competence for going public (in particular an undeniable talent for public speeches and strong personal charisma), Kechat ends up being an intermediary figure of a religious leader. On the one hand, he affirms the centrality of religious (Islamic) values and messages in social life, and of exerting an internal authority for the Muslim visitors of his Centre (and not claiming to address or to represent a larger group of Muslims). On the other hand, he secularizes in a way the internal space of the

Centre and makes of this internal secularization (separation of sacred and profane activities, relativizing his own religious authority on social issues by inviting other forms of expertise to speak next to him) the necessary condition for establishing dialogue. In the last section of the chapter, I shall return to the different aspects of Kechat's authority, spiralling in and out, and shall attempt to assess the specific interaction with the secular French context of action.

The autonomy of leadership and authority

Compared to other Muslim leaders, Kechat turns back to a more parochial conception of his own duty and role towards the community of his fellow citizens (*'mes concitoyens'*), referring to people sharing the same space and territory whether Muslims or non-Muslims. In line with his conception of the mosque's 'capacity of social control' over the neighbourhood, he assumes the dual role of local organizer and parish authority (*'curé de paroisse'*). In France, this refers to a traditional representation of the local involvement and commitment of religious leaders, in particular Muslims. From the days of managing a colonial empire to the recent urban riots, such community leaders have repeatedly been asked to intervene and mediate between 'vulnerable populations' and state authorities (Bouzar 2001). On many points, the initiatives taken by Kechat's Centre, the networks connected to it, and the nature of the projects carried out by the Centre are those of classical civic associations, at the intersection of renewal of local democracy, development of sociability, and affirmation of civic engagement of individuals (Barthélémy 2000: 81). Just as some studies illustrate the ties binding faith to rituals, Kechat's project of regular conferences and non-strictly religious activities illustrates his wish to act as a mediator between religious duties, moral obligation, and the social environment.

Kechat's authority cannot easily be assigned to any of the three ideal types that Weber distinguished; rather, it has some aspects of all three. Whereas he started on the basis of a rather rational pragmatic one, he progressively moved towards a more traditional one. Most of the regular visitors of the Rue de Tanger mosque consider him a charismatic leader,[43] besides a more traditional type of authority (Falbo, New, Gaines 1987). He can be considered as a clergyman (*un ministre du culte*), due to his personal competences, his skills and his specific training (i.e. he has legal-rational authority), not to mention the role of his family in Algeria (local authorities situating him in a traditional lineage of authority). As usefully distinguished by Abou El Fadl, Kechat both *is* an authority and *has* authority (Abou El Fadl 2001). The Saturday conferences have become proper rituals, thanks to Kechat's clergyman's legitimacy based on his skills. Larbi Kechat bridges in one unique site daily-life issues, spiritual matters, and broader topics related to nationhood and civic engagement in the public sphere. The local success of the Social and Cultural Centre of the Rue de Tanger is mainly based on Kechat's ability to carry out the dual tasks of, on the one hand, working for the education of Muslims, and on the other engaging with the social and cultural needs of the immediate neighbourhood.

His involvement in local affairs is not unrelated to his distancing himself from the national debate on Islam in France and from forms of engagement at the national level. Even though he was in one way or another also invited to the series of discussions and meetings launched by the successive Ministers of Interior since the mid-1980s, Kechat remains an independent figure among the Muslim leaders, 'a passive spectator' in his own words, and a discreet commentator. His local legitimacy and long-term presence in the field are two central elements of the fact that, notwithstanding his refusal to participate more actively, he still benefits from recognition as an important local partner by public actors. In early 2005, when the so-called '19th arrondissement network' of young radical Muslims (*'la filière du 19ème'*) was uncovered, and when it appeared that some of its members had a connection with the ad-Da'wa mosque, the mayor and senator of the 19th district, Roger Madec, made a highly public visit to the Rue de Tanger to reaffirm his trust in the Muslim leader.[44] The discourse promoted by Kechat is one of building bridges, participating, getting involved in civic action, and not at all one of claiming for exclusionary perspectives. Kechat prefers to communicate discreet and quiet signals of religious identity to the outside world. In that sense, he is in synergy with a dominant idea in French public opinion: it is much easier to deal with the ordinary Muslim next door than with an abstract Islam that remains scary. (See also Piette 2003 on 'ordinary' religion.)

Kechat is extremely critical of Muslim leaders in general, and especially of Muslims living in France.[45] The French Muslim leadership is in his own words 'defined by its intellectual poverty, which can be extended to the larger Muslim population in France'. Besides saying this, Kechat denounces the absence of a satisfactory setting for the training of Muslim leaders and authorities in the religious field and mentions the 'theological void on French soil'.

The main difficulty faced by the successive French Ministers of the Interior in charge of this item was precisely to help the emergence of a representative board in a democratic context where politics and religion coexist without further connection, the former being incompetent in what regards the activities of the latter. The implementation of the CFCM has thus been seen mostly as a symbolic and institutional gesture of recognition made by the French State towards its Muslim minorities (Zeghal 2005). The CFCM's role fits into the post-1905 French Republican representation of religion exclusively as *culte*, i.e. religions exist (and are seen by the State authorities) through their institutional settings: since 1905 the French Republic does not grant official recognition to any religion (*culte*), but it guarantees freedom of worship (*liberté de culte*) to all. In the CFCM project, Muslims are considered within the strict limits of the visible existence of Islam on French territory as a *culte*, with its double material and symbolic dimension. The term *culte* in the French context refers to two elements. The first one is subjective: faith or the belief in a deity. The second is objective: a *culte* needs a community that meets to practice this belief in the frame of ceremonies (Rolland 2005: 59). The CFCM is therefore a system of management of the practical needs related to the life of the community of Muslim believers, organized around the mosque as a reference unit, that ended up as a race for recognition of the power amplitude of Muslim leaders.

When invited to comment on the CFCM, Kechat expresses his nostalgia for the Golden Age of the 1970s:

> the world was not as complicated as today and Islam was not yet fashion. Later on, Islam became a means to do things, to obtain titles. Earlier, people just wanted to pray and learn. … It was a time of brotherhood and discretion.

Indeed, following the provisions of the 1905 law, a regime of implicitly recognized cults has been installed, slowly moving towards a regime of the 'religiously admitted', and of the 'religiously correct', with the pluralization of the religious field in France. In its dealing with Muslim religious institutions, the French state has shown a clear preference for dealing with clearly identified persons rather than with the institutions as such.[46] The need for community does not diminish with the heterogeneization of modes of believing (instable modes of identification, eclectic references to different traditions). Paradoxically, it may seem that this local and parochial significance of religious authority such as Kechat's opposes the project of public regulation of Islam by giving more opportunity to a 'personalization' of religious authority. Since the establishment of the CFCM, Muslim religious clergymen openly operate on a competition market of religious leadership and authority.

Kechat in the end is popular because of his public autonomy and his declared independence. While in many cases, the authority of Muslim leaders has benefited from either high publicity in the media (as in the case of Tariq Ramadan) or official support by Muslim states (such as Dalil Boubakeur or Soheib Bencheikh), Kechat represents a growing tendency in France among local imams whose authority stems beforehand from their capacity to create the local conditions for a certain 'spirituality' of Muslims. With regard to people who were exposed to bad experiences of interaction with French surroundings (racism, discrimination, targeting, humiliation, exclusion), the scheme of the Centre, based on the unique individual authority of its leader, may be understood as community-centred. Kechat is, for instance, extremely strict in the matter of selecting his direct collaborators, volunteers, or those remunerated by the association.

> I don't need passive volunteers, those who only run after visibility inside the Centre without being able to provide their commitment to a real spiritual and civic meaning. The youngsters in particular frighten me, especially young women: they are completely ignorant, with no culture at all of their own religion. They do not make any efforts and just express the wish to be there.

Empowering religious authority in a secular context?

The notion of authority brings together a double analytical perspective, practical and theoretical (Cochran 1977). In the French context, religious authority cannot be associated with the notion of power or coercion, or with that of legitimacy. Its meaning, as reminded by Cochran, only makes sense in a community.[47]

The different publics that regularly visit the Centre, the Muslim believers, the persons requesting help and support, and the local associations, all contribute to reinforce Kechat's spiritual authority. But in the course of action the community-belonging is challenged by the intimacy, the emotional tests, and the moral commitment that the various audiences experience while sitting together. In the Rue de Tanger, authority presents two dimensions, vertical and horizontal (Polanyi 1964). Indeed, as mentioned earlier in the text, this dichotomy is constantly presented as central by Kechat in his own discourses.

In the master narrative of secularization various strands may be discerned, emphasizing different aspects of the process (Martin 2005). One aspect that most varieties have in common but do not equally stress concerns the decline of religious authority, or at least its retreat from central public position, as a central feature of modernity and secularity. As Mark Chaves observed, 'secularization is better understood not as the decline of religion, but as the declining scope of religious authority' (Chaves 1994: 750). This emphasis differs from what used to be the dominant view of secularization as the decreasing social significance of religion (e.g. Wilson 1982; Bruce 1992), and suggests an interesting perspective on transformations of religious authority in this process, where (religious) community leaders may compensate for loss of religious authority by seeking other forms of authority.

I argue here that Kechat has integrated the requirements of his secular environment (France) and that he has become a secular religious leader. In secular contexts, the boundaries of religious authority, as compared those of other types of authority (political, bureaucratic, educational), are hard if not impossible to establish. However, religious authority, as Chaves observes, can be distinguished by a particular kind of legitimation; he defines religious authority as 'a social structure that attempts to enforce its order and reach its ends by controlling the access of individuals to some desired goods, where the legitimation of that control includes some supernatural component, however weak' (Chaves 1994: 755–6).

As we have seen earlier, Kechat is the initiator of an internal process of secularization inside his own organization, mostly based on the dissociation of ritual and profane activities. Both as citizen and as rector, he is confronted with secularization in its many aspects, from the institutional and political limitations, to the internal secularization of religious organizations and the individual ones (decline of religious beliefs and practices, distance from rituals). France is a highly secularized setting, in which local leaders such as Kechat cannot properly speak out as religious leaders, but have to develop new skills and resources to be recognized as partners for social initiatives.[48] It is in particular the case in the neighbourhood development policy, as in the local security programme (Demerath and Williams 1992). In these sensitive issues, Kechat the religious leader becomes a local social partner. In order to promote his Centre as a place where conversations can take place, encouraging people to talk to each other, to learn from each other, to get educated and instructed in order to become good citizens, thus being good Muslims, Kechat created a public stage inside his Centre. On this stage, Kechat imposes the rules and fixes the constraints (engaging in dialogue on sensitive topics), in a public local arena that offers him the possibility to perform as an imam and even 'more' (a father, a brother, a colleague, a believer, a citizen, a spiritual advisor, a friend, etc.). In front of him, as part of the public scene, the audience does not share the same views and is encouraged to make this disagreement part of the discussion. What, however, is his influence on the political outcomes? Kechat's ability to operate the conversion of social difficulties into moral issues should not give the impression of the strength of religious authority over cultural and political authority beyond the religious communities. Larbi's preaching activities for instance have no impact on other social actors than those who sit in the prayer room and listen to him. But at the same time, the output in terms of spiralling outward and affecting non-Muslims' view of Muslims is high.

Notes

1 This chapter was first presented as a paper at the Annual Mediterranean Meeting in Montecatini, March 2003. Some interviews were added in the following months, but the present chapter is mostly based on the empirical investigation that was conducted earlier. It is not supposed to be an updated description of the current situation of this specific place of worship, but rather it should offer insights into the local articulation of religious authority and social action by the time of the fieldwork (i.e. before the urban riots of November 2005 for instance). When I held the presentation in 2003, I benefited from the comments and critiques of a very stimulating audience that is also authoring chapters of this edited volume. I would like to thank them and, more particularly, Martin van Bruinessen for his meticulous and patient interpretation of my syntax, and Stefano Allievi for his accurate comments on an earlier version of this text.
2 Kechat was asked by the then Minister of Interior J.-P. Chevènement to participate in the round of discussion launched in the 1990s and known as the *Istichara*. His refusal to participate certainly added to his image as an independent leader. He nevertheless positively answered the invitation for an informal exchange at the Ministry, the invitation issued by N. Sarkozy during the months preceding the first round of elections for the CFCM in early 2003.
3 Available in English and French at www.eumap.org, and in the printed version 'The situation of Muslims in France', *Monitoring the EU Accession Process: Minority Protection, volume II. Case Studies in Selected Member States*, Country Reports (Budapest: OSI, 2002), 69–140.
4 The place is also known as the Stalingrad mosque, after the name of the nearest metro station.
5 Kechat is both the imam of the mosque and the rector of the Centre. Both labels cover different duties and imply different skills. The word '*recteur*' in French designates an academic appointed by the central education administration to run an academy or a university. In the ecclesiastical hierarchy, it is also used to refer to certain institutional authorities (for instance prelate, superior, etc.). The word has, then, a double connotation in French: religious (i.e. ecclesiastical) and secular. It is also associated in everyday parlance with the Mosque of Paris, which is directed by a rector too. In the French context, a rector is thus an imam and director of a mosque.
6 See later in this chapter the developments on the '*filière du 19ème*'.
7 For work on the representations of the mosque by Muslims and non-Muslims living in the neighbourhood, see Lejeune 2000.
8 Kechat is very vague when invited to talk of his birth and his childhood. During one of our conversations, he mentioned the fact that being born after the death of an older brother,

he inherited both his brother's name and his documents, hence the birthdate (1946). Ironically, he suggested me to contact the secret services, which would certainly be able to give me his precise birthdate!

9 The AEIF was since its inception conceived as a network of Muslim students from diverse countries. It can be said to be the first Muslim student association established in France. The association was divided into two branches by the end of the 1970s. One group followed what is called the Syrian Muslim brotherhood's leader position, 'Issam Al-'Attar based in Germany (Aachen). L. Kechat used regularly to visit this Aachen mosque to give talks there, in particular in the 1990s. A second group joined the so-called Egyptian section of the Muslim Brotherhood. From this part came later the Union des Organisations Islamiques de France (UOIF, Union of the Islamic Organizations of France). The AEIF still exists today, but does no longer has the lead as the Muslim Students Association (MSA), and stands behind the UOIF students' association Etudiants Musulmans de France (EMF, Muslim Students of France) on the French university campuses.

10 Mohammed Hamidullah (1908–2002), an Islamic scholar of Indian background, is known in France as the author of a translation of the Quran. He was one of the members of the founding board of the Islamic Centre in Geneva, together with Sa'id Ramadan, and he made most of his career as an independent leading religious authority, on issues related mostly to fiqh, in Western contexts (Europe and the USA).

11 'Our Tablighi group used to meet at 15, Belleville street in Paris', said Rachid Ghannouchi to Vincent Geisser in an interview in London, July 2001 (quoted in Ternisien 2005: 252–3). Rachid Ghannouchi is a Tunisian who lived in France during his studies at the Sorbonne and who started his Islamist activism during that stay, associating with different groups of Muslim students involved in various types of activism (including the Tabligh movement). Once back in Tunisia, he became the leader of the banned An-Nahda party (Islamic Tendency Movement), before leaving for London in 1991, where he still lives as a political refugee.

12 Since I have conducted the interviews that constitute the core of this chapter, things have changed and the mosque has been relocated to another site waiting for the final construction to be done after the newly elected City Hall socialist administration delivered the licence to rebuild the building. The city hall initiative to implement an Institut des Cultures de l'Islam (ICI) in the near 18th arrondissement and its impact on the local Muslim leadership from close areas is also excluded from this chapter.

13 I am referring here to the Centre before its modification, following the approval by the Paris municipality to rebuild the mosque and add a minaret and a dome.

14 One thousand five hundred meals are served here daily during Ramadan by an association called '*Chorba pour tous*' (Soup for everyone).

15 The socialist team of the Paris municipality has launched different 'best practice' initiatives towards the Muslim Parisians. The most recent and certainly the most ambitious one is the opening of a Fondation des cultures musulmanes in the 18th arrondissement scheduled for 2010. It will consist of a place of worship and cultural projects in the same space. The local associations are associated with this project, and a qualitative survey concerning the expectations and fears of citizens is currently being conducted by a team of social scientists.

16 Images and photos of the project can be seen on the web site of the mosque at http:// mosqueeaddawa.free.fr/. For an urbanistic assessment of the project, see Sidi Mohamed el-Habib 2007.

17 More generally, this question is not specific to Islam and also concerns other religious places, in the aftermath of the 1905 law on the separation between Church and State.

18 The order of expulsion stated that Kechat was an influential member of a political movement advocating violence and promoting hatred of the Western world.

19 From a juridical point of view, the arrested suspects were assigned a compulsory residence in complete violation of the law. Indeed, most of the persons incarcerated

in Folembray (twenty persons out of twenty-six) were expelled to Burkina Faso the day before their trial should have started (six of them are still in Burkina Faso). The six remaining persons were placed in forced residence (including Kechat). In 2005, one of them was still in this situation. See Delthombe 2005: 210–11.

20   Christian Delorme (a priest particularly active in the Muslim Christian dialogue), Monseigneur Gaillot (bishop of Evreux), and Monseigneur Deroubaix (bishop of Saint Denis) actively supported Kechat during his stay in Folembray. Dalil Boubakeur was among the persons who signed a joint statement in favour of Kechat. For an overview of the media treatment of the Folembray affair and the portrayal of Kechat, see Delthombe 2004.

21   'What my time in jail changed for me was my relation to politics. Not to culture or French civilization'.

22   'When I came out and finally discovered the entire listing, I saw all these names of scholars, intellectuals, opinion makers, clergymen, academics. And the idea came up: why don't we organize conferences here, at home, inviting these people to come and talk'.

23   'J'ai pu constater combien des notes d'une stupidité atterrante pouvaient venir sur les bureaux de ministres ou de préfets', Christian Delorme, Le Monde, 20 August 2004, quoted in Delthombe 2004.

24   For an attempt to quantify this statement that most of the qualitative research shares regarding Islam in Europe, and in France in particular, see Brouard and Tiberj 2005.

25   This can be said of other European countries and is by no means something specific to the French context. See the issue on mosques coordinated by Césari, in the *Journal of Ethnic and Migration Studies* 31(6), 2005.

26   In his intense and rather heterogeneous networking, Kechat has also been in contact with 'borderline groups', in particular those linked with extreme right movements. He is involved in the drug-fighting neighbourhood association, Les Pères de Stalingrad (see also note 35), and there have been allegations concerning the 'friendship' between Kechat and Jacques Cheminade, the leader of Solidarity and Progress (Solidarité et progrès), the French section of the US Labor Party led by Lyndon LaRouche.

27   Other Muslim leaders have developed such a position of individualized Islamic commitment in a non-Muslim environment leading to what certain scholars have called a 'civic religiosity' ('*une religiosité citoyenne*'). See Frégosi 2000.

28   'I often say to my fellows that France and Islam only co-exist geographically. The challenge to all of us, I, Muslims and non-Muslims, is to transform this geographical proximity into a historical proximity'.

29   Fourteen classes for around 400 pupils visiting the Centre on a weekly basis for one or the other classes.

30   The annual final conference usually takes place on a Saturday and is followed on Sunday by a more theologically oriented study group open to the general Muslim public. For instance, on 11 January 2003, the afternoon was entitled 'Stigmatization and discrimination: live and let people live!', as a celebration of the international day of action on HIV and AIDS. Invariably, in the first days of March, a conference is dedicated to women.

31   Travel costs for participants from outside Paris are reimbursed, and accommodation may be provided if needed. The use of French for preaching in a mosque or prayer room is not systematic. In most cases, Arabic (in a dialectal variant) is the language for preaching. In England and Wales, Urdu is the dominant vernacular language spoken in mosques, followed by Punjabi (14 per cent) and English (12 per cent) (Peach 2006).

32   In some particularly hot discussions, it can even last longer. On 14 December 2002, shortly after Nicolas Sarkozy, then Minister of Interior, had announced the signing of an agreement between his Ministry and three Muslim organizations in France, people stayed until 21:30, at the end of an afternoon discussing citizenship in Europe.

33 Evoking the conferences of the Rue de Tanger (to which he refers to as 'panel discussions'), John Bowen mentions for instance some liberties taken by a translator, who 'took it upon himself to render a very distinguished Islamic expert visitor's words in such a way as to completely reverse his meaning, in an effort to prevent divisions within the Muslim community' (Bowen 2002: 5; Bouzar and Kada 2003).

34 Dounia Bouzar, who was invited to the final June conference in 2006, is perhaps an exception. Dounia Bouzar is as difficult to classify as Larbi Kechat. By training, she is a social worker (*éducatrice*) and an anthropologist, who worked for almost fifteen years for the Protection Judiciaire pour La Jeunesse (PJJ, Judiciary Protection for Youth), in particular in the north of France (Lille, Roubaix). On the basis of this experience, she started publishing books relating her professional trajectory to broader reflections on Islam and Muslims in France (Bouzar and Kada 2003, Bouzar 2004). She has a complex multi-ethnic background with Moroccan, Algerian and French roots, and she converted to Islam in 1991. In 2003, she was asked by Nicolas Sarkozy, then Minister of the Interior, to join the CFCM board. She resigned in January 2005. In the letter she addressed to the President of the CFCM, she said her resignation was motivated by her impression that the members of this institution were more interested in their own positioning inside the Board than in discussing issues of serious concern for Muslims living in France.

35 This contrasts with the way such debates are often carried out in France: see for instance Tévanian 2005 on the gender dimension of French headscarf controversies.

36 Times are, however, changing and Kechat, who is translating his own words from one language to the other, sometimes expresses his irritation and refuses to do so because 'after all, everybody here should be speaking French' (December 2002, following the discussion on citizenship).

37 Other examples are Spain, Romania, and Bulgaria (Rouland 1998: 549, footnote 128).

38 See International Crisis Group 2006. Some indicators illustrate the difficulty of mapping the Muslim audience. In a 2001 survey of secondary schools, 85,7 per cent of Muslim pupils said that religious convictions were 'important' or 'very important' to them, without referring to a daily practice of this same religion (Geisser and Mohsen-Finan 2001).

39 This association was created by fathers of different national origins, all living next to Stalingrad square where crack and other drugs were being dealt. It came up as a very controversial initiative, criticized by several other civic associations for its methods (patrolling in the neighbourhood at night) and populist discourses. The association (*les Pères de Stalingrad*) has a website where its tone and modalities of acting in the public space are quite clearly exposed (http://www.entretemps.asso.fr/Stalingrad).

40 As indicated earlier in this text, all these data were collected before the move of the Mosque to a provisory site near Porte de La Villette while the building of the new mosque was initiated.

41 The project of public health mediation was created in Paris in 1999, inside the Institut médical d'épidémiologie appliquée in one of the Paris public hospitals (Hôpital Bichat). Neither doctors nor social workers, the health mediators were conceived as partners to improve access to health care and services for vulnerable populations. Fatma was one of the 180 newly trained mediators. Applicants for this training were asked to come with a project and were selected for their specific knowledge of vulnerable population groups. Drugs and HIV were priority topics in the training. Financially, the training session as well as the remuneration of the mediator is publicly funded.

42 A bridge represents here 'a routinized relationship that a civic group has to individuals or groups that it perceives as outside the group' (Lichterman 2005: 44).

43 The qualification of Kechat as 'charismatic' came from different comments made by Muslims and non-Muslims I met during the conferences. Journalists also refer to him as such. The use of 'charisma' brings any social scientist to relate to the concept as studied by Weber, often restricting it to part of the Weberian theory. While Weber

insists in his definition of the charismatic domination on the 'extraordinary quality' of the charismatic person, and of the exemplarity of his conduct, he also adds that the point is not to assess whether or not this 'charismatic' quality is objectively rooted, but rather to know how followers (*Anhänger*) experience and consider this extraordinary quality of the leader (*Führer*) (Weber 1995: 249). The way non-Muslim people relate to Kechat's charisma is mostly based on the perception they have of him through his physical gestures and manner of speech during the conferences. During the conferences, and only during this period of activities that take place outside of the prayer room, Kechat is perceived as charismatic, not in the loose common sense, but in the Weberian representation of 'charisma' as 'revolutionary': charisma is a rupture with tradition, a break with the representation of authority as distant. Charisma exists as a performance, here and now, in relation with a voice, a body, and all its related gestures (Kalinowski 2009).

44   Young Muslims living in the neighbourhood were being arrested because of their implication in recruiting youngsters to fight against the US army in Iraq.

45   During one of our discussions, he explained his reserve towards Tariq Ramadan's 'simplistic populism'.

46   This may be illustrated by the outcome of a 2003 court case in which Larbi Kechat sued the weekly magazine *Marianne* for slandering his Association Culturelle Islamique. In the magazine, the association was called a dangerous fundamentalist group. At the trial, Soheib Bencheikh, the mufti of the Marseille mosque, testified in favour of the magazine, qualifying Kechat's mosque as 'rigourist'. The court (the Tribunal de Grande Instance of Paris) put the Association Culturelle Islamique and Kechat in the right, and sentenced the journalist and the editor of the magazine for defamation of the rector – but not of the association.

47   With the following definition of what a community is: 'a community is a group of persons who share a basic human value and who, at least to some extent, are aware that they share it. … They may, as a church, share a faith and a hope, and a life of action in faith and hope'. Community is therefore a 'fusion of feeling and thought, of tradition and commitment, of membership and volition' (Cochran 1977: 547–8).

48   For quantitative data related to religious practices of Muslims in France, see Brouard and Tiberj 2005. For instance, on the basis of their sample, they state that Muslims in France do visit places of worship as regularly as believers of other denominations (p. 27). When comparing Muslims from sub-Saharan Africa, North Africa, and Turkey, they identify the same proportion of 'no religion' (*'les sans religions'*, p. 23) with a clear connection between religious affiliation and generation.

References

Abou El Fadl, Khaled (2001) *Speaking in God's Name: Islamic Law, Authority and Women*, Oxford: Oneworld Publications.

Amiraux, Valérie (2006) 'Speaking as a Muslim', in Gerdien Jonker and Valérie Amiraux (eds) Politics of Visibility: Young Muslims in European Public Spaces, Bielefeld: Transcript, pp. 21–52.

Amiraux, Valérie (2009) 'Suspicion publique et gouvernance de l'intime: Contrôle et surveillance des populations musulmanes dans l'Union européenne', in D. Bigo, E. Guittet and A. Scherrer (eds) *Mobilité(s) sous surveillance: perspectives croisées*, EU/Canada (forthcoming).

Barthélemy, Martine (2000) *Associations: un nouvel âge de la participation?*, Paris: Presses de Sciences Po.

Bellah, Robert, et al. (1985) *Habits of the Heart: Individualism and Commitment in American Life*, Berkeley and Los Angeles: University of California Press.

Bouzar, Dounia (2001) *L'islam des banlieues, les prédicateurs musulmans: nouveaux travailleurs sociaux?*, Paris: Syros.

Bouzar, Dounia (2004) *Monsieur Islam n'existe pas: pour une désislamisation des débats*, Paris: Hachette.

Bouzar, Dounia and Kada, Saïda (2003) *L'une voilée, l'autre pas*, Paris: Albin Michel.

Bowen, John (2002) 'Islam in/of France: Dilemmas of translocality'. Paper read at the 13th International Conference of Europeanists, Chicago, 14–16 March 2002. Online: <http://www.ceri-sciencespo.com/archive/mai02/artjrb.pdf>.

Bowen, John (2004) 'Beyond Migration: Islam as a Transnational Public Space', *Journal of Ethnic and Migration Studies*, 30(5): 879–94.

Brouard, Sylvain and Tiberj, Vincent (2005) *Français comme les autres? Enquête sur les citoyens d'origine maghrébine, africaine et turque*, Paris: Presses de Sciences Po.

Bruce, Steve (ed.) (1992) *Religion and Modernization: Sociologists and Historians Debate the Secularization Thesis*, Oxford: Clarendon Press.

Caeiro, Alexandre (2006) 'Religious Authorities or Political Actors? The Muslim Leaders of the French Representative Body of Islam', in J. Césari and S. MacLoughlin (eds) *European Muslims and the Secular State*, Aldershot: Ashgate, pp. 71–84.

Casanova, José (1994) *Public Religions in the Modern World*, Chicago: The University of Chicago Press.

Césari, Jocelyne (2005) 'Mosque Conflicts in European Cities: Introduction', *Journal of Ethnic and Migration studies*, 31(6): 1015–24.

Chaves, Mark (1994) 'Secularisation as Declining Religious Authority', *Social Forces*, 72(3): 749–74.

Cochran, Clarke E. (1977) 'Authority and Community: The Contributions of Carl Friedrich, Yves R. Simon, and Michael Polanyi', *The American Political Science Review*, 71(2): 546–58.

Delthombe, Thomas (2004) 'Quand l'islamisme devient spectacle', *Le Monde Diplomatique*, August 2004, 11.

Delthombe, Thomas (2005) *L'islam imaginaire: la construction médiatique de l'islamophobie en France, 1975–2005*, Paris: La Découverte.

Demerath, N. J. and Rhys, Williams H. (1992) *A Bridging of Faiths: Religion and Politics in a New England City*, Princeton: Princeton University Press.

Falbo, Toni, New, B. Lynn and Gaines, Margie (1987) 'Perceptions of Authority and the Power Strategies used by Clergymen', *Journal for the Scientific Study of Religion*, 26(4): 499–507.

Frégosi, Frank (2000) 'Les contours discursifs d'une religiosité citoyenne: laïcité et identité islamique chez Tariq Ramadan', in Felice Dassetto (ed.) *Paroles d'islam: individus, sociétés et discours dans l'islam européen contemporain*, Paris: Maisonneuve et Larose, pp. 206–19.

Frégosi, Frank and Willaime, Jean-Paul (eds) (2001) *Le religieux dans la commune: les régulations locales du pluralisme religieux en France*, Geneva: Labor et Fides.

Geisser, Vincent and Mohsen-Finan, Khadidja (2001) *L'islam à l'école: une analyse sociologique des pratiques et des représentations du fait islamique dans la population scolaire de Marseille, Montbéliard et Lille*, Paris: Institut des hautes études de la sécurité intérieure (IHESI).

Godard, Bernard (2005) 'Quelle formation des imams: état des lieux', in Fondation Res Publica, *Islam de France: Où en est-on?* (actes du colloque), Paris: Fondation Res Publica, pp. 29–31.

Grillo, Ralph (2004) 'Islam and Transnationalism', *Journal of Ethnic and Migration Studies*, 30(5): 861–78.

International Crisis Group (2006) 'La France face à ses musulmans: émeutes, jihadisme, et dépolitisation', *Rapport Europe*, No. 172, Brussels: International Crisis Group.

Kalinowski, Isabelle (2009) 'Le visage du charisme: Une page de Proust', *Théologiques*, 17(2) (forthcoming).

Lejeune, Marie (2000) 'L'investissement de l'islam dans l'espace public comme support des relations entre les groupes au sein d'un quartier de Paris: cas de la mosquée Adda'wa et du quartier Stalingrad dans le XIXème arr.', under the supervision of Véronique De Rudder, URMIS, Paris 7.

Lewis, Philip (2006) 'British 'ulamas and the Politics of Social Visibility', in G. Jonker and V. Amiraux (eds) *Politics of Visibility: Young Muslims in European Public Spaces*, Bielefeld: Transcript, pp. 169–90.

Lichterman, Paul (2005) *Elusive Togetherness: Church Groups Trying to Bridge America's Divisions*, Princeton: Princeton University Press.

Martin, David (2005) *On Secularization: Towards a Revised General Theory*, Aldershot: Ashgate.

Peach, Ceri (2006) 'Muslims in the 2001 Census of England and Wales: Gender and Economic Disadvantage', *Ethnic and Racial Studies*, 29(4), 629–55.

Piette, Albert (2003) *Le fait religieux: une théorie de la religion ordinaire*, Paris: Economica.

Polanyi, Michael (1964) *Science, Faith and Society*, Chicago: University of Chicago Press.

Rolland, Patrice (2005) 'Qu'est ce qu'un culte aux yeux de la République?', *Archives de sciences sociales des religions*, 129: 51–63.

Rouland, Norbert (1998) 'Les politiques juridiques de la France dans le domaine linguistique', *Revue française de droit constitutionnel*, 35: 517–62.

Sidi Mohamed el-Habib, Benkoula (2007) 'La mosquée de la rue de Tanger (Paris 19e) et son environnement socio-économique', *Urbanisme*, 357 (Nov.–Dec.): 82–5.

Ternisien, Xavier (2002) *La France des mosquées*, Paris: Albin Michel.

Ternisien, Xavier (2005) *Les Frères musulmans*, Paris: Fayard.

Tévanian, Pierre (2005) *Le voile médiatique: un faux débat: 'l'affaire du foulard islamique'*, Paris: Raisons d'agir.

Weber Max (1995) *Économie et société*, Tome 1, Paris: Plon.

Wilson, Bryan R. (1982) *Religion in Sociological Perspective*, Oxford: Oxford University Press.

Zeghal, Malika (2005) 'La constitution du Conseil français du culte musulman: reconnaissance politique d'un islam français?', *Archives de sciences sociales des religions*, 129: 97–113.

5   The pattern of Islamic reform in Britain

The Deobandis between intra-Muslim sectarianism and engagement with wider society

Jonathan Birt and Philip Lewis

Introduction

The great historian of Islam in India, William Cantwell Smith, remarked that the ulama, the guardians of Islam's religious disciplines, appeared rather late in the process of Indian Islamization, which, historically, was gradual, even in the areas of military conquest, and whose pioneers were more often than not traders and mystics.[1] This does not hold true for the Muslims of Britain, three-quarters of whom are of South Asian heritage, where some ulama arrived with the first waves of mass migration in the 1960s. For this simple reason, it is better to understand the process of Islamic reform as deeply coloured by its Sub-Continental origins, even if it is now shaped by the British context.

This chapter will map the establishment of Islamic seminaries in Britain with a particular focus on the Deoband School (*maslak*), which of all the South Asian traditions has been far and away the most successful in this regard. We will look at continuities and changes in the curriculum, as well as new social roles that young British-educated Deobandi ulama are assuming. We will also identify the conditions and contexts in which they are able to free themselves from intra-Muslim sectarian debate to engage with wider society.

The continuity of Islamic reformism

The movement takes its name from Deoband, a small town a hundred miles north of Delhi, where the first, college-level *madrasah*, *dar al-ʿulum*, was founded in 1867 (Metcalf 1982). It emerged as part of an efflorescence of religious revivalism in nineteenth-century India. Although the pattern of reform was not confined to the Deobandis, they were its most important exemplars. Their first priority was the preservation and dissemination of the religious heritage, understood in the classical sense of authentic religious belief and practice, the precondition for the transmission to new generations of a true Islamic formation. To this end, they created a network of financially independent seminaries, separate from traditional sources of aristocratic patronage – itself a diminishing asset in the new environment of British India. Their seminaries were designed for mass education and they borrowed selectively from Western educational models, making full use of print and rail to forge new trans-local solidarities.

Islam in the reform model was no longer unselfconsciously traditional, *sui generis*, but rather, in an expanded world, oppositional in character, defining itself against the popular custom of the Sufi shrines, other ulama, and non-Muslims, Hindu, and British. In such a context Deobandis were part of a sectarian environment often embroiled in what has been dubbed a fatwa-war (Metcalf 1982: 310). A sectarianism from which they have not been able to extricate themselves in Britain, but which has been exacerbated by currents from the Middle East, especially the Salafi (Birt 2005b, Hamid 2009).

Reform was 'rationalizing' in the Weberian sense of 'making religion self-conscious, systematic, and based on abstract principles' (Metcalf 1982: 12). The reform message avoided intellectual complication and local variation in belief and practice in order to appeal widely to scattered Muslim ethnic groups across an India that was opening up through mass communications and transportation. It was furthermore a pattern of self-reliance that enabled Muslims to depend upon themselves, as a newly disempowered minority, rather than upon the comforts of rule. Reformed religion was more insistently a matter of personal responsibility rather than of intercession, whether political or spiritual. The *shari*⁺*a* might no longer be enforced by a Muslim state, but, as the leading western historian of the movement noted, 'each believer was enjoined to engage in self-reflection and willed external conformity to proper behavior should desires direct otherwise' (Metcalf 1999: 220).

This legacy of reform left an interiorized reflexive religious consciousness, a this-worldly reification of mundane acts with a concomitant disenchantment of the world (the disavowal of the intercessionary power of the saints), and a symbolic religious politics of communal difference that could either focus on the individual (Tablighi Jama⁺at, Deoband, Nadwa, Ahl-i Hadith) or the state (Aligarh, Jama⁺at-i-Islami, Iqbal).[2] In other words, the Deoband reform movement, despite an insistence on tradition, was modern in important ways, if not strictly speaking modernist in its outlook. Again, in other words, in the judgement of Francis Robinson, there was a shift in all these reform movements, which was particularly true of the Deobandis, towards a 'this-worldly' or willed Islam that had four themes:

> *self instrumentality*, the idea of the individual human being as the active, creative, agent on the earth; *self-affirmation*, the autonomy of the individual, to which is connected the affirmation of the ordinary things of the self, the *affirmation of ordinary life*; and finally, the emphasis on *self-consciousness*, the reflective self, which in the Western experience is referred to as the 'inward turn'.
>
> (Robinson 2000: 112–13, our italics)

While the Deoband movement has not been slow to engage in the formal politics of Islamic republics as seen with the Taliban experiment (1994–2001) and Deobandi-inspired sectarianism in Pakistan over the last fifteen years, the Deobandis have always been able to recognize, in a *de facto* sense, the division between secular public order and the private religious sphere, and to function perfectly well as a minority in a liberal democratic context. Participants in the Deobandi movement (and its offshoots) have, for the most part, sought personal goals, aloof from formal politics, of the attainment of piety, religious self-knowledge, and even 'moral sociability', and have been more concerned to confront other Muslims than the 'West'; where the 'West' is seen as a source of corruption to Muslim individuals rather than as a supranational entity to be resisted through collective political action.[3]

The establishment of Islamic seminaries in Britain

At the heart of Islamic reform in Britain has been the emergence of Islamic seminaries (*dar al-ᶜulums*). Table 5.1 lists twenty-five seminaries in the United Kingdom from a survey we undertook in 2003, defined for our purposes here as ulama-led educational institutions training students in the traditional Islamic sciences. One was established in the 1970s, three in the 1980s, eighteen in the 1990s and three in the first few years of the new century. All except one are Sunni. This is a conservative estimate mostly compiled from seminaries that are formally registered as they provide statutory education up to sixteen years of age. However, there is no requirement of registration for those that only provide formal seminary studies for students older than 16. If this latter category is included, then there are at least four other mosques in the North of England that are training small numbers of ulama, three Deobandi and one Barelwi, and, if informal circles of higher learning are included, then the figure would increase further still.

A sectarian analysis immediately reveals the domination of the Deobandi movement – sixteen Deobandi seminaries, five Barelwi, one Azhari, one Nadwi, one Shiite, and one Ikhwani (Muslim Brotherhood) – and the list as a whole largely reflects the predominance of Muslims in Britain with roots in South Asia, 74 per cent of the total in the Census of 2001. The seminaries reflecting traditions other than the main South Asian ones have smaller constituencies and therefore struggle to find broader acceptance. The Muslim College (Azhari) enjoys an influential political role because of the national profile of its founder, the late Sheikh Dr Zaki Badawi (d. 2006). Its initial funding, some five million pounds, came from Libya, and while it has subsequently allied itself to the popular Barelwi tradition, its British Muslim intake is still small. The Muslim Brotherhood Centre in Wales uses Arabic as the medium of instruction and thus largely caters for an Islamist constituency in Britain and Europe. The director of the Nadwa centre in Oxford admits that it is as yet more a virtual Islamic seminary without a permanent building. Its clientele are full-time students at Oxford who spend their spare time studying, 60 per cent of whom are women. The Hawzah Ilmiyyah in Willesden, London, established in 2003 (growing out of the Imam Hussain Institute founded in 1998) intends to develop a comprehensive eight-year course for students over the age of eighteen. Affiliated with the Islamic College for

Table 5.1 Survey of Islamic seminaries, 2003

No.	Est.	Name	Location	Gender	No. of students	Affiliation	Notes
1	1975	Darul Uloom al-Arabiya al-Islamiya (DUAI)	Holcombe near Bury	boys	410	Deobandi Saharanpuri	Mother *madrasah* to five other UK seminaries
2	1981	Institute of Islamic Education	Dewsbury	boys	300	Deobandi Tablighi	Centre for Tabligh in Europe
3	1987	Jamia-tul Imam Muhammad Zakaria	Kidderminster then Bradford (1993)	girls	488	Deobandi Saharanpuri	Affiliated to DUAI
4	1987	The Muslim College	London	boys/girls	50	Azhari	Dr Zaki Badawi's institute
5	1991	Islamic Education Institute	Crowborough, East Sussex	boys	50	Deobandi	Principal a murid of DUAI principal
6	1991	Darul Uloom London	Chislehurst	boys	131	Deobandi	
7	1993	Madinatul Uloom Al-Islamiya	Kidderminster	boys	202	Deobandi Saharanpuri	Affiliated to DUAI
8	1994	Darul Uloom School	Leicester	boys	87	Deobandi	
9	1994	Hijaz College	Nuneaton	boys	90	Barelwi	
10	1995	Al-Jamiyah al-Islamiyah Darul Uloom	Bolton	boys	165	Deobandi	
11	1995	Darul Uloom Jamia Arabia Islamia	Birmingham	boys	20	Barelwi	
12	1995	Al-Karam School	Retford, near Nottingham	boys	123	Barelwi	Sends students to al-Azhar to complete studies

		Name	Location		Students	Orientation	Notes
13	1995	Jamea al-Kauthar	Lancaster	girls	222	Deobandi Saharanpuri	Affiliated to DUAI
14	1996	Jamia al-Huda	Nottingham	girls	166	Deobandi	Affiliated with Jamia al-Huda in Sheffield
15	1997	Jamiatul Ilm wal-Huda	Blackburn	boys	246	Deobandi Saharanpuri	Affiliated to DUAI
16	1997	Jame'ah Riyadul Uloom	Leicester	boys	100	Deobandi	Principal is DUAI graduate
17	1997	Dar al Uloom Leicester	Leicester	boys/girls	110	Deobandi	Principal is murid of DUAI principal; non-boarding
18	1997	Sultan Bahu Trust	Birmingham	boys	32	Barelwi	
19	1998	Jamia Madinat ul-Uloom	Plaistow, London	boys	90	Deobandi	
20	1999	Dar al Uloom	Oxford	boys/girls	20	Nadwi	
21	1999 [?]	Kanzul Uloom	Birmingham	boys	20	Barelwi	Sends students to Syria to complete studies
22	1999	European Institute for Human Sciences	Llanbydder, Wales	boys	60	Ikhwani	Affiliated with EIHS in France, est. in 1992
23	2001	n/a	Blackburn	girls	150	Deobandi Saharanpuri	Principal is a DUAI graduate
24	2002	Jamia al-Huda	Sheffield	boys	20	Deobandi	Affiliated with Jamia al-Huda in Nottingham
25	2003	Hawzah Ilymiyyah	Willesden, London	boys/girls	100	Shi'i	Sends students to Qom to complete studies

Sources: *Muslim Directory 2001/2*; Register of Muslim Independent Schools in England; Athar 2002; *Muslim News* (London); telephone interviews.

Advanced Studies in London, it offers BAs, MAs and PhDs in Islamic Studies including a year of Arabic in Syria and three years at the premier centre of Shiite learning at Qom in Iran.

The Barelwi alliance, formed of multifarious Sufi orders from South Asia, has taken longer to address the need to train a new generation of English-speaking ulama. Pir Marouf Hussain Shah (b. 1936), an early pioneer who arrived in Bradford in 1961 and who has become an influential patron, reflects an older set of attitudes. His main concern is to preserve community languages, and he accuses the younger generation of making excuses about not understanding either Urdu or the Punjabi dialects. Pir Marouf, whose organization controls seventeen mosques, set up three seminaries in Mirpur (the first in 1965), and claims to have directly or indirectly sponsored three hundred Pakistani ulama and placed them in imamate positions at Barelwi mosques. Yet even he admits that many have used this conduit of migration as a means to find gainful employment elsewhere once permanent residency status has been achieved, usually after four years. To date, his Islamic Missionary College in Bradford (est. 1974) has produced fifty-five *huffaz* (Qur'an memorizers) but no ulama (Athar 2002: 21–38).

Yet it is evident that his viewpoint is no longer widely shared either among the younger generation or even among many ulama of his generation. Under the guidance of the Siddiqi family of ulama and *pirs*, the Hijaz College, an £18.5 million project established in 1994, is to date the only Barelwi institution to offer the full traditional, South Asian curriculum – *dars-i-nizami* – taking nine years, combined with accredited BA and MA courses in Islamic Law, Islamic Studies, and an LLB in Law. Taught in the medium of English, some sixteen ulama have completed the nine-year *dars-i-nizami* course, many of whom have stayed at the College to form part of the teaching staff. None of the other Barelwi *dar al-ʿulum*s offer the full *dars-i-nizami* course and it appears that only two of these have well-organized programmes that ensure their students complete their studies at an institution of higher learning in the Muslim world, the al-Karam School with the al-Azhar of Egypt and Kanzul Uloom with various ulama of Damascus. The Barelwi *dar al-ʿulum*s also teach the older Persianate form of the *dars-i-nizami* syllabus that places a greater emphasis upon logic, theology, and Persian language and literature, elements that have been largely discarded or reduced by their Deobandi equivalents.[4] Many young British-born Barelwis have responded to this lack of institutionalization by going abroad to study the traditional Islamic sciences on their own initiative, not just in the Sub-Continent as might be expected, but also in the Yemen, Syria, Egypt, Morocco, and Mauritania.[5]

Discounting the numbers of women being trained, there are nearly 2,500 young men studying in such seminaries. Considering that roughly half of these students normally go on to purse the full *ʿalim* course of six years after completing the memorization of the Qur'an (*hifz*), and that the *dar al-ʿulum*s established after 1997 have yet to produce full graduates, a reasonable estimate is that currently around 140 ulama graduate in Britain every year, a small proportion of whom, having come from abroad, will return home to serve their communities. The potential capacity of the sector is approximately 250 a year, which could be achieved by 2010. Around 80 per cent of the current graduates are Deobandi – well out of proportion to the size of their natural constituency – and this clear majority is likely to be even more dominant given the fact that, with a single exception, the Barelwi *dar al-ᶜulum*s function more as preparatory schools for further basic and advanced study abroad. By contrast, Deobandi graduates study abroad in order to further a specialization having already completed a full course.

This enables us to draw two broad conclusions. First, despite the recent trend for larger mosques to employ a second, younger English-speaking imam to complement the first one who speaks the community language, there are far more graduates being produced than available imamate positions allow. Teaching in supplementary schools normally affords only ten to fifteen hours of usually ill-paid work per week with a hiatus for Ramadan. Thus the graduates, the vast bulk of them Deobandi, have and will continue to have to look outside the traditional forms of employment and explore new social roles (see below). Second, there will still be a shortage of English-educated imams in Barelwi mosques for the foreseeable future – the sectarian division between British Deobandis and Barelwis means it is unlikely that Barelwi mosques will employ many Deobandis, even English-speaking British-trained ones.

Ethos and curriculum of the Deobandi seminaries: continuities and changes

In response to the failure of the 'Mutiny' against the British rule in 1857, the Deobandi tradition emphasized the importance of popularizing Islamic law and legal decisions (fatwas) as a bulwark against non-Islamic influences. In reaction to the bifurcation of education into secular and religious strands in British India, its curriculum deliberately excluded English and Western subjects. One of its luminaries, Ashraf ᶜAli Thanawi (d. 1943), insisted that 'to like and appreciate the customs of the infidels' was a grave sin (Saroha 1981: 23). In the nineteenth century, it sought to maintain social, cultural, and intellectual distance from non-Muslims, an orientation that changed somewhat with the entry of some of its ulama into national politics in the 1920s, when they formed an alliance with the Hindu-dominated Congress party in order to campaign for independence from British rule, but crucially as a separate party in an attempt to retain their status as independent moral arbiters. It also generated a revivalist tradition – Tablighi Jamaᶜat (the Preaching Movement) – which adopts a strategic anti-political stance and seeks to win back lapsed Muslims, as well as traditional Muslims whose practices are shaped by non-Islamic norms (Masud 2000).

The first seminary in the Deobandi tradition in Britain was established in 1975 in Holcombe, a sleepy village near Bury in the North of England, and enjoys a decisive influence among British Deobandis. Its founder is a Gujarati Indian scholar, Sheikh Yusuf Motala (b. 1946), referred to affectionately by one young imam as 'the Pope' of the Deobandis in Britain. As of April 1995, this institution had produced 260 ulama, 250 Qurᶜan reciters (*qurra'*), and 290 Qurᶜanic memorizers (*huffaz*) (Sikand 2002: 246). The Darul Uloom al-Arabiya al-Islamiya, or 'Bury' in a widely used shorthand, runs five other seminaries of good size in the United Kingdom with significant informal ties with three others, so that it either directly or indirectly informs the ethos and curriculum of half of Britain's Deobandi seminaries. The second seminary, established in Dewsbury in 1982, is also the European headquarters of Tablighi Jama‘at.

Both seminaries are in large part the heirs of a distinctive strand of the Deobandi reform movement identified with the Mazahirul Uloom of Saharanpur (est. 1867), Uttar Pradesh, in North India, 'in size and influence ... second only to Deoband itself ... [it] came to be considered less intellectual and more Sufi in orientation than Deoband' (Metcalf 1982: 128, 133), known for its expertise in Hadith commentary and for attempting to remain aloof from the controversy that split the Deoband movement in the 1920s over the desirability of participation in national politics. In the later twentieth century, its central figure was Muhammad Zakariya al-Khandhalwi (d. 1982), known for his piety, his writing of the Tabligh manual for its preachers and his learned Hadith commentaries. He was also the teacher and Sufi guide of Sheikh Yusuf, himself a graduate from Saharanpur in 1968, the year he migrated to England.

Bury is felt by Deobandis to occupy a unique position for more than merely mundane reasons of influence. Of great significance were two visits made by Muhammad Zakariya shortly before his death in 1980 and 1981, which were attended by thousands. Because this luminary inaugurated its Hadith studies programme with his first visit and gave his last lecture on Hadith on his second, this amounts to the claim that Bury is a direct heir of the Saharanpuri tradition. Motala's account captures the exalted mood of the last visit well:

> Maulana Muhammad Salman Sahib talked about the Imam of the People of Sufism, Shaikh Ibn ‘Arabi. Upon hearing this, the gathering, including Hadrat [Muhammad Zakariya], wept. Thereafter, the recitation of *ahadith* began. Little was it known that this was to be the final teaching of *ahadith* in the blessed life of Hadrat Shaikh *may God have mercy on him*. ... The spectacle of this was beyond imagination. ... [A] congregation of tens of thousands was found respectfully seated in all directions. ... Hadrat's seat was raised so that from all four sides his beloved enthusiasts could easily observe his radiant face.
>
> Hadrat *may God have mercy on him* spoke briefly: ... 'Imam Bukhari began his book with the Hadith, 'Actions are based on their intention' and ended with the Hadith, 'Two expressions are beloved to God Most High. ...' The moral of all of this is that there are only two things in the world: sincerity of the heart [and] praise of God by the tongue. This is the aim of Imam Bukhari *may God have mercy on him*'.[6]

It is this pietist, anti-political, and Sufi-orientated strand of the Deoband school that has predominated in the United Kingdom due to the influence of Muhammad Zakariya upon the 'mother *madrasah*' of the United Kingdom and upon Tablighi revivalism in general.[7] Of lesser influence have been the followers of Ashraf ᶜAli Thanawi, and those of Husain Ahmad Madani (d. 1957), one of the founders of the Jamiᶜatul ᶜUlama-i Hind, the chief political wing of the movement in India (Metcalf 2009; Zaman 2008).

Until very recently, students who attended these seminaries were socialized in a relatively self-contained world. Locations are often remote from centres of population – or on the edge of such; there was no structured interaction with wider society and informal meeting discouraged; and TV and radio were not allowed. Islamic study dominates the morning taught through the medium of Urdu, while a minimal English curriculum is taught in the afternoon for pupils from twelve to sixteen to conform to the dictates of English law. Students who complete the entire programme of study often lack good English and the interpersonal skills to relate to wider society. The structure of study indicates that students live in two unconnected intellectual, linguistic, and cultural worlds (Lewis 2002: 90–4).

The *dars-i-nizami* curriculum taught at Bury was initially developed in the eighteenth century by the famous Lucknow dynasty of scholars known as the Farangi Mahall. An historian of the movement describes the Farangi Mahall scholars as 'the great consolidators on Indian soil of the rationalist tradition of scholarship derived from Iran' (Robinson 2001: 2). Their syllabus with its enhanced significance given to logic and philosophy alongside the traditional subjects of the Qurᶜan, Hadith, and *fiqh* (Islamic jurisprudence) was congenial to the Muslim elites who would become the lawyers, judges, and administrators of the Mughal Empire.

> The study of advanced books of logic, philosophy and dialectic sharpened the rational faculties and … brought to the business of government men with better trained minds and better formed judgement … the emphasis on the development of reasoning skills meant an emphasis on the understanding rather than merely rote learning … It could help … to develop opposition to dogmatic and extreme religion … [and] bring the continued possibility of a truly understanding interaction with other traditions … whether Shia or Hindu.
>
> (Robinson 2001: 53–4)

Farangi Mahall offered an expansive and innovative curriculum: one of its great nineteenth-century luminaries, Maulana ᶜAbd al-Hayy, was unusual in embodying in his scholarship a highly developed historical sense. He sought to contextualize the classical texts, especially the great works of *fiqh*, studied in the seminaries.

> He was deeply concerned that the lack of such a sense [of history] amongst his contemporaries meant that they were using all the elements of the Islamic tradition … in a wooden and inflexible fashion which made them increasingly less serviceable guides to Islamic behaviour in the present. 'On account of this state of things', he declared somewhat waspishly, 'our ulama have become riders of a blind animal' and fell into a dry well.
>
> (Robinson 2001: 121)

However, with the emergence of the Deobandi tradition in South Asia in the nineteenth century this tradition of rational sciences and emerging historical contextualization of classical Islamic texts was largely eroded in favour of a renewed emphasis on the revealed sciences of Qurʿan and Hadith and the production of legal verdicts focused upon the moral reform of the individual. There are various reasons for this development: the influence of the great Indian reformist scholar, Shah Wali Allah of Delhi (d. 1762) (Rahman 1982: 40–1), the disappearance of the old centres of patronage and demand for the Farangi Mahall education with the collapse of the Mughal Empire, and the reduction of the *shariʿa* to the status of personal law. Western education was now the route to positions in British India, which left the ulama, the erstwhile educators of the ruling elite, with the task of immediate preservation of the core Islamic sciences in what they viewed as a hostile climate.

The syllabus in the British seminaries offers a somewhat attenuated *dars-i-nizami* course. The first few years include the study of Arabic literature and language – the precondition for any serious study of the key Islamic texts. There is some minimal study of the life of the Prophet, and his companions, and an elementary review of the history of early Islam. Apart from the canonical Hadith collections forming the apex of study, a selection of medieval texts drawn from the historic *dars-i-nizami* syllabus is included: the short Qurʿanic commentary by Suyuti (d. 1505), *Tafsir al-Jalalayn*; a short text on the articles of belief by Nasafi (d. 1143); and a Hanafi *fiqh* text, the *Hidaya*, written by Marghinani (d. 1196). The teaching methods remain traditional: the aim is to initiate the student into the accumulated wisdom of a religious tradition, personalized in the life and teaching of a respected teacher. Teaching is one way – with opportunity for questions to clarify rather than challenge the contents of these revered texts. The aim is the mastery of key texts rather than the systematic and critical exploration of subjects; successful completion of the course entails the permission (*ijaza*) to teach these texts to others.

In the last decade, Bury has made internal changes, and furthered its links with outside educational institutions, following the lead of graduates who have gained expertise in the wider world. Talk radio is now allowed and some newspapers and weeklies, excluding the tabloids. Many students are opened up to wider currents in Islamic thought by going on to complete specialisms elsewhere: comparative *fiqh* and Arabic at the al-Azhar in Egypt, Hadith studies at the Islamic University of Medina in Saudi Arabia, and training as jurisconsults (*muftis*) in the Hanafi legal school in the Sub-Continent under such luminaries as Justice Taqi Usmani in Karachi. In the 1990s the more able students were encouraged to get further qualifications from British universities. Initially such studies were pursued in Islamic disciplines, including Arabic studies and law – two Bury alumni now have PhDs from Manchester University and the School of Oriental and African Studies (SOAS) in London respectively. In 1998, the first cohort of five Bury students were accepted to study in the BA course in applied theological studies offered by Westhill College of Higher Education in Birmingham, qualifying them to teach religious education in schools. This innovative scheme majors on Islam and is largely taught by Muslim scholars, two of whom were themselves Bury alumni. This prepared the way for a new development in 2000 whereby some thirty graduates from Bury went on to study a range of degrees at a local university where another of its alumni now lectures.

Bury has also begun to open up a little to the outside world. The new Muslim Adviser to Prisons was encouraged to visit and talk about prison chaplaincy. Some schoolchildren studying religious education are allowed to visit. There has also been a realization since September 11 that Muslims are under close scrutiny. To address fears and misconceptions the Principal invited a local Bishop, MP, and a few others to visit and talk to students on the anniversary of 9/11. This reflects both a growing confidence in the institution and an awareness that many students will not go on to become imams in mosques, and so will need other qualifications to earn a living. The minimal attention given to the English curriculum is also changing. A local college is providing science and computing facilities on site and some personnel to teach examination subjects: mainly GCSE level but some at AS or 'A' level in Arabic, Urdu, and Islamic History. Such people could also begin to teach in the proliferating private Muslim school sector (about one hundred). It is clear that the principal of Bury, Sheikh Yusuf Motala, has given active support and blessings to such developments that should enable many of his alumni to engage more confidently with wider society.

New social roles for imams and ulama

In 1989, the first Deobandi imam from Bury appointed to a Bradford mosque identified the functions of an imam as follows: to lead the five daily prayers; to teach the children in the supplementary school; to give the Friday address in Arabic (*khutba*) and the accompanying sermon in Urdu; to preside over the rites of passage – at birth to whisper the call to prayer, *adhan*, into the child's ear, to solemnize the marriage contract, *nikah*, and to prepare the dead for burial; to prepare amulets –*ta⁵widh* – for those fearful of the evil eye (*⁵ayn*); and to offer advice within his competence on the application of Islamic teaching and law, and on a range of general issues put to him (Lewis 2002: 117).

The first generation of mosque congregants did not expect an imam to have a role in the wider community. However, there is a growing impatience with such a limited understanding of the imam's role. With 52 per cent of Muslims under the age of 25, there is already a high level of expectation from the first generation of British-born Muslims, who are now in their thirties, that imams should lecture and teach in English, address pertinent issues of concern to them, and take up wider roles in society outside the mosque, especially pastoral youth work.

In the 1990s, the first generation of British-educated ulama began to respond to these challenges. Some set up independent Islamic academies outside the constraints of the more conservative mosque committees; others work full-time or part-time as chaplains in prisons and hospitals; and others have become state school teachers, but continue to teach in mosques in their spare time while applying the new teaching methods they have learned. The new roles available to these young ulama can be illustrated by referring to the activities of four Deobandi imams: one serves part-time as a prison chaplain; another has developed a flourishing audio cassette ministry; the third has trained as a *mufti* and has developed an Islamic magazine as a vehicle for teaching; and finally the fourth is an imam who has assumed a range of social roles in the community, locally and nationally.

Khalil Ahmed Kazi, a Gujarati, was one of the first imams appointed to a prison chaplaincy in 1996. He initially assumed that his role would simply be an extension of his preaching and teaching role in the mosque. Recently qualified from Bury, he had few transferable work or social skills: he had to master the art of writing complex letters on behalf of inmates to probation officers and review boards; to organize religious festivals in the prison; to develop managerial skills to equip him to work within a complex hierarchical institution; to acquire the knowledge and confidence to relate to Christian colleagues; to perform a pastoral role for disoriented Muslim prisoners and intercede with fathers whose first response was often to wash their hands of their sons who had brought shame on the extended family; and to build a network of support within the Muslim community for those released. As a chaplain he had a generic role and therefore wider responsibility for all prisoners. Initially, his role as a prison chaplain was met with incredulity within the Muslim community, which was initially in denial about the soaring numbers of Muslim prisoners.[8] Even when they acknowledged the problem, they were still unconvinced of the need for a Muslim prison chaplain. That he has a generic role that covers all prisoners is still not deemed important by many in his congregation.

The lessons he has learned as chaplain are being applied in Batley, West Yorkshire, where he is General Secretary of an Institute of Islamic Scholars. Their first biannual report for 2000–2002 makes clear what new social roles imams are beginning to fulfil in that town. There are reports from groups with responsibility for religious education in the mosques; a chaplaincy group reporting on their work in prisons and hospitals; work with local schools and colleges; a *daʿwa* (invitation to Islam) and publications department; lecture and youth programmes; a community services network working with the police, MPs and policy makers; lectures on Islam delivered in a variety of venues, including an Inter-Faith Council; and a support group for drug and alcohol abuse.

The report is notable for bringing formerly private debates into the public domain: the ulama are urged to 'come forward to direct, motivate, create ideas, initiate new projects and take up responsibilities'. Only then will they be in a position to 'provide direction to the masses'. Their innovative approach has met with 'much criticism from some quarters' but the rejoinder is that 'every new idea is a threat'. In the section on Islamic education (*dini taʿlim*), the report notes that 'the student, after spending a good part of the day at school, comes exhausted both mentally and physically to the *madrasah* [supplementary religious school]. If the [teacher] then conducts his lesson without any preparation, planning or using relevant methods, how would that then capture the imagination, attention and hearts of the students?'

To meet such needs they are looking to South Africa, which has 'one of the most advanced and refined madaris [plural of *madrasah*] systems in the world. Textbooks have been written [in English], regular teacher development workshops take place, examiners visit the madaris on a regular basis and uniform examination papers have been … introduced'. The report admits that we are 'a few light years behind', yet their example remains a practicable model for reform in method, content, and organization of mosque teaching.

One major concern clearly articulated in the report is the limited expectations parents have from Islamic education. 'Their idea of Islamic education is no more than the ability to read the Qur'an … under the pretext of flimsy excuses, such as increased school workload or attending weddings' they deprive them of basic education:

> Consequently when pupils reach adolescence, when they are in a position to appreciate the beautiful teachings of Islam, when they need to be guided through the difficult period of teenage-hood, they are taken out of madaris. This great injustice is going to create an identity crisis, an ignorant rebellious Muslim.
>
> (Institute of Islamic Scholars, 1st Bi-annual Report, 2000–2002, Batley)

Khalil, as a prison chaplain, is also aware of the growing disaffection of young Muslims with the mosque. In Batley, where he serves as a part-time imam, he has started meetings for these disenchanted young Muslims in a community centre, a neutral space outside the mosque.

British-educated ulama are very much aware of the need to connect with streetwise British Muslim youth. Two such Bradford scholars reflect two overlapping sets of responses. Mufti Saiful Islam serves a largely Bangladeshi community and Maulana Ahmed Ali a Pakistani constituency, although their work cuts across such ethnic divides. Both have established independent Islamic academies, staffed and run largely by British-educated ulama from Bury and its associate seminaries. Both continue to have good relations with local mosques, and the Mufti runs some of his teaching sessions in a local mosque.

The aim of such independent academies is to get away from the somewhat negative associations mosques carry with Muslim youth. Both run a range of activities for Muslim youth intended to maintain their interest through adolescence – the major problem Khalil identified. Maulana Ahmed Ali runs additional educational classes on the weekend in computing, English, and maths, as well as homework clubs. Everything is studied through the medium of English. In all, he and his colleagues seek to supplement and consolidate state education.[9] In the summer Ahmed takes youngsters camping, as well as organizes day trips to local theme parks. In cooperation with youth workers they provide soccer at weekends and competitions in the summer. They will take groups of young men between the age of fifteen to thirty to the annual *tarbiyah* camp organized by Bury since 1998, where they listen to addresses in English delivered over a period of three days, and live under canvas. Ahmed is quite clear that his Islamic Academy is to be understood as a 'social centre' generating a wide range of activities not normally associated with a mosque.

Ahmed's particular strength is as a charismatic speaker who has developed an audiotape ministry. He has over fifty titles and sells over forty thousand a year. He does not avoid controversial issues. One of his best-selling tapes is entitled, *Drugs, the mother of all evils*. It is clear why he is popular. He can speak the language of the street and his tapes are larded with local phrases drawn from the drug culture. The message, however, remains very traditional. Shape up or else hell fire awaits you. He is a textual scholar not a social scientist.

If audio tapes are Ahmed's main medium of communication to a wider constituency, Mufti Saiful Islam prefers the popular format of magazine and pamphlet. Like Ahmed, he initially went straight into an imamate at a local mosque, after completing his ʿ*alim* training at Bury. While Ahmed went off to Cairo to complete his training at al-Azhar, Saiful Islam was in the first group to complete a newly developed *ifta'* course begun in Bury in 1995 to train Hanafi muftis. Like Ahmed he soon became aware of the limited impact of the traditional mosque on Muslim youth increasingly being drawn into a range of anti-social and immoral behaviour. For this reason, he too has established an independent Islamic academy.

Saiful Islam, in addition to the normal pattern of teaching, runs a weekly session of Qurʾan exposition followed by a question-and-answer session. It is clear in his publications that simply rehearsing what the Qurʾan and Sunna say about issues is no longer enough. In a pamphlet entitled, *Alcohol, the Root of All Evil*, after the section on Qurʾanic verses and Hadith, he notes that 'these traditions should be sufficient to display the corruption and evils of alcohol. Unfortunately in this "advanced age" … one may be more influenced by medical and scientific research'. So he includes material on the intellectual, physical, psychological, and social costs of alcohol, drawing on a range of popular sources, including the *Reader's Digest*!

He is clearly worried about the inroads of Christian cultural practices. In a booklet entitled the *Prophet Jesus* (1999), he cites a number of Hadith which condemn the imitation of *kafir* – 'unbelievers who are condemned to eternal hellfire' – not least those who 'say Jesus is Son of God': 'buying or accepting Christmas presents, putting up decorations, sending Christmas cards and buying sweets linked with the occasion are all forbidden. All come under the category of imitating and following the kafir'. Other young Deobandi scholars, like Mufti Muhammad ibn Adam al-Kawthari of Leicester, are more realistic and relaxed about the Anglicization of Muslim custom and have developed criteria enabling a more discriminating response.[10]

Mufti Saiful Islam's bi-monthly magazine, *Al-Mu'min*, is a polished production. It includes sections on *tafsir* (Qurʾanic commentary), Hadith, religious and historic personalities central to Islam, a women's section, poems, children's corner, and a question-and-answer page where the mufti gives *fatawa* on everything from clones to contraception. There is no embarrassment at asking difficult questions: for example, a questioner asks whether a man's marriage is still valid if he has had an affair with his wife's sister. The mufti answers that the marriage remains valid and points to the prevalence of such immoral behaviour as rooted in not maintaining strict segregation (*purdah*) between close relatives within the family.

The articles self-consciously seek to connect with the world of Muslim youth with such catchy titles as: 'Football: a religion?', 'Designer clothing', 'Benefits and harms of the Internet'. The latter notes that:

> 'Dating' is a curse freely practised on the net and by email. Remember that communicating with a *non-mahram* [marriageable adult] before *nikah* [marriage] is *haram*: notwithstanding the foolish excuse presented by some Muslim youth of discussing and propagating Islam to others, especially *Kafir* (disbelieving) young women! ... [While] it is *haram* to view movies, documentaries, cartoons, news and sporting events on the net just as on TV ... viewing and playing is so rampant ... that Muslim students at school and even *madrasah* discuss and exchange such animated games to the loss of both deeni and secular studies ...
>
> (May/June 2001, vol. 2: 3)

The article is concerned to draw attention to some of the dangers of the Internet while urging Muslims to make use of it 'in a truly constructive and educational manner'.

One innovation Mufti Saiful Islam has pioneered is that of teaching part-time the *dars-i-nizami* syllabus to a number of local adults. He realized that they wanted to study the course but as married men, or those already working, they could not afford to study full-time. This pattern of formal Islamic studies for adult Muslims has become a feature of many Deobandi mosques in the North, the Midlands, and the South East, as well as in many of the other sectarian groupings.

The final case study profiles Sheikh Ibrahim Mogra, a Gujarati, who works in Leicester in the East Midlands. Originally from Malawi, he was sent to the UK to train as a doctor. However, he decided to become an ʿalim. His educational formation covers Bury, al-Azhar and an MA at the School of Oriental and African Studies in London. Ibrahim has worked part-time in mosques and taught in one of the three Islamic seminaries in the city. Alongside these traditional roles, he has pioneered work in the wider community. He runs Radio Ramadan, which, like two-dozen similar ventures across the country, is granted a licence for this period. If a traditional imam has a congregation of some two hundred on Friday, Radio Ramadan gives him a constituency of thousands for his teaching and preaching. He invites imams from Deobandi and Barelwi traditions to participate. He also delivers the Friday *khutba* at three local universities on consecutive weeks.

Ibrahim is unusual in being prepared to talk to and work with the local media, as well as pioneering inter-faith relations. He did not want to be limited to the traditional role of imam, so preferred to be part-time rather than full-time, but his boldness has not won approbation from all sides. His designation as 'associate imam' to a prestigious local mosque, a term borrowed from a local priest, has been dropped because he is viewed in conservative quarters as controversial. His local community work has won him a measure of national recognition. He has been appointed an area representative for a national umbrella organization, the Muslim Council of Britain (MCB), and acts as a shari⁺a consultant for them. He chairs their mosque and community committee. The MCB has very few active ulama as members and, of these, Ibrahim is the only *ʿalim* of his generation educated in a British seminary. Aware of the increased media exposure of Muslim communities in Britain since 2001, he hopes to convince mosques to have an open day every year when they would invite local non-Muslims into the building and extend hospitality to them. Since mosques have nothing to hide, this would begin to break down suspicions and misunderstandings.

Between pragmatism and rejectionism

Three of the four scholars participated in the annual Youth Tarbiyah [Education] Conference of 2002 – held in the summer under canvas in the spacious grounds of a Deobandi seminary near Kidderminster, at an attractive rural location in the Midlands. This represents the major public interface between the Deobandi imams and British Muslim youth. The conference is testimony to the imagination and influence of Bury's principal, Sheikh Yusuf Motala, the driving force behind it. All but two of the ulama are of Gujarati heritage. For the 2002 camp two had travelled from the USA and Zimbabwe. Most are the spiritual disciples (*murids*) of the Sheikh.

Over three days, the leaders among the new generation of young, British-educated ulama delivered eighteen addresses on a wide range of pressing issues (for a list of topics see Table 5.2). These included Sheikh Riyadhul Haq – the *khatib* imam of the prestigious Central Mosque in Birmingham (1991–2003) and the Principal of the Madinatul Uloom al-Islamiya at Kidderminster since 1993 – and other Bury alumni who, having completed their Islamic formation at Bury, have gone on to further education in secular establishments: two talks on education were given by an *ʿalim* who also teaches in a state school in Birmingham; another on 'globalization and Islam' was delivered by an *ʿalim* with an MA from Manchester University; the talk on 'the Terrorist Act 2000 (UK)' was given by Ibrahim Mogra; the lecture entitled 'the Prophet's Image in the West' was delivered by an *ʿalim* with a PhD from SOAS; the talk on Muslims and education was given by another PhD from Manchester.

An analysis of these talks provides an illuminating insight into the concerns of these young scholars and an indication of the creative connections being developed between classical scholarship and modern concerns: those on education by Maulana Imran Mogra seek to marry insights from the great Al-Ghazali (d. 1111) with those drawn from contemporary educational thinking, with the books of popular children's writers like Roald Dahl and J. K. Rowling commended! The talks also contain references to social abuses in the community which need addressing: amidst an interesting exploration of the meaning of the central Islamic terms *iman* (faith), *islam* (practice) and *ihsan* (spiritual excellence), Maulana Bahauddin

Table 5.2 Youth Tarbiyah Conference 2002

Actions (a‘mal) of the Inner and Outer Self Maulana Bahauddin Sayyid	**Safeguarding the Tongue** Maulana Rafiq Sufi	**The Prophet's Image in the West** Maulana Ashraf Patel
Status of Women Maulana Anas Uddin	**Education** Maulana Imran Mogra	**How to Practice Islam in this Day and Age** Maulana Ibrahim Madani
Advice from a Great Scholar on Education Maulana Imran Mogra	**Zikrullah – Remembrance of Allah** Maulana Ahmad Patel	**Faith (*iman*)** Maulana Ahmed Ali
Globalization and Islam Maulana Rashid Musa	**Obedience to the Prophet** Maulana Saeed Peerbhai	**Muslims and Education** Maulana Mahmood Chandia
The Terrorism Act 2000 (UK Legislation) & Our Responsibilities as Muslims Sheikh Ibrahim Mogra	**The Nur [Light] of Allah and the dark deeds of Kufr** Maulana Abdur Rahman Mangera	**Elements of Qur‘anic Medicine** Maulana Shabbir Menk
Sira of the Prophet Maulana Khalil Kazi	**Important Role of Youth in the Mosques** Maulana Shoayb Desai	**Steadfastness in the Days of Fitna [sedition]** Shaikh Riyadhul Haq

Sayid can digress about the high incidence of wife battery within Muslim families in his neighbourhood.

However, what is most striking is an evident tension in many of the talks between those who are urging wide ranging engagement with non-Muslim society and those who seem content to keep their spatial, social, and intellectual distance from an infidel (*kufr*) society, often painted in lurid colours. Not surprisingly, those who are most open are often those who have gone on to study in secular academies and work outside the mosque as teachers or chaplains. Here they have developed new social and intellectual skills, as we saw with Khalil, the prison chaplain.

The difference is seen most clearly if we compare two talks, one by Dr Mahmood Chandia, who now lectures in Islamics at the University of Central Lancashire, UCLAN, and that delivered by Sheikh Riyadhul Haq. Mahmood's presentation points to the necessity for Britain's youthful Muslim population to consider the importance of education. He insists that if they are to have influence in society they must raise their educational aspirations, for only thus will they be able to recapture that time in medieval Spain where they coexisted creatively with Christians and Jews and made significant additions to the store of knowledge in a whole range of disciplines. Time and again he repeats that historically Muslims integrated but did not assimilate. The respect in which they were held turned on the pen not the sword. He regrets that with other ethnic minorities in Britain so few go into education and teaching – 4 per cent compared to 25 per cent in IT and 10–12 per cent in medicine for all ethnic minorities. A good education is presented as a passport to influence in the key professions that shape the nature of society: academia, law (especially judges), politics, civil service, and the media.

Muslims are urged to engage in all these areas not simply out of narrow sectional Muslim interests – 'because it serves our needs' – but in 'the interests of wider society'.

He then worries about the attitudes in the Muslim communities. Drawing on his own experience as a lecturer, he notices that many students do not complete their examinations in science, medicine, law, or journalism and use the 'excuse' that we must give priority instead to revivalist tours of forty days', four months' or one year's duration – a central component of the activities of Tablighi Jama⁀at. Mahmood is scathing about such attitudes. Islamic Spain – medieval Andalus – is presented as teaching the important lesson that Muslims adopted a balanced attitude with regard to secular and religious learning and sought to contribute to the common good. He notices that because Muslim students 'do not know how to handle that freedom they enjoy on the university campus, [their] rate of drop outs ... is highest [amongst all communities] and still rising'.

Mahmood remarks that the most popular disciplines in university are politics, philosophy, economics, and law and the number one students are from the Jewish community. He then asks rhetorically: 'What of Muslims? Not interested in politics ... philosophy? ... [we] do not know what the word means ... economics? ... [where is the need?] I have my corner shop and petrol station ... law? I make up my own rules ...'. In all, Mahmood attacks the complacency and low educational aspirations within the Muslim communities. He points out that there is an open door in British society to influence its future shape but that they must engage at every level, whether as school governors or judges, academics or journalists.

Sheikh Riyadhul Haq's talk, 'Steadfastness in the days of *fitna* (discord)', suggests another set of attitudes. He has no truck with the 'propaganda' that all has changed since 9/11.

> Nothing has really changed. The persecution of the Muslims ... enmity, hostility, hatred of the *umma* ... ridicule and vilification of Islam [is] part of a constant battle between *haqq* and *batil*, truth and falsehood, which did not start on 9/11 but [was] present from the beginning [of Islam].

The sheikh argues that all this was promised by Allah as a test to his people. A number of supporting Hadith are cited to the effect that a time would come when men would prefer to be in the grave than living; that to be steadfast to their faith would be like holding fast 'to a burning cinder'. Muslims stand 'in awe of US fire power and economic might ... their technology ... [enabling] them to spy on the whole globe and [seemingly] bomb anywhere at will ... [as well as] their culture of MacDonald's ... their fashions, music ... their apparent liberty and democracy'. They have even begun to 'doubt the Word of Allah and the supremacy of Islam over all other faiths, cultures and ways of life'. Faced with the Western world's 'blind passion for retaliation' post-9/11 some Muslims have begun to change their names and avoid dressing according to the Sunna and want to dissolve into wider society. 'Not just out of fear but doubt about the truth of Allah's promises when they see non-Muslims straddling the globe'.

This jeremiad continues with stirring stories of exemplary Muslims standing up to the superpowers of their day. The Prophet himself was not spared such hardships in the Battle of the Trench but prevailed. When he prophesied that the wealth and glory of Abyssinia, Rome, and Persia would fall to Islam he was mocked by the doubters. He did not see it come to pass but it did.

Riyadhul Haq seeks, then, to reassure Muslims that Allah has not abandoned his *umma*. He has promised that they will know glory, liberty, and liberation. However 'demoralized and divided and doubting' Muslims are, Allah will reward their steadfastness and patience. In all, Muslims must not despair: 'Allah's light will not be extinguished ... Allah's truth and guidance are such that "His religion will prevail over all other religions ... [even though] the *mushrikin* [those who associate a creature with the Creator] detest it" '.

This lachrymose reading of contemporary history is almost Manichean. Reality is presented in terms of binary opposites, the undifferentiated *kuffar* – no mention here of the People of the Book – intent on humiliating Muslims. Such an essentialist vision provides little room for Muslims to engage openly with wider society. It is significant that in his diatribe he conflates integration with assimilation, a distinction Mahmood Chandia was careful to draw.

Theorizing the Deobandi pattern of reform in the British context

While it is tempting to explain these reactions – pragmatism and rejectionism – solely by reference to the context of minority status in a non-Muslim country, there are equally important, less visible factors at play, most importantly that the Deobandi movement is primarily concerned with the moral reform of the Muslim individual. As we have seen, the Deobandi movement works to a pattern of reform that relies on creating networks of grassroots support that acquiesce to its basic message. A paradox arises however that in order to gain that support in changed social contexts, the reformers have to answer, and often adapt to, pockets of resistance to their message and criticisms from within the Muslim community at large.

The irony of migration has been to transform Deoband's North Indian scriptural universalism into a South Asian 'ethnic' parochialism in the multi-ethnic British Muslim context, which includes an even wider potential constituency (see Table 5.3), which has no prior knowledge or understanding of its message, even in polemical terms. How is it to universalize its appeal in this more polyglot milieu?

As has been widely remarked, the core support for the movement, whether for its ulama or lay preachers, comes from the Indian Muslim communities (Gujaratis, East African Asians, and some North Indians), who form a fractional part of the British Muslim community as a whole, less than 9 per cent; although it has support also from Bangladeshis and to a much lesser extent Pakistanis (King 1997: 129–46; Sikand 2002: 226–30). Even if the two movements are formally separate, the Tablighi Jama'at has been essential in supporting the rapid institutionalization of

Table 5.3 Muslims of England and Wales by ethnic group or regional origin, 2001

Ethnic group or regional origin	(thousands)	percentage of Muslim total
Asian	**1,139**	**73.6**
Pakistani	658	42.5
Bangladeshi	260	16.8
Indian	132	8.5
Other Asian	90	5.8
Non-Asian	**408**	**26.4**
Arabs and Iranians*	130	8.4
Black African	96	6.2
Mixed	64	4.2
Turks and Eastern Europeans*	60	3.9
Unidentified or other	41	2.7
Far East*	12	0.7
Black Caribbean	4	0.3
All	**1,547**	**100.0**

*Only foreign-born figures are available.

Source: 2001 Census; rounded figures do not total up exactly.

the Deobandi movement, an observation borne out if we compare the geographic spread and preponderance (vis-à-vis other local Muslim ethnic groups) of Indian Muslims and the *dar al-ʿulum*s (see Table 5.4), whose community make up the core leaderships for both movements in the United Kingdom.

The 2001 Census allows us to move away from generalizations about British Muslims and Islamic movements towards a more nuanced appreciation of the various local contexts within which these young ulama operate and which decisively shape the manner of their response. The centres of Deobandi influence are the mill-towns of the North West, Bolton, Preston and Blackburn, Leicester in the East Midlands, and West Yorkshire (Dewsbury and Batley in particular).[11] Hafiz Muhammad Ishaq Patel, later the *amir* of Tabligh in the UK and himself a Gujarati, was called over to Dewsbury from India by local Gujaratis who 'did not

Table 5.4 Geographic spread of Deobandi seminaries and Indian Muslims

Region	Deobandi seminaries	percentage of Indian Muslim total for England and Wales	percentage Indian Muslims as a proportion of regional Muslim total
NW	6	27	17
East Midlands	4	15	29
London and SE	3	31	6
Yorkshire	2	12	8
West Midlands	1	8	5

Sources: Survey of British Dar al-ʿUlums 2003; 2001 Census.

have a mosque and ... were [not] regular in their prayers ... [and] had little knowledge of the fundamentals of Islam', 'to guide them in religious matters' (Sikand 2002: 225). The case of Leicester in the 1970s was similar. Yet today these towns have become centres of learning, and nodes for the dissemination of the Deobandi message nationally and even abroad, in which the ulama are at the centre of the Gujarati community and are able to determine the scope and direction of the further Islamization of these communities.

Leicester is a case in point. Out of a population of 31,000 Muslims, 59 per cent are of Indian origin or heritage. A pioneer of multiculturalist policies since the late 1970s (Singh 2006), Leicester has the third highest ethnic minority population after Slough and parts of London (36 per cent), and the second largest Hindu population after the capital. In this religiously diverse environment, twenty mosques have been established (over half are Deobandi), three *dar al-ʿulum*s (all Deobandi), eight day schools, and numerous supplementary schools. Thus the core institutions have already been established, and there is little discernible religious radicalism among younger Indian Muslims in Leicester; groups like Hizb ut-Tahrir struggle to make inroads into the Deobandi community. The youth are captured while young in the *madrasah*s (mosque supplementary schools), which are large, streamed by age, and well-supported, and have pioneered well-thought-out syllabuses based on South African Deobandi models. There is a register of 130 Deobandi ulama in the city, a quarter of whom have been trained in Britain. As such, younger ʿ*ulama* like Sheikh Ibrahim (see above) who operate as mild critics of the establishment ulama in the city, are forced to find new roles, and innovate novel ways of working. In this context, we find that younger ulama inaugurate or advise projects like a Muslim community counselling helpline, a national pro-Palestinian lobbying group, fund and build orphanages in Albania and propose an accredited BA Islamic Studies degree through a local university. They contemplate drug rehabilitation projects and Muslim-only sports centres. Arguably then, such local 'centres' produce a concern to engage with wider society among younger well-educated ulama, like Ibrahim Mogra, Mahmood Chandia, and Khalil Ahmed Kazi.

By contrast, Birmingham is dominated by the Barelwi tradition, and so is a Deobandi outpost compared with Leicester. Its 140,000 Muslims are dominated by Pakistanis (Mirpuris and Punjabis, around 97,500) – linked mostly to the large South Asian Sufi orders that opposed Deobandi reform – along with significant Bangladeshi and Yemeni minorities. It contains the liveliest Islamic sectarianism in the United Kingdom as it represents in many ways the meeting point between the visible, established South Asian groups and the first port of call for the Arab-based movements like the Salafis and Hizb ut-Tahrir that began to spread from the capital after the first Gulf War in the early 1990s. This environment has produced radical reactions against what might be called the Barelwi status quo: the Ahl-i Hadith and the pro-Saudi Salafis have their headquarters here, and the Jamaʿat-i Islami also has a strong presence, as do the newer Islamist movements like Hizb ut-Tahrir and al-Muhajiroun. Therefore, the Deobandi message has had to compete in a maelstrom of religious argument, which, in a youthful population, has tended to strengthen the appeal of oppositional and radicalized discourses. Thus young Deobandi ulama in Birmingham find themselves on the periphery, with less than 4 per cent of the population being Indian Muslim, and so have to work hard to establish basic networks of support.

Sheikh Riyadhul Haq's rhetoric and positioning has been largely shaped by this context. He is self-consciously a pioneer, struggling to bring the reform message to an often sceptical, even cynical Muslim constituency. *Wa⁵z* (admonitory preaching) is central, with the goal to establish basic love and attachment to God and His Prophet and aversion to un-Islamic influences. Sheikh Riyadh has arguably begun to overcome the perceived parochialism and limitations of the older style Deobandi preaching. In reaction to the critique of *taqlid* (following a legal school) and by extension the received authority of the ulama by the Salafis, the Ahl-i Hadith, and the Jamaᵉat-i Islami, he has focused upon adducing proof-texts for all arguments. In a Muslim youth culture where Sufism is heavily contested, he has taken care to recast a particular Sufi tradition – the Sabri-Chishti sub-order – in the universal language of the Sunna. And with the rise of popular pan-Islamist rhetoric in Britain, he has, perhaps uniquely among his peers, ventured to comment publicly and trenchantly upon geopolitical matters such as the 'war on terrorism', while always taking care to emphasize the need to protest within the norms of democratic dissent.[12]

He makes almost no explicit reference to the virtues of the Deobandi elders, a staple element in places like Leicester, but instead refers to the revealed sources and the classical ulama, especially the traditionists (*muhaddithun*), who are accepted by most Sunni Muslims. Running a successful cassette ministry like Ahmed Ali's in Bradford, he has been able to appeal to young Muslims across ethnic and sectarian lines. His followers, found nationwide, include Pakistanis, Bangladeshis, Arabs, Africans, and Turks. Such pioneers among the Deobandi ulama can be critical of their peers who have, in their view, taken the easier option of preaching to the converted, many preferring to remain underemployed in the Deoband 'centres'. There is little time in Birmingham for the niceties of engagement; more pressing is the work of basic reform. With some attention to local variation, Bradford may similarly be characterized as a Deobandi 'outpost' and the rhetoric of Ahmed Ali and Mufti Saiful Islam understood in like manner. Muslim London's pluralism is of an altogether different order, and represents an even greater challenge than either Bradford or Birmingham.

As the Deobandi reform movement works from particular locales, it, unlike the Islamists, rarely addresses the national stage, and has not, to date, established a national body that claims to 'represent' the interests of British Muslims. Its chief interests, as we have suggested, are more inwardly directed towards universalizing its appeal among all British Muslims. The Youth Tarbiyah Conference provided the first national platform for the younger generation of Deobandi ulama; but with the exception of the efforts of Sheikh Riyadh, the main attendees have come from the 'centres' of Deobandi influence rather than from its 'outposts'. One Bury graduate maintains that the annual conferences were inaugurated in 1998 to counteract the emerging Saudi Salafi polemic, and inspired in format by comparable youth conferences organized by other sectarian tendencies. There is no evidence as such to prove that these conferences are designed to establish a political presence at the national level, but rather to endorse a younger generation of leaders who are able to take the reform message to new constituencies in a radically changed context. Yet it is evident that there is as yet no consensus among these younger ulama as to how to universalize the appeal of the reform message, whether the priority is moral reform or upward mobility, or whether to engage with or retreat from the complexities and challenges of wider society.

The ulama in the lens of public policy and legislation

Up until 2005, the ulama, with the exception of the late Sheikh Zaki Badawi, had little or no direct input into public policy, even in areas that directly concerned their interests. This has been, in part, because of their own sectarian differences, which often disable collaboration. As they have often been stereotyped by British Muslims and others as obscurantist, ill-educated foreigners who retard the integration of the Muslim communities, they were historically rarely consulted about such matters. But most importantly, the majority are still very much largely, as we have suggested, either apolitical or even anti-political.

With the 'securitization' of the Muslim communities, a feature of European policy discussions throughout the 1990s (a trend greatly intensified after autumn 2001), the ulama, seen through the prism of a few assorted radicals, have come under suspicion of collusion with and support for terrorist networks and jihadist causes. Even the Deobandis have not been unaffected by this suspicion, one notable example being the brief detention of Sheikh Yusuf Motala at Heathrow airport while on an *ʿumra* trip, which was widely protested by the Muslim community (for more detail see Birt 2005a). Muslim lobbyists at Whitehall and Westminster, normally from the moderate Islamist movements which have tenuous links with British ulama, have given little attention to a handful of policy proposals that have sought to address the 'problem' of British imams. Before 9/11, and for some time thereafter, central and local government and some state institutions had by default (for there is no evidence of 'joined-up' thinking in this instance) undertaken a twin-track approach: to curb the 'importation' of ill-qualified foreign imams as a subset of immigration policy; and to provide limited alternative pastoral opportunities in hospitals and prisons for British-born ones (see Birt 2005a, Lewis 2007: 89–118).

The key perceived 'problem' has been that of the 'imported imam'[13] – the phrase itself suggestive of an undesirable commodity rather than a human being. However, it appears that little was done about it until after the terrorist attacks of 2001, despite discrete lobbying by influential Muslims to tackle the issue since the 1970s. A recent survey of three hundred British imams (Geaves 2008) showed that 92 per cent were foreign-born and trained, that only 6 per cent spoke English as a first language, and that there was still a considerable turnover, with 39.1 per cent arriving in the last five years. In the 1970s, imams enjoyed, in theory, free employment permit, although after 1980 entry clearance for foreign ministers of religion was made compulsory. The public policy argument after 9/11 has been that foreign-born imams, unable to connect effectively with British Muslim youth, by default leave them more vulnerable to isolation or extremism. First, a number of measures were undertaken to reduce sharply the numbers of foreign imams taking up positions in UK mosques. Certain loopholes in immigration policy were tightened up to prevent easy entry for foreign ministers of religion, such as stopping temporary visitors from switching their work status to 'minister of religion' in 2004. Entry standards were made much higher, so that from 2006 onwards, ministers of religion applying to work in the UK had to speak the same level of English as would be expected of a foreign student applying for a postgraduate course (an exception was made for ritual officiants). Steps were taken to bar 'preachers of hate' from entering the country – between 2005 and 2008, seventy-nine were banned from entering the UK. Finally, the government has supported the formation and development of the Mosques and Imams National Advisory Board (MINAB) since 2005, which the government is hoping will act to provide additional checks and assessments on the bona fides of foreign imams in cooperation with the immigration service.

The second development in the last fifteen years has been the proliferating opportunities for British-educated imams to find paid employment in education, chaplaincy work (in prisons and hospitals), and Muslim organizations, as has been seen with the case studies above. The Lancashire Council for Mosques – and similar organizations – have local authority-funded posts for Muslim develop-ment officers. Ulama of Dr Mahmood Chandia's abilities can begin to find here positions commensurate with their talents.

The process of integrating Muslim chaplains into state-funded pastoral roles began with the Prison Service during the mid-1990s in response to rising numbers of Muslim inmates. In 2003, there were thirty-one paid Muslim prison chaplaincy positions (six of which are part-time), with wages of £25,000 per year, far outstripping those offered by most mosques; by 2008, there were 198 Muslim prison chaplains (forty-one were full-time) (Gilliat-Ray forthcoming). Most of these positions have been taken up by young Deobandi imams. The National Health Service has been slower to follow the example of the Prison Service as it employed its first full-time Muslim 'Faith Manager', Yunas Dudhiwala (himself a Gujarati graduate of Bury) in 2003, at the Newham Health Authority in London, but it still relies on voluntary services by imams or part-time paid positions for the most part. In 2007, there were forty-three Muslim hospital chaplains (four of whom were full-time) (Gilliat-Ray forthcoming). In other sectors, paid chaplaincy posi-tions are unlikely to become available in the short term. The numbers of Muslims serving in the police and the armed forces remain relatively low, but the Armed Forces appointed their first civilian chaplain, Asim Hafiz, in 2005 (Gilliat-Ray forthcoming). There are also a number of Muslim chaplains in higher education.

Structural issues which dissuade able young men training as ulama have been poor salaries and lack of contractual security; a recent estimate in 2003 put the average weekly wage at £150, well below the national minimum wage (Gilliat-Ray forthcoming). In 2003, the exemption of 'ministers of religion' from statutory employment legislation, as part of a process to harmonize British law with

European Union legislation, was lifted. The Muslim College, the leading Shiite organization, the al-Khoei Foundation, and the lobby group FAIR – 'Forum against Islamophobia & Racism' – in a joint submission in December 2002 supported the change, on the grounds that the conditions of employment for imams were clearly unsatisfactory:

> As the salaries of imams are often paid for by the community, they can receive less than the minimum wage while being subject to having to follow all the demands of the community with few, if any limitations. This can have the effect of undermining the role of the imam in providing leadership and providing protection to the vulnerable (e.g. women).
>
> Sole economic dependence on the communities served by imams leaves the possibility of low salaries, poor and undefined working conditions and unfair dismissal, that without the protection of employment law, is often ad hoc and capricious, frequently being driven by factional politics within the mosque committee. And even where cases of dismissal are justified, dismissal processes take place behind closed doors with no transparency or real accountability ... The extending of employment status to imams therefore has enormous symbolic as well as practical value ... in bringing imams into the mainstream with other public servants ...
>
> (FAIR 2002)

While the authors of the submission hoped at the time that this harmonization with EU law would 'encourage a readily available pool of younger generation imams trained in the UK to take up positions', further research is needed to find out if it has made a discernible impact on the employment conditions of imams. Within the remit of MINAB is a commitment to ensure a good standard of 'corporate governance' for mosques, which includes providing proper terms of employment and training (www.minab.org.uk).

After the London bombings of 2005, two further strands have emerged with respect to government policy on imams. The first has been the official encouragement of the 'good imam' to 'wage a jihad against extremism' (Birt 2006). One flagship project that has received public funding has been the Radical Middle Way (www.radicalmiddleway.co.uk), which has brought prominent international scholars and imams to preach against extremism and in favour of engagement with mainstream society, and provided specialist training to British imams. In its first phase of operation between 2005 and 2007, it reached over 30,000 young Muslims: over 80 per cent were under the age of twenty-five and over 60 per cent were women. Another strand has been the Foreign and Commonwealth Office's Projecting British Islam, which, as part of the government's counter-terrorism strategy, has been designed to work against the narrative of a clash between the West and Islam by showcasing British Muslims as being an integral part of UK life. Between 2005 and 2009, over thirty trips have been organized to Muslim countries, in which some younger imams and religious leaders like Dr Usama Hasan have participated. In 2009, the government sponsored a discussion forum under the auspices of the University of Cambridge, 'Contextualizing Islamic Thought in Britain', featuring imams, activists, and academics, to deliberate on theological questions within the British context.

The second new strand since 2005 has been a state-led attempt to work more closely with the major Islamic institutions – the mosques, the *madrasahs*, and the *dar al-ʿulums* – to implement high professional standards, improve their capacity as integrative institutions, and to increase their resilience against extremism. As mentioned previously, MINAB has been set up to improve the standards of governance in mosques (including the development of policies on equality of opportunity, racial and religious harassment, health and safety, hygiene, and child protection) as well as to provide an additional check on the suitability of foreign imams seeking to work in the UK. Additionally the Faith and Social Cohesion Unit (part of the body that regulates charities in the UK, the Charities Commission) was launched in 2008; its first director, Ghulam Rasool, is heading up its first project to ensure that mosques are properly registered under UK charity law (if collecting amounts over £5,000 per year). In 2007/8, 19 per cent of all preventing violent extremism funding was given to projects run by mosques, some fifty in all. These included English-language training for imams.

Much more so than the Muslim faith schools, which only cater for a minority, approximately 1,600 *madrasahs* are estimated to educate up to 200,000 Muslim children. In 2007, in association with the Bradford Council of Mosques, the Nasiha pilot project was tasked with designing and delivering citizenship classes at *madrasahs* in West Yorkshire. Currently the government-funded Islam and Citizenship Education project (ICE) has developed an Islamic citizenship curriculum with a multi-denominational panel of imams, which is being piloted in Bradford/Kirklees, Leicester, Bristol, Oldham/Rochdale, and East and West London (www.theiceproject.com). The government has also commissioned a report looking at ways to build the capacity of the *dar al-ʿulums*, considering matters like accreditation in the public education system and which is due to appear in 2010.

Conclusion

The Deobandi tradition has been most successful in establishing its seminaries in Britain. Further, some of the graduates of their mother seminary, Bury, have sought to broaden the appeal of the reform message, re-imagining it anew outside its original South Asian context and scripturalizing it further; others have attempted to bridge the professional and educational gap between the seminary and the university and between the mosque imamate and the new educational and pastoral careers available in the public sector.[14] Both these developments have been encouraged by the Deobandi elders, who have always married religious conservatism with pragmatic engagement. The movement as a whole has proceeded cautiously, as Bury has only established formal links with other institutions by following the lead of its graduates.

Given their overall preponderance, British Deobandi graduates are now well placed to capitalize on the new career opportunities that local and national state institutions have opened up, along with the prospects of greater contractual security, improved salaries, and in-service training, even within the traditional mosque imamate. As the government multiplies bureaucratic hurdles to deter ill-qualified imams from abroad, the other non-Deobandi traditions, notably the largest one of the Barelwis, face the immediate challenge of developing adequate parallel institutions of higher Islamic learning in Britain. At the same time, in a globalized age, many Deobandi imams are unlikely to enjoy the luxury of disengaging from new intra-sectarian debates, imported from the Muslim world, to multiply and deepen their interactions with wider society.

In the long term, the most interesting question is to what extent imams exposed to a new professionalism – in terms of new social skills, a public service ethos, and distinct intellectual formation in Western institutions, whether university, teacher training college, or chaplaincy training centres – will form a critical mass able to influence and shape the religious formation in the *dar al-ᶜulum*s themselves. A more expansive curriculum, which once characterized the Farangi Mahall *dars-i-nizami* syllabus, could, theoretically, be retrieved and built upon, to include a greater use of reason and historical context in the parsing of venerable texts. Such, arguably, is the precondition for developing a new hermeneutic equal to the task of engaging confidently with contemporary challenges.

Notes

1 Smith 1963: 42. The basic historical research proving the gradual nature of Islamization is summarized in Winter 2000.
2 For Aligarh, see Lelyveld 1978 and Troll 1978; for Tablighi Jamaᶜat, see Masud 2000; for Deoband, Ahl-i Hadith, and Nadwa, see Metcalf 1982 and Sanyal 1996; for Jamaᶜat-i-Islami see Nasr 1994; and for Iqbal, see Schimmel 1989.
3 Metcalf 2002 argues convincingly for this pragmatism with regard to political processes, which can incorporate strategies of engagement, isolationism, and opposition.
4 See Sufi 1981 [1941] for a clear account of the development of the *dars-i nizami*, which demonstrates that this syllabus encompassed a wide diversity of versions within a basically traditional orientation.
5 See Athar 2002: 39–61, 77–87, 88–127, 401–17, 443–9.
6 Motala 1998: 44–5, with some modification to the spelling and grammar, and with some translation of Arabic terms.
7 Sikand 2002: 156–57, argues that, after 1965, Muhammad Zakariya successfully consolidated a broad influence over the Tablighi Jamaᶜat when his preferred candidate was appointed as the third *amir* of the worldwide movement.
8 The figures for 2002 are about 6,000 Muslim prisoners, which compares to just over 2,000 in 1993. This represents some 8 per cent of the prison population while Muslims account for 3 per cent of the population. The size of the Muslim prison population may partly be explained by the youthfulness of British Muslims as a whole. Over 90 per cent of all inmates in England and Wales are between the ages of 16–49 (95 per cent of all Muslim inmates). Fifty-five per cent of Muslims but only 46 per cent for England and Wales as a whole are in the same age range. Figures are derived from the 2001 Census, and Guessous, Hooper, and Moorthy 2001: 15/01, Table 4b.
9 Such additional work is vital given the alarming levels of educational underachievement amongst sections of British Pakistani students. In Bradford, for example, in 1999, they obtained 21.8 per cent target of the benchmark five or more GCSEs at Grades A–C taken when 15 or 16 years old. The citywide figure for all communities was 34 per cent

and 46 per cent for the country at large. If disaggregated into male and female, the results become even more disturbing with boys obtaining 16.7 per cent and girls 27.8 per cent. The national picture, across the different Muslim ethnic groups, is more variegated.

10 See Mufti Muhammad al-Kawthari, 'Is it permitted to celebrate birthdays?', *The Sunni Path*, at www.sunnipath.com, accessed 4 September 2003.

11 The great exception is London. Despite the presence of a large natural constituency, the Deoband reform movement has been less able to build the full range of institutions found elsewhere as it has struggled to appeal successfully to London's truly diverse Muslim population that has a significant intellectual component.

12 The view among British Deobandis is that Britain is *dar al-ʿaqd* (the domain of covenant), which obliges Muslims, in return for security and the freedom to practise their religion, to respect the laws of the land, unlike the radical Islamist groups who have insisted that Britain is *dar al-harb* (the domain of war), arguing that to follow or to support the law of the infidels is unbelief (*kufr*). For example, Sheikh Riyadh condoned the participation of his followers in the Anti-War Coalition marches (held from 2001 onwards) whereas Hizb ut-Tahrir boycotted them.

13 The Home Office estimated that between thirty to forty imams were entering the UK annually in the late 1990s and early 2000s. As it only keeps total numbers of 'ministers of religion' per country, rather than breaking them down into different faiths, these figures are estimates drawn from Pakistani and Bangladeshi figures with a small addition made for India. Recent restrictions are likely to have reduced this figure.

14 A similar flexibility among Deobandi scholars in adapting pragmatically to new social and public roles in India and Pakistan is confirmed by Zaman 2002. South Africa provides another instance whereby the movement has wrested moral and religious leadership from mosque committees by re-contextualizing the message of reform, see Tayob 1999: 60–76.

Bibliography

Athar, Khalid (2002) *Ulama-e-ahle sunna, mashaikh & Sufis in U.K.*, Islamabad: PPA, Vol. I.

Birt, Jonathan (2005a) 'Locating the British *Imam*: The Deobandi *ʿUlama* Between Contested Authority and Public Policy Post-9/11', in J. Cesari and S. McGloughlin (eds) *European Muslims and the Secular State*, Aldershot: Ashgate, pp. 183–96.

Birt, Jonathan (2005b) 'Wahhabism in the United Kingdom: Manifestations and Reactions', in Madawi al-Rasheed (ed.) *Transnational Connections: The Arab Gulf and Beyond*, London: RoutledgeCurzon, pp. 168–84.

Birt, Jonathan (2006) 'Good Imam, Bad Imam: Civic Religion and National Integration in Britain after 9/11', *The Muslim World*, 96 (4): 687–706.

FAIR, Muslim College and al-Khoei Foundation (2002) *Employment Status in Relation to Statutory Employment Rights*, London.

Geaves, Ron (2008) 'Drawing on the Past to Transform the Present: Contemporary Challenges for Training and Preparing British Imams', *Journal of Muslim Minority Affairs*, 28 (1): 99–112.

Gilliat-Ray, Sophie (forthcoming) *Muslims in Britain: An Introduction*, Cambridge: Cambridge University Press.

Guessous, Farid, Hooper, Nick and Moorthy, Uma (2001) *Religion in Prisons 1999–2000*, London: Office of National Statistics.

Hamid, Sadek (2009) 'The Attraction of Authentic Islam: Salafism and British Muslim Youth', in Roel Meijer (ed.), *Global Salafism: Islam's New Religious Movement*, London: Hurst.

King, David (1997) 'Tablighi Jamaᶜat and the Deobandi Mosques in Britain', in Steven Vertovec and Ceri Peach (eds) *Islam in Europe: The Politics of Religion and Community*, London: Macmillan, pp. 129–46.

Lelyveld, David (1978) *Aligarh's First Generation: Muslim Solidarity in British India*, Princeton: Princeton University Press.

Lewis, Philip (2002) *Islamic Britain: Religion, Politics and Identity Among British Muslims*, London: I.B. Tauris.

Lewis, Philip (2007) *Young, British and Muslim*, London: Continuum.

Masud, Muhammad Khalid (ed.) (2000) *Travellers in Faith: Studies of the Tablighi Jamaᶜat as a Transnational Islamic Movement for Faith Renewal*, Leiden: Brill.

Metcalf, Barbara Daly (1982) *Islamic Revival in British India: Deoband, 1860–1900*, Princeton: Princeton University Press.

Metcalf, Barbara Daly (1999) 'Weber and Islam', in Toby E. Huff and Wolfgang Schluchter (eds), *Max Weber & Islam*, New Jersey: Transaction Publishers, pp. 217–29.

Metcalf, Barbara Daly (2002) 'Traditionalist Islamic Activism: Deoband, Tablighis, and Talibs' [ISIM Papers, No. 4], Leiden: ISIM.

Metcalf, Barbara Daly (2009) *Husain Ahmad Madani: The Jihad for Islam and India's Freedom*, Oxford: Oneworld.

Motala, Yusuf (1998) *Hadhrat Shaikhul-Hadeeth (Moulana Muhammad Zakaria* rahmat-ullahi alaihi*) & I*, Bradford: Jamia-tul Imam Muhammad Zakaria.

Nasr, Syed Vali Reza (1994) *The Vanguard of the Islamic Revolution: The Jamaᶜat-i Islami of Pakistan*, London: I.B. Tauris.

Rahman, Fazlur (1982) *Islam and Modernity: Transformation of an Intellectual Tradition*, Chicago: University of Chicago Press.

Robinson, Francis (2000) *Islam and Modern History in South Asia*, Delhi: Oxford University Press.

Robinson, Francis (2001) *The ᶜUlama of Firangi Mahall and Islamic Culture in South Asia*, Delhi: Permanent Black.

Sanyal, Usha (1996) *Devotional Islam and Politics in British India: Ahmad Riza Khan Barelwi and his Movement, 1870–1920*, Delhi: Oxford University Press.

Saroha, M. (1981) *Heavenly Ornaments: Being an English Translation of Maulana Ashraf Ali Thanawi's Bahishti Zewar*, Lahore.

Schimmel, Annemarie (1989) *Gabriel's Wing: A Study into the Religious Ideas of Sir Muhammad Iqbal*, 2nd edition, Lahore: Iqbal Academy.

Sikand, Yoginder (2002) *The Origins and Development of the Tablighi-Jamaᶜat (1920–2000): A Cross-Country Comparative Study*, New Delhi: Orient Longman.

Singh, Gurharpal (2006) 'A City of Surprises: Urban Multiculturalism and the "Leicester Model"', in N. Ali, V.S. Kalra and S. Sayyid (eds) *A Postcolonial People: South Asians in Britain*, London: Hurst, pp. 291–304.

Smith, William Cantwell (1963) 'The Ulama in Indian Politics', in C.H. Philips (ed.) *Politics and Society in India*, London: George Allen and Unwin, pp. 39–51.

Sufi, G.M.D. (1981) [1941] *Al-Minhaj: Being the Evolution of the Curriculum in the Muslim Educational Institutions of Indo-Pakistan Subcontinent*, Lahore: Sh. Muhammad Ashraf.

Tayob, Abdulkader (1999) *Islam in South Africa: Mosques, Imams and Sermons*, Gainsville, FL: Florida University Press.

Troll, C.W. (1978) *Sayyid Ahmad Khan: A Reinterpretation of Muslim Theology*, New Delhi: Vikas.

Winter, Tim (2000) 'Conversion as Nostalgia: Some Experiences of Islam', in Martyn Percy (ed.) *Previous Convictions: Conversion in the Real World*, London: SPCK, pp. 93–111.

Zaman, Muhammad Qasim (2002) *The Ulama in Contemporary Islam: Custodians of Change*, Princeton: Princeton University Press.

Zaman, Muhammad Qasim (2008) *Ashraf ʿAli Thanawi: Islam in Modern South Asia*, Oxford: Oneworld.

6 Transnational ulama, European fatwas, and Islamic authority

A case study of the European Council for Fatwa and Research

Alexandre Caeiro

Introduction: *mufti* and fatwa

In Islam, the Law is a privileged means of access to the sacred. For many believers, adherence to Islamic normativity (shariᶜa) is an essential part of being a Muslim. The passage to Europe has produced many discontinuities, but normative concerns (even when the norms are not strictly followed) seem to remain an integral and under-researched part of Muslim life in non-Muslim lands (Waardenburg 2000). One mode of social expression of normative Islam occurs in the form of fatwas, the demand and production of authoritative opinions. It has been argued that fatwas 'circumscribe the mental and moral universe of their day, always balancing around the boundaries of what is conceivable, legitimate and right' (Skovgaard-Petersen 1997: 13). They are thus particularly useful instruments for studying social dynamics in Muslim communities. The relationship between the *mufti* (the person who issues a fatwa) and the *mustafti* (the person who requests one) is one of authority: in the eyes of many questioners, the *mufti* speaks in God's name (Abou El Fadl 2002), acting as the 'heir of the Prophets'. The questioner is therefore highly encouraged to follow the fatwa, even if s/he will not be punished for ignoring the answer, for fatwas, unlike the judgements delivered by the *qadi*, are not legally binding. In Europe, where Islam is disconnected from both the state and mainstream society, the institution of the fatwa has been considered the only useful mechanism in dealing with issues related to Islamic normativity (Oubrou 1998). Perhaps more so than elsewhere, the fatwa's *enforcement* depends on the charisma and authority *socially* conferred upon the *mufti*.

Islam in Europe: the historical context

It has become a commonplace to assert that the Muslim minority presence in Europe – as the fruit of voluntary migration – is unprecedented in the history of Islam.[1] Muslim migrants started acquiring visibility in the early 1970s in Europe and, soon afterwards, in the Muslim world. Driven primarily by economic reasons, they raised from the perspective of Islamic Law the problematic issue of their minority status in non-Muslim lands. Acting as 'guarantors of continuity'

(Zaman 2002), the ulama initially did not wish to support this migration. Considering it as a challenge to the 'proper' Islamic way of life and to the hegemony of state-applied shariʿa, many emphasized the commitment to an Islamic territory to fully practise one's religion, and reiterated this through a number of fatwas. The position became more difficult to maintain as Muslims progressively acquired European citizenship, loosened ties with the countries of origin, and abandoned the idea of return. Traditional Muslim scholars have responded variously to the new configuration. In a famous 1992 meeting a group of ulama gathered in France for a fiqh seminar on the topic of 'Muslims in the West' organized by the Union des Organisations Islamiques de France (UOIF).[2] In a summary of the discussions written by one of the participants, the late Shaykh Sayyid al-Darsh, one can read the main lines of the arguments:

> 'We have to consider the question of settlement [in non-Muslim countries] in its totality, together with the implications it has for all those who are affected by it, [in order to think of] how to remedy its sad implications. Facing such a difficult situation, some people may say, 'is it not better to go back, instead of losing our Islamic identity?' For the majority [of Muslims in Europe], this question is irrelevant, even if it is supported by a religious edict, for the majority do not bother about its implications. For the conscious minority, if they accept the fatwa it will mean the abandoning of those who are in need of protection.
>
> (al-Darsh n.d.: 4)

The reasoning perhaps put 'reality' ahead of 'the legal rule', as one participant feared,[3] but ultimately led to a legitimization of the Muslim presence in the Western World through a hierarchization of religious priorities known, in contemporary Islamic legal thought, as the fiqh of priorities (*fiqh al-awlawiyyat*).[4] Moreover, the traditional Islamic geo-strategy was revised: the dichotomy *dar al-islam/dar al-harb* was contextualized and finally dropped, since it no longer seemed adequate to understand a world under 'the United Nations', where even in Muslim countries the areas where shariʿa applies are 'shrinking' (Darsh n.d.: 6). The Lebanese scholar Faysal Mawlawi proposed the term *dar al-daʿwa* – a concept that he believed no longer separated Muslim lands from non-Muslim countries.[5]

This group of ulama considered that the classical positions of Islamic Law in relation to Muslim minorities had become increasingly disconnected from the reality of Muslim settlement in Europe. While they assumed that the discursive tradition of shariʿa continued to be central to Islam, if not its very embodiment, they believed it needed to be re-imagined, defended, and modified, in order to remain relevant for Muslim minorities in the West. One answer was the institutionalization of fatwa (*iftaʿ*) in a collegial body symbolizing the consensus (*ijmaʿ*) of Muslim scholars.

The European Council for Fatwa and Research

The European Council for Fatwa and Research (*al-majlis al-urubbi li-l-iftaʿ wa-l-buhuth*) was formed in London in March 1997 at the initiative of the Federation of Islamic Organizations in Europe (FIOE).[6] The Council's annual meetings are funded by the Maktoum Charity Foundation of Shaykh Rashid Hamdan Al-Maktoum of Dubai, a foundation based at Dublin's Islamic Cultural Centre of Ireland where the headquarters of the ECFR are also set. According to the president of the FIOE, Ahmed Rawi, the ECFR was conceived as an interim stage to fill the authority gap until *muftis* trained in Europe, fluent in the native languages and knowledgeable of the local contexts, could take over. In his opening speech delivered in London in 1997, Rawi outlined in detail the reasons for the Council:

> Having arrived with the waves of emigration, the Muslim preachers, imams and scholars of different tendencies, ethnic and social backgrounds did not really know the European society; they ignored the language and had difficulties communicating. The fact that they came from another [older] generation increased the conflicts with the new generations raised in the Western society. Without taking into consideration the circumstances of the new generations, the fatwas that were issued carried great contradictions and striking differences, despite the uniformity of life in the West. These divergences had immediate repercussions on the cohesion of Muslim communities in Europe.

Thus,

> waiting to train the first (European) scholars, [the FIOE] has not spared efforts to establish the European Council for Fatwa and Research, gathering distinguished ulama known for their piety and knowledgeable of the European reality. These scholars have the mission of orienting and counselling European Muslims on how they should behave daily with their co-citizens, at the individual, collective, or institutional levels, in the field of politics, society and economics; they will also help them to solve typical problems facing Muslims in European societies, such as those related to the Muslim headscarf. We wish the Council will become an essential reference for European Muslims, representing them and carrying their aspirations at the institutional level on the whole of the European territory, so that it can solve the problems and participate with the rest of the Islamic organizations in the promotion and dissemination of Islamic values in Western societies. Only in this way can we pretend to truly integrate Muslims in Europe, rooting the culture of social peace and the necessity of civil security in the society to which they belong.
>
> (Rawi, opening speech, 1997)[7]

The formation of the ECFR was also the materialization of an aspiration formulated by Yusuf al-Qaradawi and Faysal Mawlawi, respectively chosen as the ECFR's president and vice-president. In France during the early 1980s, Mawlawi was a popular preacher who helped form the UOIF, and on his return to Lebanon in 1985 he remained unofficially one of the spiritual guides of the French Muslim organization. Qaradawi, a former member of the Muslim Brotherhood trained at

Al-Azhar, emigrated to Qatar in the early 1960s where he became one of the foremost ideologues of the 'Islamic Movement'. Partly due to his weekly appearances in the Al-Jazeera show *al-shariᶜa wa-l-hayat* (Shariᶜa and Life), a favourite among Arabic-speaking Muslims living in Europe (Roald 2001), he developed into one of the world's most respected Islamic scholars.[8] Qaradawi's personal investment in the issues of Muslim minorities in Europe and North America highlights the symbolic – and, in numerical terms, quite disproportionate – importance of Muslims in the West in the religious imagination of contemporary Islam. The two leading figures of the ECFR, alongside religious scholars such as the Mauritanian ᶜAbd Allah Bin Bayyah based in Saudi Arabia and the Qatari deputy-director of <http://www.IslamOnLine.net>, ᶜAli al-Qaradaghi, contribute to give the ECFR a distinctively transnational flavour.

Membership of the ECFR

Islamic scholars need more than formal qualifications to issue fatwas legitimately. In the definition of the *mufti* retained by the ECFR, 'shariᶜa studies at university level' precede the granting of *ijazas* (teaching licences) in the conditions to be met by prospective members, and in this sense diplomas can be assumed to represent the norm. There are five conditions that the European *mufti* must fulfil:

1   Possess the appropriate legal (*sharᶜi*) qualifications at university level, or have been committed to the meetings and circles of scholars and subsequently licensed by them, and have a good command of the Arabic language;
2   be of good conduct and committed to the regulations and manners of Islamic shariᶜa;
3   be a resident of the European continent;
4   be knowledgeable in Islamic jurisprudence (*fiqh*) as well as being aware of the current social surroundings;
5   be approved by the majority of [the Council's] members.

(ECFR 2002: 4–5)

Implicit in the third and fourth conditions is the idea of a *mufti* actively engaged in the life of the Muslim communities of Europe. But if the ECFR is testimony to the desire to relocate religious authority in the West, Islamic scholarship is still largely rooted in the Muslim world. Thus exceptions can be made for those who do not live in Europe but nevertheless 'carry the worries and anxieties of their fellow Muslims in Europe, visit them on a frequent basis and appreciate their conditions and living situation' (ECFR 2002: ix). Their number should not exceed 25 per cent, according to the statutes adopted in 1997. While some of the non-resident scholars in the ECFR have lived in the West for some periods (Muhammad Mansur from the UAE), others seem to have been chosen primarily because of their close relations with the ECFR's leadership (Issam al-Bashir from Sudan, ᶜAjil al-Nashmi from Kuwait). Given the religious credentials and charisma of these scholars based in the Muslim world, their impact in the

Table 6.1 Members by country of residence

Country of residence	Members
United Kingdom	6
France	5
Germany	3
Austria, Bosnia, Canada, Ireland, Netherlands, Norway, Switzerland, United States	1 each
Saudi Arabia	3
Qatar, Sudan	2 each
Egypt, Kuwait, Lebanon, Mauritania, UAE	1 each

Source: Personal observations and ECFR official website.

collective discussions goes beyond their internal minority status. Just as it is possible to inhabit Europe in multiple ways, the manners in which scholars from the Arab world approach the issues of Muslims in the West differ widely.

The internal statutes stipulate that the four Sunni schools of jurisprudence and the size of the Muslim populations of European countries must be proportionally represented in the Council.[9] Currently, Britain and France accordingly provide the largest contingent of scholars (see Table 6.1). While all the French-based scholars come from North Africa and work or have worked closely with the Union des Organisations Islamiques de France (UOIF), the scholars in the UK exhibit greater heterogeneity. They include a leading Tunisian Islamist exiled in London (Rachid Ghannouchi), a self-avowed member of the Muslim Brotherhood who was until recently the president of the FIOE (Ahmad al-Rawi), an Iraqi *hadith* specialist living in Leeds (Abdullah Judai), the Manchester-based Lybian scholar Salim al-Shaykhi, and two South Asian scholars of Deobandi and Ahl-i Hadith orientation (Bradford's Ismail Kashhoulvi and London's Suhaib Hasan). Milli Görüs Europe is currently represented by two Turkish scholars. The Bosnian Grand Mufti Mustafa Ceric and Muhammad Sadiq, a German convert who joined the ECFR in the early 2000s, are the only native Europeans (if we discount Turkey). Countries such as Austria, the Netherlands, Norway, and Switzerland provide one member each – while Italy, the Iberian Peninsula, and Eastern Europe outside Bosnia-Herzegovina are absent.[10] There are also two members from the Fiqh Council of North America (Jamal Badawi and Salah Sultan) sitting in the ECFR. Despite the FIOE's professed effort to include the diversity of Islamic tendencies present in Europe (Rawi, personal communication, Leicester 2002), the all-male ECFR remains exclusively Sunni, overwhelmingly Arab in ethnicity, and close to the 'middle-ground' (*wasatiyya*) ethos of Yusuf al-Qaradawi and the Muslim Brotherhood.[11]

Lacking organic legitimacy, the ECFR has pursued a threefold policy of recognition, aimed at the Muslim world, the European authorities, and the Muslim communities of the West. The leadership of the ECFR has consistently stressed its non-competitive character towards the centres of Islamic learning in the Muslim world. Rather than short-circuiting the well-established councils of *fiqh*, the ECFR pretends to 'complement them by contributing to a reflection on the *fiqh* of minorities'. It thus takes 'full advantage of the fatwas and research' issued by these other councils, whose members are regularly invited to attend the ECFR meetings. However, since Islamic rulings vary 'according to time and place', and there is no greater difference than that 'between the Land of Islam and any other', Muslim minorities are deemed to be in need of a specialized institution to deal with their specific *fiqh* issues (ECFR 2002: X).

The negotiations with European authorities have proved delicate. In its 'relentless efforts with the official authorities in European countries to acknowledge and officially recognize the Council, and to refer to the Council in reference to Islamic judgements' (ECFR 2002: 2), the ECFR is confronted with the progressive insti-tutionalization of Islam at the national, rather than European, level. Certainly, in the post 9/11 world, the emphasis put on 'loyalty' and on respecting the European legal frameworks has been welcomed. Nevertheless, the transnationalism of the ECFR and the recent assimilationist turn of European debates on the integration of Muslims have proved to be major obstacles in the way of any sort of official recognition.[12] Internally, the status quo – disengagement from European states, if not European politics – seems to have become widely accepted.

Towards the Muslim communities of Europe, the ECFR has attempted to portray itself as a moderate body, marketing its fatwas as the embodiment of taysir (facility). In the contemporary world, often described by Islamic scholars as *ᶜasr al-darura* (the age of difficulty), *taysir* 'within the boundaries of the shariᶜa' is the trademark of Yusuf al-Qaradawi. In his introduction to the ECFR's First Collection of Fatwas, Qaradawi specifies his vision: 'The message of this Council is to bring ease to its fatwa for those Muslims [living in Europe], rather than difficulty and hardship ... to include people in the circle of Islam rather than exclude and alienate them' (ECFR 2002: X). This is not only 'the true spirit of Islam', but also 'a necessity' imposed by the nature of the present times: speaking about the Muslim world, Qaradawi argues that Muslims today 'are in dire need of facilitation ... their determination has weakened ... while the obstacles in the path of goodness and their desire for committing evil have increased' (Qaradawi 2000: 141). For the Muslim minorities in the West, the need for *taysir* is, if anything, greater: many Muslims have gone astray and need to 'flock back to their umma and message' (ECFR 2002: VIII). Facility in fatwa can thus be a means of protecting the identity of Muslims while ensuring they also remain concerned with Islamic normativity and connected to the authority of the ulama.[13]

The 'market' for fatwas

The migration of highly diverse Muslim populations to Western Europe has starkly revealed the multiplicity of Islamic practices and beliefs, creating conditions conducive for revisiting received notions of Islamic orthodoxy. The distinction between (Islamic) religion and (Arab, Pakistani, Turkish) culture, everywhere a contested issue, acquired great importance. In this context, the act of *plausibly* deciding in Europe which shariᶜa norms belong to the universal message of Islam, and which are contingent expressions of local traditions liable to be discarded, may be said to constitute one crucial form of religious authority. Islamic scholars may pretend to a monopoly of interpretation, which they seek to reaffirm partly through the production and dissemination of fatwas. By choosing *taysir*, the ECFR is 'marketing' its fatwas to a segment of the Muslim population, challenging more conservative and more liberal interpretations alike. Gathering in secluded locations to search for God's Law, and disseminating their findings through the mass media, the ECFR is ostensibly *performing* religious authority. Since the field of Islamic normativity is always inserted in a broader context, the social and political conditions in which the ulama operate also have an impact on their deliberations. The real practices and expectations of the petitioner(s) are also taken into consideration, for ultimately – as the *muftis* know only too well – the fate of the fatwa will depend on the favourable echo it gets among Muslims; in other words, on its consumption.

The demand for fatwas

There is a perception among Islamic scholars in Europe that *muftis* are kept busier here than in the Islamic world, either because they are in shorter supply, or because the needs are greater. A number of indicators seem to confirm that Muslims in Europe are avid consumers of fatwas.[14] The demand for fatwas in Europe is fuelled by a number of factors, including the discontinuities in the transmission of Islamic knowledge; a turn towards Islam as a comprehensive mode of life; the growing desire among the youth to adapt Islamic normativity to European contexts; the need, in particular for women, to elaborate strategies of survival and to navigate skilfully between different normative orders (including the traditions of the parents and the hegemonic discourses of mainstream society). Fatwas, because of their pragmatic outlook, can be effective and rather costless tools in the construction of an Islam suited to the life experiences and aspirations of European Muslims in a post-migratory context.

The questions typically put to the ECFR relate to the adaptations of Islamic norms to the European context, both at the level of *ʿibadat* (How to determine the prayer timetable in European countries? When to start the month of Ramadan?) and at the level of *muʿamalat* (What is the status of meat products in the West? Is it permissible to participate in European elections? What about marriage contracts and divorce certificates issued by non-Muslim judges?). Some questions appear to be universal, such as those related to doctrine or biomedical issues, but even then many take on a special significance in the context of Muslim minorities and life in pluralistic societies. Criticism by 'Europeans' or 'atheists' informs a number of fatwa petitions. Catering for an alcohol-drinking clientele (ECFR 2002: 50) is a multicultural dilemma. A doctrinal question on performing the Friday prayer before or after its stipulated time (ECFR 2002: 18) highlights the work constraints on religious practices in a non-Muslim setting; an inquiry into the obligation or otherwise of sticking to one *madhhab* (ECFR 2002: 31) demonstrates the crisis of the traditional *fiqh* schools among the heterogeneous Muslim communities of the West; another question on the orthodoxy of praying in absentia for the deceased (ECFR 2002: 39) hints at the splitting of families and the pangs of migration; one fatwa on the language of the *khutba* illustrates the acculturation of Muslims in Europe; a further enquiry into the modalities of distributing *zakat* to the needy ones (ECFR 2002: 42) tells a story of seasonal work and precariousness, just as it provides a glimpse of Muslim life without Muslim institutions. Furthermore, underlying the *istifta'* related to women is the latter's position as metaphors and crucibles of Muslim identity in Europe.

The single greatest number of questions received by the ECFR pertains precisely to women's issues – which seems to indicate that the status of women is the most politicized issue for Muslims in Europe. This is in line with Qaradawi's general observation that women demand more fatwas than men – supposedly because of women's greater religious sensibility (Qaradawi 1999: 36), but perhaps more importantly because women's issues are the domain where the discrepancies between classical fiqh and modern expectations appear to be the widest. Out of the forty-three rulings published in the ECFR's *First Collection of Fatwas*, no less than twenty-one concern the position of women in Islam. In the *Second Collection of Fatwas*, this rate decreased to thirteen out of thirty-seven. The number and nature of questions emanating from women has propelled the exclusively male members of the ECFR into the ambivalent role of arbiters of women's rights and duties. The questions range from basic daily matters (Can a woman cut her hair without the husband's permission? Can she attend Islamic circles in the mosque?) to crucial contemporary fiqh issues (Can she marry without a tutor? Does she have the right to divorce? What is the status of her marriage to a non-Muslim?). Often the formulation of the question indicates clearly the answer that is sought: the woman who asks whether her husband has 'the right' to prevent her from visiting her parents, like the wife who enquires whether it is permissible for the husband to live off her income, and the mother who wonders if she has 'the right' to rest after giving birth, are all seeking an authoritative fatwa that will allow them to make an Islamic claim in a domestic dispute.[15]

Converts to Islam also make up an important segment of the petitioner population. In the first three sessions of the ECFR, six questions (and perhaps more) out of the forty-seven that were answered came specifically from them. Their concerns extend from questions as to which *madhhab* to follow, to guidelines on answering external criticisms of Islam and, especially for women, ways of regulating family conflicts arising from cultural differences. A number of questions are also sent by Muslims seeking to repent from past misdeeds, revealing a wide range of actual religious practice among the *mustafti* population. The ECFR is expected to act here as a sort of absolver, determining the amount and character of the penitence: to a young Muslim who had an illicit relationship with a girlfriend, it counsels prayer and steadfastness; to a mother guilty of abortion, it recommends repentance and charity.[16]

The queries have often been mediated by imams residing in Europe, both member and non-member, suggesting that imams delegate to the ECFR for expert advise in a number of fiqh issues: 'A couple has lived outside marriage for many years but now they wish to ratify an Islamic marriage. May we write such a contract for this couple?', 'When people die in the home country, may we pray for them in absentia?', or 'Can we collect and distribute *zakat*?'. In contrast to the fatwa councils of the Muslim world, the ECFR has not had to respond directly to questions put forward by government bodies or courts. Some members have, however, relayed questions arising from dealings with local or national authorities (for example on the kinds of burial practices that do not contravene Islamic teachings) while other scholars are regularly solicited by judges to explain the Islamic position on certain behaviour. The *istifta* comes therefore mostly from Muslim individuals. When questions have been received from organizations, they are usually Muslim. In a single instance, the World Health Organization Regional Office of the East Mediterranean in Cairo requested a fatwa from the ECFR.[17]

The production of fatwas

The ECFR convenes once or twice a year to answer what it considers to be the most pressing questions facing Muslims in Europe.[18] Since the institutional framework of the ECFR does not allow all questions to be answered within the limited time of each session, a selection is carried out by the secretary general; questions directly relayed by the members stand a greater chance of being chosen than those sent by letter, fax or email. Any remaining questions may be sent to a member or to the two regional commissions set up in France (Dar al Fatwa of the UOIF) and in Britain (under Abdullah Judai at the Leeds Grand Mosque). There has been a gradual shift towards more research, which has led to the production of more 'resolutions' (*qararat*), and correspondingly less fatwa-issuing.[19] This has allowed the ECFR to set the terms of the discussion and to participate more actively in the public debates on Islam in Europe. Sometimes a fatwa issued previously by one of the main councils of *fiqh* (Al-Azhar, the International Islamic Fiqh Academy of the Organization of the Islamic Conference, or the Muslim World League's Fiqh Council in Mecca) is the starting point of the discussion, but the ECFR does not hesitate to give different rulings, usually towards greater permissiveness. As the Mauritanian scholar Abdullah Bin Bayyah argued during one discussion on the merits of investing in the stock exchange, 'if you want to forbid it, then just ring [the International Islamic Fiqh Academy in] Jeddah and let us all go home'.[20]

After the presentation of any relevant research papers and an initial discussion, the first version of the fatwa is drafted by a volunteer member, and then debated. According to the internal statutes, an absolute majority decides. In practice actual voting is seldom necessary, because the largest possible consensus is sought. Textual modifications are introduced to accommodate individual requests. Inevitably the most innovative or controversial ideas are the first to be dropped. In divisive issues each word, including the title of the fatwa, is negotiated. The text that is finally published as the ECFR's fatwa is thus the result of numerous drafts and revisions that may sometimes transform the spirit of its initial drafter. This multiple authorship creates ambiguities and explains the different tones and literary styles adopted by the ECFR in answer to apparently similar questions. This is very clear in women's issues. In one fatwa the ECFR argues in a detached manner that a woman should ask for the husband's permission to cut her hair if he is bound to notice the change;[21] but in the answer to whether the husband can prevent his wife from attending Islamic women's gatherings, the tone changes:

> The problem with many Muslims who lack sufficient Islamic knowledge is that they impose their moods, mentalities and personal views upon Islam. Therefore we often find someone who is rough and merciless, treating those around him, including his wife and children, in a very aggressive way and rough manner and may go to lengths of claiming that this is part of Islam.[22]

The sources quoted by the ECFR are standard: Qur'anic verses, *hadith*, as well as opinions of Hanafi, Maliki, Shafiʿi, and Hanbali jurists, used in a discretionary way. Reference is occasionally made to principles such as ʿ*urf* (custom), *maslaha* (what is beneficial), *maqasid al-shariʿa* (objectives of the law), *darura* (necessity), *haja* (need), as well as 'logic', 'common sense', 'good taste', 'human rights', and even poetry. In general the answers are long, and systematically include the reasoning that underlies the ruling – conventionally a sign that the fatwa is also addressing a specialist audience alongside the specific *mustafti*.

The formulation of the question often indicates that the issue is a frequent one, confronting the European Council for Fatwa and Research with other opinions ('some claim that' and its variants are recurrent). The members of the ECFR are therefore aware that in answering the query – and publishing the fatwa – they are also collectively taking a position in a public debate on the meaning and relevance of Islamic law. They draw on the *continuities of conflict* which characterize the discursive tradition of the shariʿa (Zaman 2002: 6). Their expectations in relation to the use and spread of the fatwa influence their decision. The publication of the fatwa can be negotiated within the ECFR and on occasion the members have decided not to publish the fatwa or refrained from issuing a collective answer altogether. Usually, however, the imperative of spreading the ECFR's '*ijtihad*' and 'academic methodology' is considered a fundamental part of its work. The fatwas of the ECFR are aimed at mass consumption: a complex Islamic *mediascape* disseminates them in print and HTML language, including – since 2002 – the official website <http://www.e-cfr.org>.[23] Through the fatwas the members seek to educate the community as much as to guide the individual *mustafti*. This *tarbiya* (didactic) component is explicitly mentioned in the internal discussions. In keeping with the tradition of the early twentieth-century reformists, the fatwas of the ECFR are thus not simply pragmatic answers to dilemmas faced by Muslims but also the expression of the *mufti*'s missionary zeal.

Specifically taken into consideration, contested, and negotiated during the discussions are also questions of unity of the Muslim community and the need for reform; the difference between the roles of the *mufti* and the *qadi*; the media impact of a fatwa under globalization; the implications and philosophical underpinnings of scientific advances; the reception of the rulings in Europe among Muslim leaders and the non-Muslim authorities; the European legal frameworks and the boundaries of national political discourses; the promotion of shari⁼a as an evolving and yet divine legal system; and *taysir* as the proper *fiqh* methodology.

'Integration without assimilation': the general thrust of *fiqh al-aqalliyyat*

The fatwas of the ECFR are collectively contributing to the development of the Muslim *fiqh* of minorities (*fiqh al-aqalliyyat*). This new concept, used to justify the foundation of the ECFR, is an attempt to theorize the simultaneous belonging to the Muslim *umma* and to the local non-Muslim society within an Islamic framework. Members of the ECFR define it as having two components: the re-actualization of old juridical opinions forgotten in history (selective *ijtihad*) and the resolution of the new emerging problems arising from modern societies (new *ijtihad*). Despite the efforts of the ECFR's leading authorities to locate it within the shari⁼atic tradition by claiming it is just another branch of *fiqh*, like the *fiqh* of economics or the *fiqh* of medicine (Qaradawi 2001), its very idea has sparked a controversy among the ulama and Muslim public intellectuals (Masud 2003; Caeiro 2004). The debate is partly about what departures from the tradition are to be allowed in the modern world, but it also concerns the nature of those changes, and to what extent they should attempt to bridge gaps and minimize differences with dominant Western discourses and practices (Ramadan 2003; Khan 2004). As understood and applied by the members of the ECFR, this new *fiqh* seems to aim at the integration without assimilation of Muslims in Europe.

This double concern often translates into an initial exhortation towards the creation of Islamic institutions: the Council has thus expressed the need for Islamic banks (in order to avoid interest-bearing mortgages), for *halal* slaughter-houses (in order to provide licit meat), for quasi-Islamic courts (to administer Muslim personal law), and for Islamic cemeteries (to bury the dead properly). But these demands are eased by the subsequent permission to take part in the domi-nant system, adapting as a minority group to conditions in mainstream society: the use of high-street mortgages is allowed (Caeiro 2004), and so is the consump-tion of certain meat products slaughtered by the People of the Book, or the burial in non-Muslim cemeteries. As for civil marriages and divorces, they are recog-nized as Islamically valid. The integration that is desired for Muslims in Europe is above all legal: Muslims are generally urged to follow the state law, and even when the ECFR calls for the establishment of communal institutions, it warns that due consideration must be taken of national laws. In each case the argument is predicated on the idea that residing in the West amounts to an acceptance of the legal framework by virtue of an implicit contract. On the other hand, Muslims are exhorted to maintain a distinctive cultural identity, not sharing in Christian cele-brations (ECFR 2002: 97), preserving the 'unique and independent character' of youngsters (ECFR 2002: 13), donning the *hijab* in order to be 'distinguished from the non-Muslim and the non-obedient' (ECFR 2002: 35).[24]

A thorough analysis of the whole production of the ECFR is beyond the scope of this chapter. In the section that follows I will focus on two fatwas that have contributed significantly to on-going debates about shariʿa in the West. Although the fatwas are somewhat untypical, their interest lies in what they reveal in terms of the institutional possibilities and constraints within the ECFR.

The fatwa on political participation in the West

One question related to the integration of Muslims in Europe is that of their political participation in non-Muslim countries, through either voting or standing for elections. While the once-problematic issue of naturalization seems now to be de facto settled,[25] the question of political participation remains at the fore of intellectual debates, if not always Muslim concerns, in Western countries. The debate is revived when elections approach, with fatwas and counter-fatwas circulating quickly through the Islamic cyberspace. Democratic participation divides Muslim activists and scholars in the Islamic world, on both the theoretical and practical levels. In Europe, at least six different positions have been rehearsed across the Islamic spectrum (Hussain 2004). There have been attempts to stay outside the system and condemn democracy as un-Islamic: the radical group Al-Muhajiroun disseminates a fatwa stating that 'any Muslim who votes for a person knowing that the Parliament is a body of legislating law is an apostate'.[26] There is a certain consensus among Salafi movements that democracy amounts to *kufr* (unbelief) since God is the only Legislator. A different position has been the effort to create an alternative system: the short-lived Muslim Parliament of Britain is the perfect illustration. Some Muslims have opted for a third way, that of joining political parties, while others have established Islamic parties – which have usually proved a failure. Other options have included lobbying, and the establishment of Muslim councils and federations.

The position of Qaradawi is characteristic of his general adoption of 'middle-ground' views. For the Egyptian scholar, the Muslim is a *political animal* by definition: 'the true character of a Muslim as required by Islam obliges him to be a man of politics. Every Muslim is required to fulfil the Islamic obligation of commanding good and forbidding evil'. Questioned on the compatibility between democracy and Islam, Qaradawi has argued that 'the content of democracy [is] in harmony with the essence of Islam', since 'mutual consultation (*shura*) is one of the bases of Islamic life',[27] although, according to the Muslim scholar, Islam takes precedence over democracy in setting the bases of the system. In the Muslim world, this thinking translates into fatwas that encourage Islamic movements towards participation in elections in order to 'lessen evil and oppression' (Qaradawi 1998: 277). In the West, Qaradawi holds that it is an obligation for local Muslims to join existing political parties and to express their voting power (Roald 2001; Shadid and van Koningsveld 2003). In both cases, Qaradawi's reasoning is based on what he calls the '*fiqh* of balances' or 'the *fiqh* of priorities'. Qaradawi's view on political participation is broadly accepted by the member organizations of the FIOE.[28] However, during the second session of the ECFR, in October 1998, the issue was not straightforward.

The question was twofold:

> Is it permissible for a Muslim to participate in the council elections in a European country, or to vote for a non-Muslim party which may not serve the interests of Muslims?

The answer was uncharacteristically brief:

> This matter is to be decided by Islamic organizations and establishments. If these see that the interests of Muslims can only be served by this participation, then it is permissible on condition that it does not involve the Muslims making more concessions than gains.

Out of the two questions, only the first one seems to be addressed. The answer places 'the interests of Muslims' as the foremost criterion, but it falls short of encouraging outright political participation – contradicting the president's own opinion. This fatwa illustrates the balance between different tendencies within the ECFR itself, tendencies that are broader than those represented in the FIOE. By delegating the decision to local Islamic institutions, the ECFR is deferring the authority and undoubtedly seeking to avoid criticism. The fatwa allows multiple readings, conveniently creating *spaces of dissension*:[29] one member, favourable to the political participation of Muslims, stressed that 'what needs to be remembered is the [theoretical] permission to participate' (Tahar Mahdi, personal communication, Paris 2003). But others, differently inclined, have argued that this involves making 'more concessions than gains' and is therefore to be avoided.

In order to understand this ruling one needs to look at the context of its formulation. The fatwa was issued during the second session of the ECFR, a meeting dominated by another question: a Muslim immigrant in Brussels asked about the Islamic view on the Muslim presence in the West. In the internal discussions, the ECFR heard from a minority of members 'extremely strict views which call for all Muslims to leave these countries immediately ... views [which] caused great difficulty and inconvenience' (ECFR 2002: 23). The issue seems to have occupied most of the session, and in the end the ECFR's fatwa – adopted by the majority – rejects that call, allowing Muslims to live in non-Muslim countries as long as the environment does not threaten their life, religion, and family.[30] In order to establish itself as the primary reference in Europe, the ECFR needs to keep different tendencies in its midst, including those opposed to the 'middle-ground' ideology of Qaradawi and the FIOE. The members know that the legitimacy of the ECFR is derived from its perceived inclusiveness; the need for consensus has therefore been all the greater, particularly in the first years. In the case of political participation, this led to an open-ended fatwa as a form of compromise.[31]

A woman embraces Islam and her husband does not

One of the most controversial questions yet to be dealt with by the ECFR originated in a question from Ireland through its headquarters in Dublin. It concerned
a married woman who had converted to Islam and was enquiring about the status
of her marriage. This issue has been debated throughout the Islamic history and
the contemporary fatwa literature testifies to its recurrence and social significance. In the case of the ECFR, the question, formulated in apparently neutral
terms by a third party, is a typical example of how the *mustafti* 'not only initiates
the *mufti*'s interpretative activity but also constrains it' (Masud, Messick and
Powers 1996: 22), and therefore deserves a detailed analysis. The question starts
with an observation: 'In the West it has been noticed, as a definite phenomenon,
that women more often than men come to embrace Islam'. The issue is simple,
the petitioner continues, when the woman is single, but a problem arises when she
is married, particularly if the couple have children and a relationship based 'on
mutual love, intimacy, understanding'. The *mustafti* is learned; he or she knows
what the conventional answer is: 'generally, most scholars issue a fatwa which
forces her to divorce immediately'. Despite the same detached tone, the *mustafti*
then tries to move the *mufti* emotionally by arguing that 'having to sacrifice the
life she had established is, practically, a very hard thing to do for a newly
converted woman'. By relating the precise issue to a sociological observation on
the frequency of conversions, and hinting at the difficulties facing newly
converted women, the *mustafti* is seeking to impact on the *mufti*'s own hierarchy
of Islamic duties: 'some women in this situation truly wish to embrace Islam, but
this forced separation from their husbands and the consequent family breakdown
constitute obstacles in the way of their conversion'. Far from expecting an answer
that removes the traditional interdiction of marriage between Muslim women
and non-Muslim men, what is requested is a sympathetic understanding of the
exceptional nature of the problem, and a fitting answer. The questioner concludes:
'Is there any proper solution for this complicated problem from a shariᵉatic point
of view in the light of the Qur'an, the Sunna and the finalities (*maqasid*) of
the shariᵉa?'. The final invocation of the *maqasid al-shariᵉa*, which often allows
for the departure from the textual limits of *fiqh*, shows once again the degree of
learning of the petitioner.

The secretary-general sent the question to Qaradawi, whose conclusions
fuelled the debate within the ECFR.[32] Qaradawi starts by acknowledging that, for
many years, his opinion was that the woman must separate from her husband
either immediately or after her ᵉ*idda* (waiting period). But after reviewing a
dozen historical opinions on the matter, Qaradawi comes to the conclusion that
the woman has the right to remain married and, crucially, to have sexual relations
with her non-Muslim husband (the whole meaning of marriage, according to
Qaradawi), provided two conditions are met: that the relationship 'does not have
a negative impact' upon the woman's faith, and that she 'has hope he will convert'
to Islam too. However, by ostensibly not defining the 'negative impact' upon the
faith, and by not issuing a time limit for the husband's conversion, Qaradawi

effectively gives the woman the possibility to keep her marriage indefinitely. His fatwa is based on secondary sources, mainly opinions of the two Companions and Caliphs, ʿUmar ibn Khattab and ʿAli ibn Abi Talib, and one Successor, al-Zuhri, who are known to have given women the same option. Building upon these sayings, Qaradawi invokes the concepts of 'necessity' and 'removal of hardship' to justify his decision.

In his reply, Mawlawi tried to refute Qaradawi's arguments by contending that the opinions mentioned by the Egyptian scholar have never been followed by the *fuqaha'*. The Lebanese scholar conceded that non-Muslim countries abide by international conventions such as the declaration of Human Rights, and therefore women need not fear persecution on religious grounds, but he argued against Qaradawi that in these cases sexual relations are a violation of the shariʿa, and that the preferable course for the woman is to divorce and marry a Muslim man (al-Saify 2004). The discussions in the ECFR spanned three sessions, starting in Dublin in 1999. The research papers were read, the evidence was reviewed; the hadith-based idea that Islam 'builds and does not destroy' (already invoked during a question on mortgage) was debated and contested. A full issue of the academic journal of the ECFR was devoted to this issue. Finally in Valencia in 2001, unable to reach a consensus, the ECFR issued a final declaration that states the two opposing views:

> According to the four main schools of jurisprudence, it is forbidden for the wife to remain married with her husband, or indeed to allow him conjugal rights once her period of waiting has expired. However, some scholars see that it is for her [to decide whether] to remain with him, allowing him and enjoying full conjugal rights, if he does not prevent her from exercising her religion and she has hope in him reverting to Islam. The reason for this is for women not to reject entering into Islam if they realize that they are to separate from their husbands and desert their families by doing so.
>
> (ECFR, Final Statement, The 8th Ordinary Session, 2001)

In spite of not taking sides, the message is clear: the ECFR implicitly leaves the woman the choice of the preferred answer, and therefore it enables her to remain married with her non-Muslim husband. In the current European context, this was arguably the first time that a positive answer to this question became available to the public. Arguably, this was also the first time in the ECFR that European ʿ*urf* (custom) – recognized as one source of legislation by the ECFR's charter – has had a decisive impact on the scholars' understanding of Islamic law. Whereas Mawlawi recognized the specific position of women in the West, Ahmed Rawi argued that 'the fatwa is only possible in the West because here the woman is respected, and this is a crucial difference' (personal communication, Leicester 2002). This decision does not question the prohibition of marriage between a Muslim woman and a non-Muslim man, which is nevertheless increasing in Europe. But in the internal discussions another distinction was introduced: according to another member, Muhammad Mansur, the members realized that 'marriage in Islam is a civil contract, not a religious one, for the Prophet did not remarry his Companions after their conversion to Islam' (personal communication, London 2001).

Conclusion

It is now widely recognized that fatwas have been a productive instrument in the development of Islamic law, allowing the *fuqaha'* to Islamize, regulate, and incorporate in the legal corpus new developments occurring in the wider society (Hallaq 2001; Johansen 1999; Skovgaard-Petersen 1997). Until recently, the power relation between *mustafti* and *mufti* underlying the process of *istifta'* echoed wider differences between the literate and the illiterate (Masud, Messick and Powers 1996: 21). With the spread of literacy and the liberalization of access to sacred knowledge, this relation has started to change. Mass education and new media have contributed to the displacement and fragmentation of religious authority, while modernity has challenged the very credibility of the ulama's discourses (Zaman 2002: 1). The ulama have in turn attempted to re-imagine the shariʿa in the modern age, seeking to find ways to maintain their authority and expand their audiences. They also have continued to issue fatwas, a genre that authorizes interventions in the Islamic tradition at the same time that it reasserts the ulama's claim to be the sole interpreters of the foundational texts.

This chapter has looked at how the ulama have responded to the challenges of Muslim migration to Europe through the institutionalization of *ifta'*. It has studied the processes underlying the demand for fatwas as well as the mechanisms of their production. The success of a contemporary fatwa however depends greatly on its media impact – and therefore the media professionals who disseminate Islamic *responsa* are at least as important as the religious scholars who issue them in the first place. The publishers of fatwa collections, the editors of Muslim magazines, and the website managers make important editorial choices regarding the materials, translating – often literally and metaphorically – the opinions of Islamic scholars to Muslim publics in Europe. A study of the motivations and aspirations of these media professionals is needed in order to gain a better understanding of how Islamic norms are constructed and disseminated today. In a unique illustration of the competing claims to religious authority made by traditional scholars and eclectic Muslim intellectuals, Tariq Ramadan prefaced and critically commented the French translation of the ECFR's fatwas (Conseil européen des fatwas et de la recherche 2002). It was through this bestselling edition, rather than through the rougher translation made by the UOIF's own publishing company, that most francophone Muslims came into contact with the work of the ECFR.

The ulama seem caught in a predicament. Producing fatwas for mass consumption is one way of entering the public sphere and participating in the public debates about Islam. Publication 'converts a form of highly personalized interpretation … into more generic messages for a mass audience … thereby shift[ing] part of the burden of interpretation to the listener/reader' (Eickelman and Anderson 2003: 3).

Given the fluidity of Islamic authority, it also contributes towards the proliferation of conflicting religious opinions, creating the conditions for market differentiation. Frowned upon in theory, the fatwa wars played out in different media between Islamic authorities effectively force the Muslim individual to make a choice and select the most convenient answer. This appears as a paradox of publicity: seeking to enhance their claim to religious authority though public fatwas, the ulama end up marketing their work and contributing to the religious individualization of Muslims.

Notes

* This article is a revised version of a paper first presented at the workshop 'The Production of Islamic Knowledge in Europe', Fourth Mediterranean Social and Political Research Meeting, Florence 2003. I thank Martin van Bruinessen, Jean-Loup Herbert, Baber Johansen, Frank Peter, and Mathias Rohe for their insightful comments. The usual disclaimers apply.

1 This view has been prominently articulated in Lewis and Schnapper 1994 and contested by, among others, Khaled Abou El Fadl, Tariq Ramadan, and Olivier Roy, who note that Muslims have often lived as minorities throughout history. Abou El Fadl (1994) also discusses the fact that Muslim minorities in the West today are the result of *voluntary* migrations, but he dismisses this as irrelevant from the perspective of Islamic law.

2 The meeting was attended by a number of prominent Muslim scholars close to the Muslim Brotherhood, including the late Mustafa Zarqa and ʿAbd al-Fattah Abu Ghudda (both from Syria), as well as a number of individuals who became, in 1997, founding members of the ECFR, such as Yusuf Qaradawi, Faysal Mawlawi, the Kuwaiti ʿAjil Nashmi, and the members of the UOIF Ahmed Jaballah and Ounis Qurqah.

3 In the seminar Dr. Abdul Aziz As-Suhaibani remarked, 'I expect our learned scholar first to give the Shariʿa rule dealing with ordinary circumstances [and only] then considering the de facto position' (al-Darsh n.d.: 10).

4 This mode of reasoning does not seem exclusive to Islam: Hervieu-Léger (2003) speaks about the developments of Catholic thinking in France in similar lines.

5 In practice, however, distinctions between Muslim and non-Muslim countries continue to be important for the ulama, leading to geographically bound, context-specific formulations of Islamic norms. See for one example Caeiro 2004.

6 The FIOE is the umbrella organization of the European associations close to the Muslim Brotherhood. The UOIF is its semi-autonomous French branch.

7 Ahmed Rawi, opening speech of the President of the FIOE during the founding session of the European Council for Fatwa and Research (in Arabic), London 1997. Not published. A copy of the speech, given by Mr Rawi, is in possession of the author.

8 Described by Western scholarship alternatively as 'neo-fundamentalist' (Olivier Roy) or 'progressive thinker' (Peter Mandaville), the personality and work of Yusuf Qaradawi have only started to receive due attention recently. For an attempt to provide a comprehensive analysis of Qaradawi's 'phenomenon' see Gräf and Skovgaard-Petersen 2009.

9 The juristic school in which each individual member was primarily trained is known to the others and is taken into consideration in the discussions. However, differences between Hanafi, Hanbali, Maliki, and Shafiʿi scholars appear considerably less important today than in the past due to the wide acceptance of inter-school reasoning or *talfiq* (Krawietz 2002). For the leadership of the Council, borrowing from different schools is a key instrument for facilitating the lives of Muslims (*taysir fi-l-fatwa*): *talfiq* has become inextricably linked to *taysir* (Qaradawi 1995). By contrast, the members known

in the Council for being against 'facilitation' seem to care more for the *madhhab* than their counterparts. Yousouf Ibram, for example, has hailed the inclusion of Hanbali scholars from Saudi Arabia in the European *fiqh* council as an improvement which redresses the imbalance between 'easy' and 'rigorous' trends within the ECFR (Yousouf Ibram, *Le Conseil Européen de la Fatwa. Rôle et objectifs*. Audio cassette available at Editions Tawhid in Lyons, France).

10 A scholar from Belgium (Mujahid Hasan) and another from Spain (ᶜAbd al-Rahman al-Tawil) attended some of the early meetings of the ECFR but have since retired. A scholar based in Denmark (Fu'ad Barazi) resigned over a disagreement on the question of buying a house on an interest-bearing mortgage (Caeiro 2004). In relation to the Balkans, the late chairman of the Islamic Community in Albania Sabri Koçi and the then Grand Mufti of Bulgaria Mustafa Illish Hajji were invited to be members of the ECFR. They were removed from the Council's membership list for failing to attend the collective meetings and have not been replaced by those who succeeded them at the head of their respective Islamic communities in Albania and Bulgaria.

11 The basis for these calculations is the ECFR's official website. There are discrepancies between the Arabic and English membership lists posted there, partly because membership of the ECFR is continuously evolving as old scholars retire or move on and new *muftis* join. Although neither of the lists bears a date, I have used here the Arabic list of thirty-four members because it seems to be the most recently updated one. The English list of thirty-eight scholars includes a number of *muftis* who have not attended the sessions for a number of years (Muhammad Taqi ᶜUthmani from Pakistan, ᶜAbd Allah ibn Sulayman al-Maniᶜ, and Nasir ibn ᶜAbd Allah al-Mayman from Saudi Arabia, as well as the two retired scholars from Belgium and Spain mentioned previously) and it does not include Hamza Sharif (also from Saudi Arabia), who joined recently.

12 The ECFR's stance on the Arab–Israeli conflict has been a particularly contentious point. The support of Qaradawi and Mawlawi for Hamas and its martyrdom operations in Israel, which they describe as forms of 'legitimate terrorism', is well known. For a study of the role played by the conflict in the Middle East in shaping the reception of Qaradawi in the West see Caeiro and al-Saify 2009.

13 This ideology of *taysir*, broadly adopted by the European Council for Fatwa and Research, is actualized differently in the various European countries. In Britain, it is portrayed as a struggle against *taqlid* (imitation) and 'extremism'; in France, it is usually a cry for 'authenticity' against the modernist interpretations of liberal thinkers which, encouraged by the state and the intellectual elites, hold the high ground in national public debates.

14 Although we are lacking systematic studies, a superficial glance is enough to realize that a disproportionate amount of the questions put to Islamic scholars in satellite TV programmes such as Al-Jazeera's Al-Shariᶜa wa-l-Hayat come from the West. Likewise, according to the information given to the author by Mawlawi's personal secretary, around two-thirds of the fatwa petitions sent by e-mail to Faysal Mawlawi (<http://www.mawlawi.net>) come from Europe and America.

15 In one instance it is actually the husband who is seeking a fatwa in order to counter his wife's claims: 'Is it compulsory upon a husband (father) to attend educational courses which teach how to solve children's problems?' (First session, ECFR 2002: 79).

16 It is interesting to note in this regard what Ben Achour has written: 'L'islam a son Eglise, qui "sait", interprète, mais surtout, et c'est ce qui échappe à la plupart des observateurs, "intercède" … [l]e Faqih indique la voie, et le simple croyant … se sent lié par la parole du Faqih' (1992: 21–2).

17 The question related to a vaccine against poliomyelitis that contained trypsin, a product derived from pigs (Fatwa 11/6, Stockholm 2003, available online at <http://www.who.int>). The fact that the fatwa was not related to Muslim minorities suggests that the ECFR has acquired a certain level of global authority.

18 During the first three years (1997–9) the ECFR convened once a year. Since then it has convened twice a year, usually around December and July. In order to meet local communities and popularize the work of the Council the members decided in 2001 systematically to hold one of its annual sessions outside Dublin: thus sessions were held in Valencia (2001), Paris (2002), Stockholm (2003), and London (2004). Before then, the Council had also convened in Sarajevo (1997) and Köln (1999), with the remaining meetings taking place in its Irish headquarters.
19 In the last sessions, only the last day was dedicated to questions and answers.
20 Ninth session, Paris, July 2002.
21 But not if he does not notice it (sic) Fatwa 21, 1st session. *First Collection of Fatwas*, p. 69.
22 Fatwa 25, 1st session. *First Collection of Fatwas*, p. 76.
23 Hacked for a long period, the original website of the ECFR <http://www.ecfr.org> has recently been restored at <http://www.e-cfr.org>. The fatwas, resolutions, and research papers of the Council are available there in Arabic and (partially) in English.
24 Dealing lovingly with dogs and keeping one's original name after converting to Islam provide two counter-examples where a level of cultural integration is actually desired (ECFR 2002: 37, 90–1).
25 Contemporary fatwas on the subject contradict one another, but the fact that more than half of the Muslims living in France and the UK – to mention just these two countries – hold citizenship there renders the juristic discussions highly irrelevant.
26 <http://www.almuhajiroun.com/fatwas/20–06–2001.php> (accessed 19 March 2003).
27 Undated fatwa delivered in answer to a question from Algeria, included in Qaradawi 1998: 195–223.
28 In May 2002, after the French presidential elections were won by Jacques Chirac, the UOIF very openly appealed to Muslims to vote for the socialist party in the legislative elections. Unusually, the UOIF's Dar al Fatwa published a fatwa on political participation on its website, www.uoif-online.com..
29 For this concept, which originates in Foucault, I am indebted to Bowen 1993.
30 While the text of this fatwa demonstrates a clear willingness to legitimize Muslim settlement in the West, the implicit shared assumption is that this presence is indeed problematic. As Frank Peter has pointed out in an unpublished manuscript (Peter n.d.), by insisting on the need to preserve an Islamic identity and to fulfil a number of (unspecified) Islamic duties, the ECFR is actually 'suspending the judgement on this question ad infinitum', making the Muslim presence in the West 'durably dependent on their approval'.
31 In a subsequent resolution issued in July 2006, the ECFR develops the same approach further. It states that 'Originally it is permissible for Muslims living in Europe to take part in politics. Nevertheless, sometimes it can be permissible or recommended or prohibited ... Adhering to Muslim morals ... is one of the foremost criteria of Muslim participation in politics' (*al-Majalla al-ʿIlmiyya li-l-Majlis al-Urubbi li-l-Ifta' wa-l-Buhuth* no. 10–1, part 2: 331).
32 For a detailed analysis of Qaradawi's opinion and a comparative study of contemporary fatwas on the issue, see al-Saify 2004.

Bibliography

Abou El Fadl, Khaled (1994) 'Islamic Law and Muslim Minorities: The Juristic Discourse on Muslim Minorities from the Second/Eighth to the Eleventh/Seventeenth Centuries', *Islamic Law and Society*, 1 (2): 141–87.
Abou El Fadl, Khaled (2002) *Speaking in God's Name: Islamic Law, Authority and Women*, Oxford: One World.

Ben Achour, Yadh (1992) 'Islam et laïcité – propos sur la recomposition d'un système de normativité', *Pouvoirs*, 62: 15–30.

Bowen, John R. (1993) *Muslims through Discourse: Religion and Ritual in Gayo Society*, Princeton: Princeton U.P.

Caeiro, Alexandre (2004) 'The Social Construction of shariʿa: Bank Interest, Home Purchase, and Islamic Norms in the West', *Die Welt des Islams*, 44 (3): 351–75.

Caeiro, Alexandre and al-Saify, Mahmoud (2009) 'Qaradawi in Europe, Europe in Qaradawi: The Global Mufti's European Politics', in Bettina Gräf and Jakob Skovgaard-Petersen (eds) *The Global Mufti: The Phenomenon of Yusuf al-Qaradawi*, London: Hurst, pp. 109–48.

al-Darsh, Sayyid (n.d.) 'Muslims in the West – a Fiqh Seminar in France. Summary by Dr. Sayyid Al-Darsh', unpublished typescript.

Conseil européen des fatwas et de la recherche (2002) *Recueil de fatwas: Avis juridiques concernant les musulmans d'Europe – Série n° 1*, preface and comments by Tariq Ramadan, Lyon: Editions Tawhid.

Eickelman, Dale and Anderson, Jon (eds) (2003) *New Media in the Muslim World: The Emerging Public Sphere*, Bloomington and Indianapolis: Indiana University Press.

ECFR [European Council for Fatwa and Research] (2002) *First and Second Collection of Fatwas (Qararat wa fatawa li-l majlis al-urubi li-l-ifta' wa-l-buhuth)*, translated by Anas Osama Altikriti and Shaikh Nasif Al-Ubaydi, Cairo: Islamic INC/Al-Falah Foundation.

Gräf, Bettina and Skovgaard-Petersen, Jakob (2009) *The Global Mufti: The Phenomenon of Yusuf al-Qaradawi*, London: Hurst.

Hallaq, Wael (2001) *Authority, Continuity, and Change in Islamic Law*, Cambridge and New York: Cambridge University Press.

Hervieu-Léger, Danielle (2003) *Catholicisme français: la fin d'un monde*, Paris: Bayard.

Hussain, Dilwar (2004) 'Muslim Political Participation and the "Europeanisation" of Fiqh', *Die Welt des Islams*, 44 (3): 376–401.

Johansen, Baber (1999) *Contingency in a Sacred Law: Legal and Ethical Norms in the Muslim Fiqh*, Leiden: Brill.

Khan, Asif (2004) *The Fiqh of Minorities: The New Fiqh to Subvert Islam*, London: Khilafah Publications.

Krawietz, Birgit (2002) 'Cut and Paste in Legal Rules: Designing Islamic Norms with Talfiq', *Die Welt des Islams*, 42(1), 3–40.

Lewis, Bernard and Schnapper, Dominique (eds) (1994) *Muslims in Europe*, London: Pinter.

Masud, M. Khalid (2003) 'Islamic Law and Muslim Minorities', *ISIM Newsletter*, 11: 17.

Masud, M. Khalid, Messick, Brinkley and Powers, David (eds) (1996) *Islamic Legal Interpretation: Muftis and their Fatwas*, Cambridge, MA: Harvard University Press.

Oubrou, Tareq (1998) 'Introduction théorique à la chari'a de minorité', in *Islam de France*, 2: 27–39.

Peter, Frank (n.d.) 'Crisis of Laïcité and Reformist Discourses in France: The Case of Muslim Debates on Citizenship', unpublished manuscript.

Qaradawi, Yusuf (1995) *Al fatwa bayna al-indibat wa-l-tasayyub*, Beirut, Damascus, and Amman: Al-Maktaba al-Islamiyya (2nd edition).

Qaradawi, Yusuf (1998) *State in Islam (Fiqh al-Dawlah fi al-Islam)*, Cairo: El-Falah.

Qaradawi, Yusuf (1999) *Contemporary Fatawa (Fatawa mu'asira)*, vol. 1, New Jersey: Islamic Book Service.

Qaradawi, Yusuf (2000) *The Priorities of the Islamic Movement in the Coming Phase*, London: Awakening Publications.

Qaradawi, Yusuf (2001) *Fi fiqh al-aqalliyyat al-islamiyyah: hayat al-muslimin wast al-mujtam'at*, Cairo: Dar al-Shuruq.

Ramadan, Tariq (2003) *Les musulmans d'Occident et l'avenir de l'islam*, Paris: Sindbad/ Actes Sud.

Roald, Anne-Sofie (2001) 'The Wise Men: Democratization and Gender Equalization in the Islamic Message: Yusuf al-Qaradawi and Ahmad al-Kubaisi on the Air', *Encounters*, 7(1): 29–55.

al-Saify, Mahmoud (2004) 'Fiqh for Muslim Minorities: A New Era of Islamic Jurisprudence', MA thesis, Leiden University.

Shadid, W.A.R. and van Koningsveld, P.S. (2003) 'Religious Authorities of Muslims in the West: Their Views on Political Participation', in W. A. R. Shadid and P. S. van Konigsveld (eds) *Intercultural Relations and Religious Authorities: Muslims in the European Union*, Leuven: Peeters, pp. 149–68.

Skovgaard-Petersen, Jakob (1997) *Defining Islam for the Egyptian State – Muftis and Fatwas of Dar al Ifta*, Leiden: Brill.

Waardenburg, Jacques (2000) 'Normative Islam in Europe', in Felice Dassetto (ed.) *Paroles d'islam*, Paris: Maisonneuve et Larose, pp. 49–68.

Zaman, M.Q. (2002) *The Ulama in Contemporary Islam: Custodians of Change*, Princeton and Oxford: Princeton University Press.

7   Cyber-fatwas, sermons, and media campaigns

Amr Khaled and Omar Bakri Muhammad in search of new audiences

Ermete Mariani

Introduction

The spread of the new communications media (information and communications technology, or ICT) and the reduced cost of travel are increasing the mobility of individuals and information, and altering the relationship people have with the space that surrounds them, especially in Europe. In order to evaluate the consequences of the implementation of ICT on the production and diffusion of Islamic knowledge, I have chosen to compare the careers and communication strategies of two Arab interpreters of contemporary Islam who have spent an important part of their professional lives in Europe: Amr Khaled, a young Egyptian preacher who currently lives in London, and Omar Bakri Muhammad, the Syrian leader of a Salafi-inspired movement, al-Muhajiroun, who was also based in the British capital until August 2005, when he moved to Lebanon.

These two men of religion do not represent a single school of thought; what they do have in common, however, is their Arab origin, a sophisticated knowledge of the communications media, and the fact that they are both active on the Internet. Also, both men chose to live in London, though for quite different reasons. The Muslim community in Great Britain has a substantial Arab component, but the majority of its members hail from the Indian subcontinent and was attracted to the UK not only by the prospect of work but also in search of political asylum (Kepel 1994; Lewis 1994). London in particular is a meeting point for Muslims of different origins and backgrounds, as well as an important centre for the production of Muslim knowledge (Thomas 2005).

This chapter is based on website analysis and field research that I conducted in London between the Twin Towers attacks of 11 September 2001 and the London bombing of 7 July 2005. In this particular lapse of time the Islamist discourse online was seriously scrutinized by intelligence services, but radical preachers, such as Omar Bakri, were still free to operate. Actually, it was only after the London bombing that 'Londonistan' was largely dismantled, and Omar Bakri was strongly advised to leave British territory.

The process of communication is always the result of a continuous negotiation between authors, the political and economic requirements of the contexts in which the message is produced and received, and the level of development of the ICT. Therefore, I underline in this article how much the European technological and sociological context enabled Khaled and Bakri to implement original communication strategies to reach new audiences on the Internet too. Consequently, from these two cases studied it emerges how designers, webmasters, and sponsors of websites (in other words, the entire editorial apparatus) all participate in defining communication strategies and in formulating their contents. In this context, we will give some attention to the definition of *fatwa* as well as the birth of new religious figures like the 'cyber counsellor' and probably what we may call 'Muslim campaigner'.

What also emerges here is how, for Amr Khaled, Europe represents an object of study and a new market for his religious products, while Omar Bakri, through his various activities, sought to create an Islamic community with local roots in London, but also having strong transnational links. Moreover, as regards Amr Khaled, it could be argued that the effect of the religious information market itself encourages him continually to increase his audience, even to non-Muslims, and to seek to be present in all available media, in order to reach the widest possible public and gain some independence from satellite TV.

Website analysis

The Internet is not considered anymore as a novelty by technicians and users because it is almost thirty years old, but for social scientists it is still a rather new phenomenon. As there is not yet a common methodology to analyse the social consequences of the use of the Internet to produce and diffuse contents, I developed my own one, drawing inspiration from the reading of Roland Barthes (1985), Roger Chartier (1990), and Michael Benedikt (1991). From Roland Barthes I borrowed the conceptual tools to interpret hypertexts, while Chartier's work is crucial to analysing the link between cultural production, means of communication, and social phenomena. Finally Benedikt's pioneering job is fundamental to inquiry into the interrelations between technical infrastructures and virtual reality, as well as in conceptualizing cyberspace architecture.

From a technical point of view, the Internet brings smaller communication networks into contact with one another, making it possible to exchange e-mails and instant messages, use graphic interfaces to access data banks (World Wide Web), to exchange text and voice messages publicly and privately (chat room, forum, and VoIP[1]), to share audio and video files, and eventually to transfer money. This is the infrastructure of cyberspace, in other words, the artificial world that is given shape and form by those who use it.[2]

I have sought to define the space occupied by Amr Khaled and Omar Bakri Muhammad within this world; in other words, the area of cyberspace they occupy and how they define that space (be it religious, lay, commercial, or entertainment). To this end, I have gathered all information available online from the sites they run, and from other sites in which they participate: owners,[3] location of the Internet Service Provider (ISP),[4] traffic rank,[5] links in and links out,[6] and visibility.[7]

Finally, I have sought to reconstruct the development of the design and contents of the sites in question.[8]

Having completed this information-gathering phase, I conducted non-directive interviews with the authors, and attended their lectures and work sessions with the aim of evaluating their knowledge of the communications media, understanding the motives behind their decision to publish their messages on the Internet, and studying what (if any) communication strategies they adopted. Finally, I sought to understand the political, cultural, and religious constraints they have had to face, and how they worked. I interviewed Amr Khaled several times in London during the spring/summer of 2003 and 2004, and have also interviewed Omar Bakri Muhammad on a number of occasions. For three months, I followed Omar Bakri's lessons at his London School of Sharia, and attended lectures and audiences at his Sharia Court of Great Britain.

Finally I analysed the message of these two authors, in particular their Internet publications. For Amr Khaled, I analysed the English and Italian translations of a number of episodes of his television programme *Sunna᷄ al-hayyat* (Life Makers) – which are also available in video and audio form, in Arabic, on his site – and the answers to *'as'al al-shabab* (questions from young people), the transcription of a weekly column published in the Egyptian paper *Kull al-nas*, available online at the site, Gn4me.[9] With regard to Omar Bakri Muhammad, I studied his Internet sites and the PDF-format publications contained thereon, as well as a number of printed works. In reading these texts, I extracted cultural references and analysed the style of the language, because my aim is not to evaluate the theological value of the interpretations they give, but to understand the public to whom they are directed, and the methods used.

Amr Khaled: an itinerary in global communications

Amr Khaled was born to an upper middle-class family in Alexandria, in Egypt, in 1967. His grandfather Ibrahim Abd al-Hadi Pasha, was prime minister at the time of King Farouk. Until the year 1988, Amr Khaled studied business and accounting at the University of Cairo, before going on to follow courses at the Institute of Islamic Studies, also in the Egyptian capital, whence he emerged with a diploma two years later. He then signed up to do a PhD at the University of Wales at Lampeter (UK). Until the middle of the 1990s Khaled worked as an accountant, even creating his own consultation company; then his activities as a preacher became his true mission – and his new career. Khaled began 'speaking about religion' in an almost informal way, on Saturday afternoons at the Dokki Shooting Club, a sports centre in Cairo where he would go to play football. Having met with a good public response, he continued his activities in two mosques belonging to the al-Hussary Association[10] (though never as *imam* or *khatib*) and by giving private courses on religion.

After some years of preaching in mosques, sports clubs, and private houses of the Egyptian middle classes, Emad Eddin Adib, a famous small-screen journalist and president of the Gn4me media company (Atia 2001), offered him the chance to present a television programme on the new Egyptian satellite channel, Dream TV.[11] Thus, from his very first television appearances the former football player became a famous *téléqoraniste*,[12] and thanks to another weekly programme on the satellite channel Iqra TV,[13] his audience soon extended well beyond the frontiers of Egypt.

He has now been living in Great Britain for a number of years (in the wealthy neighbourhood of Notting Hill in London), having signed up to do a PhD at the University of Lampeter (Wales). As he himself says, 'the next years will be strategic' for his future, because it is a period he intends to dedicate to 'understanding the western society'.[14] Amr Khaled also hopes to learn English in order to address his sermons to the largest possible number of Muslims, because the majority understands English better than Arabic. For the moment his media activities (television, lectures, public and private classes, and Internet) continue smoothly and without problems, as he always seeks to maintain 'good relations with the Arab and Muslim world ... and that's not an easy thing to do!'[15] It is for this reason too, if we take him at his word, that he deliberately avoids speaking about politics and giving juridical opinions, i.e. *fatwas*, on particular religious questions.

Nonetheless, his modern views – delivered 'from the heart'[16] and seeking to promote social commitment – have certainly caused him some difficulties. Indeed, the boards of trustees of the mosques that invited him to speak have had to face enormous difficulties in managing the crowds coming to see and listen to him. His success did not take long to arouse suspicion and envy, to the point that some people claimed his stay in Great Britain was not entirely the result of choice (Kovach 2002). Rather, it appears to be a form of voluntary exile (though one that does not prevent him from exercising a kind of intellectual influence on the Arab world); an exile to some extent imposed by the Egyptian authorities, who always seek to control Islamist debate, both moderate and extremist, on their national territory (Shahine 2002; Kepel 1984).

The existence of someone like Amr Khaled must also be interpreted as a function of the Egyptian Islamist media scene, in which many preachers of varying political and religious tendencies have appeared. Making use of all available means, figures such as the Shaykhs Sha'rawi (Gonzalez-Quijano 2000), Kishk (Kepel 1984), Ghazali, and al-Qaradawi (Anderson 2008; Mariani 2003; Gräf and Skovgaard-Petersen 2009) have often attained great success. The last-named is considered to be the greatest star of contemporary Islam, above all for his appearances on satellite channels and the Internet, and for his opinions on Islamic finance (Galloux 1997; Moore 1997). In his own way, Amr Khaled continues this nascent tradition of communicators, introducing, however, certain important stylistic changes: he is the first to have conquered such a large public so quickly, thanks to his passionate and amusing delivery, as well as to his youthful image (even though he is in his forties), and decidedly removed (clean-shaven, casual dress, with an elegant blue suit and tie for television wear) from the classical look favoured by traditional *ulama*, including those who appear on the modern media.

With great rapidity, his preaching has managed to capture young Egyptians of both sexes (his female audience seems particularly receptive to his charm), who have finally discovered that religious discourse is possible even for young people who enjoy sports and having a good time, that it is possible not only to lay down the law on *haram* and *halal* (the lawful and the unlawful), but also to enjoy life in accordance with divine commandments, and invite others to participate in one's happiness (Haenni 2002; Haenni and Holtrop 2002; Bayat 2003). It is clear from the translations of his programmes for Iqra TV, *Sunnaᶜ al-hayat*[17] that our *téléqoraniste* addresses his public informally, not *ex cathedra*, presenting a pleasant and entertaining interpretation of religion, while at the same time invoking real moral and social values. Indeed, he invites his listeners to commit themselves to a rediscovery of the true meaning of Islam, and to invest their personal, intellectual, and material resources in a series of small gestures capable of improving the lives of the less fortunate. According to the interpretation of Patrick Haenni and Tjitske Holtrop, Amr Khaled 'dessine sans doute le chemin de l'une des formes possibles d'innovation religieuse dans l'Égypte de demain. Non par la voie royale d'un nouveau discours théologique, mais par les chemins de traverse de l'interaction entre mutations culturelles et pratiques religieuses' (Haenni and Holtrop 2002).

Amr Khaled's originality also lies in his work methods. As he explained to me, every six months he chooses a subject on which to work, seeking all available references on CDs, audiocassettes and videotapes, as well as in books.[18] During his research he takes notes, on the basis of which he builds up his discourse, which once finished he transcribes into a large exercise book. When I met him he had around ten such exercise books, which he carries with him everywhere because they contain all his lessons. Once a month he visits Lebanon, where he records four episodes of his television programme at the studios of the Lebanese TV station LBC. The programmes are then transmitted once a week on Iqra TV.

In keeping with the format used by many Islamic preachers in the contemporary media, Khaled's transmissions take the form of an imaginary dialogue with his listeners. At the end of certain episodes, he offers questionnaires and assigns 'homework', and through his Internet site gathers feedback and reaction from his public. In order to be as clear as possible, he uses many examples taken from the classical age of Islam, from modern history, and from the lives of famous people, still living and not necessarily Arab or Muslim. These examples are chosen as a function of his line of argument, and at times historical reality is adapted to rhetorical or ideological requirements.[19] His preaching and his lessons become television programmes, audiocassettes, DVDs, CDs, videotapes, and audio and video files available on the Web. A lot of this material is for sale in Islamic shops throughout the world, as well as on the Internet, whence it can be downloaded free of charge.[20] His only economically profitable occupation remains his television work,[21] while his other activities serve above all to put him in the public eye, increase his popularity, and bring him face to face with his public. Indeed, given the non-application of laws safeguarding copyright in the Arab world, Amr Khaled, like other media figures of this type, cannot hope to make a great profit from the direct sale of his products. This explains, perhaps, why ICT occupies such an important position in his communication strategy, though being secondary to his television work.

Amr Khaled and the institutional world of Arab cyberspace

Amr Khaled is not so well integrated into the institutional world of Arab cyber-space as the Shaykh Yusuf al-Qaradawi (Mariani 2003; Gräf 2007), who has his own website besides dedicated spaces in the most visited and traditional websites which provide Muslims with information and services. Apart from his own websites and the one managed by his fans, Amr Khaled has got a dedicated space only on Gn4me, an information web portal online since 2001 and headed by Emad Eddin Adib.

Adib is a famous Egyptian journalist and publisher, who runs a daily newspaper in Arabic, *al-ʿAlam al-Yawm*, two radio stations *Nujum FM* and *Nile One Radio*, and two weekly magazines *Kull al-Nas* and *ʿAdam al-Yawm*. As a journalist he is well known throughout the Arab world, as a presenter of the programme *ʿAla-l-Hawa* transmitted by Orbit – one of the biggest Arab satellite pay TV channels – and presenter on the new and successful channel, Dream TV. In the eyes of its founder and director, Gn4me is not simply a dot-com firm, but a complete media company whose 'core business' – Adib says – 'is content syndication, not only putting sites on the net' (Atia 2001). Gn4me is also an Internet access provider in Egypt, and Emad Eddin Adib has developed a partnership with the American media group MSNBC (which launched its Arabized information portal at the end of 2001, at exactly the same time as Dream TV began its transmissions), to develop a shared website, which is currently inactive.

The portal presents all the group's specialized fields: the production of general and specialist information (finance, economics, and 'good news'), religious questions, radio, and entertainment.[22] In the first version, which came online in July 2001, *fatwas* occupied an important position, with a rolling bar in Arabic proudly announcing that this was the first site offering *fatwas* in audio format.[23] In November 2000 the company had already acquired the URL <http://www.gn4fatawa.com> (currently inactive), in which it could store all the *fatwas* that it had been putting online from July 2001. In reality, this address was never used because the relevant pages were located at the main address of <http://www.gn4me.com/fatawa/index.jsp.htm> and, since the beginning of 2003, the site Gn4fatawa has disappeared completely. At the time, it was possible to ask for *fatwas* directly by e-mail and enter into dialogue with the *muftis*. In principle, Shaykh Sayyid al-Sabah and Amr Khaled checked the content of the website personally and guaranteed its 'Islamicity'.[24] Al-Sabah was available for two hours every Wednesday for discussions with web users, while Khaled was responsible for all the audio files, though he did not sign any *fatwas*.

The Gn4me portal and all its associated sites have undergone at least two profound revisions, of style and of editorship, as well as a number of smaller modifications. In September 2002, the portal was extremely simple with a central image surrounded by links to other sites, officially autonomous and with a specific design of their own. Since the beginning of 2003, all the associated sites have become sub-pages presented on the homepage with an icon and a brief description, except Party radio, which still has a different address.[25] In May 2006

Gn4me created a YouTube Channel as well.[26] The Gn4fatawa site became the page *is⁺al al-mufti* (ask the mufti) which presented Amr Khaled, even though the requests for *fatwas* were always answered by Shaykh Sayyid al-Sabah,[27] who was not presented in the open access web pages.[28] In March 2003, the structure of the portal's homepage was simplified with a more sober choice of colour: grey and blue on a white background. Khaled was still present in the section marked 'services' – *khadimat* – under the heading 'religion' (in English on the site). Since July 2003 he has had a special section of his own with no specific title. He is, nonetheless, still present in the page *fatawa* in the online version of the weekly magazine, *Kull al-nas*, published by the Gn4me group.

Judging by the technical characteristics of the site and by the Gn4me company's publicity investments in Egypt, we may deduce that the target public is Egyptian.[29] However, the nature of the company itself, specialized in supplying website content, enables us to hypothesize that the principal function of the portal is to highlight all the group's capacities and activities in the Arab information market.

The limited space currently given to religion on the Gn4me site seems to reflect the publishing group's communication strategy, as it seeks to present itself as an information site and to find a space in that sector of the market. The choice of bringing Amr Khaled into the project may, then, be seen as being essentially linked to his popularity among young Egyptians and Arabs in general, as well as to his friendship with Emad Eddin Adib, president of Gn4me, and one of the promoters of Amr Khaled's media success.[30]

Since the beginning of 2003, Amr Khaled's participation in the portal has diminished considerably;[31] there is no longer an archive with his lessons and sermons, but only interviews already published by *Kull al-nas*. Until March 2004 he maintained a kind of virtual dialogue via e-mail with visitors to the site (an activity that Khaled himself admits took up very little of his time!).[32] This evolution is probably due to the fact that, since the beginning of 2003, despite much investment in publicity, the site has not had a large enough audience to justify the commitment of a celebrity of media Islam. Nonetheless, the portal has attained a good position in the statistics in terms of numbers of visitors. Perhaps for this reason, Amr Khaled remains associated with Gn4me, even though he dedicates himself above all to his own personal site.

Amr Khaled's homepage and network

Amr Khaled's more passionate fans were the first to put his lessons online, on sites that also supplied personal information about the young man of religion. Since 1999, it has been possible to find it on the site For Islam (<http://www. forislam.com>) – audio files in English and Arabic of 'Shaykh Amr', though the pages were only in English.[33] Actually, at that time, it was technically very difficult to realize webpages in non-Latin alphabets (Atia 2003–4). In 2002, one Abd Allah Abd al-Rahman[34] opened the site 'Amr Khaled home page' (<http:// www.amrkhaled.net> and <http://www.amrkhaled.com>) entirely in Arabic, also because in the meantime the most important browsers and software to create websites were completely arabized. The new site was <http://www.amrkhaled.net> registered in the Mohandessin neighbourhood of Cairo, which went some way to taking the place of the For Islam site. Abd Al-Rahman was webmaster and administrator of the new site. Amr Khaled welcomed the change because the first site, by its very title (For Islam), had the defect of limiting the reach of the message that the young preacher wanted to transmit, a message not limited to Islam, but covering all aspects of life. Moreover, 'it was too militant and focused on the Palestinian issue'.[35]

From the beginning, the new personal website appeared as a neutral space where a young Muslim talks directly to his peers about matters of life and faith. Because of its great success and the great quantity of e-mail addresses it managed to supply, the URL <www.forislam.com> has not disappeared altogether, but automatically connects to <www.amrkhaled.net> in which some of the content of the old site has been transferred and the 'name@forislam.com' accounts have been maintained.[36] The choice of using an URL that does not end in '.com', as tends to be the case with commercial sites, but in '.net', which is characteristic of more generic sites registered by associations and private citizens, is another way to underline the neutrality of the virtual space he wanted to create: neither religious, nor commercial.

Since it was first opened, the Amr Khaled homepage has undergone various modifications, even though the style has always remained basic, with no religious symbols. Images and sophisticated technology (such as Flash) have been used only rarely as they could reduce compatibility with older browsers, which are more widespread in the Arab world, and make the download of pages slower. Despite these measures, the server hosting the site is described by Alexa as 'very slow',[37] and hence the download of audio files takes a long time, especially for users linked to the Internet by an analogue telephone line, as is the case in most of the Arab world at the time of writing (2009).

The visibility of this site has increased considerably over the last year. In a Google search in September 2003 with the words 'Amru Khaled' or 'Amr Khaled', the first result was a commercial site where it was possible to buy books and other multimedia material by Amr Khaled, while the link to his official site did not appear before the third page. The same search undertaken in February 2009 brings up the official site in first place. According to Alexa, <http://www.amrkhaled.net>'s ranking fluctuated a lot: the site was in 7,220th place among the most-visited sites in September 2003, in August 2004 it was 591st, while in March 2009 it was 5,228nd. At the time of writing, 63.6 per cent of its visitors use the discussion forums, while 32.2 per cent navigate through the webpages, and 3.2 per cent use the e-mail accounts provided free of charge.[38] So it seems that Amr Khaled is right to pronounce himself 'satisfied of my website's audience success'.[39] According to his own estimates 60 per cent of those who visit his site are Egyptians between the ages of 15 and 30; the rest live in Syria, Jordan, the United States, and Saudi Arabia.[40] According to Alexa in February 2009 there were 1,428 sites with a link in to <http://www.amrkhaled.net>. These include religious sites, search engines, forums, chat rooms and Arab directories, but there are also many journalistic and scientific articles with links to the pages of Khaled's site. According to Alexa, which can also follow the movements of Web users in cyberspace, visitors to the Khaled site also frequent other religious sites such as that of the Kuwaiti sheikh Tareq Al Sawaidan (<http://www.suwaidan.com>), Muhammad Jebril (<http://www.jebril.com>), Yusuf al-Qaradawi (<http://www.qaradawi.net>), as well as Islamic portals such as Islam Today (<http://www.islamtoday.net>), and Islamway (<http://www.islamway.com>).

The current site has a very clear and simple style. The information is presented in three columns against a white background (not green, as is the case in most of the Islamic websites). Since the month of Ramadan 2008, there is an additional page before the usual homepage where the latest web projects are presented: 'Radio Sotcom' (in Arabic *radio sawtkum* – radio your voice); '*Toot*' a website entirely dedicated to children; '*bayt sunnaᵉ al-hayyat*', a forum about the homonymous television programme; and '*mujaddidun*', where Amr Khaled presents his programme of lectures worldwide promoting a renewal of the Islamic message.

The site header contains a photograph of Khaled with the current slogan: 'together we build life …' (in Arabic *maᵉan nasnaᵉu al-hayyat* …), taken from his most famous cycle of TV programmes *Sunnaᵉ al-hayyat* – Life Makers. The centre of the page is dedicated to the novelties of the site: the latest episodes of his TV show, his speeches, articles about him, and caricatures. To the right is the list of all the sub-pages of which the site is composed, subdivided into three categories: 'main list' – *al-qaᵃima al-raᵃisiyya* – including speeches, official visits, photograph albums, caricatures, and discussion forums as well as the collected episodes of *Sunnaᵉ al-hayyat*; then 'with voice and images' – *bi-l-sawt wa-l-sura* – presenting the conferences attended and the lectures delivered; finally, a part dedicated to *Sunnaᵉ al-hayyat* containing audio files and written translations in nineteen languages.[41] The left-hand column contains the internal search engine and highlights certain campaigns, such as that against smoking, as well as the latest survey. At the bottom of the page are small publicity icons.

An analysis of content, graphic style, behaviour of visitors, user statistics, and its position in cyberspace reveals a site that appears to be a neutral, almost secular space, even though it talks a lot about religion. Amr Khaled himself is generically termed *ustadh* (an Arabic word that means teacher or master, but that is also used as a sign of respect) and deals with religious questions in a tone that strives to be light and amusing, while at the same time remaining serious. The author and administrator have not created links to exclusively religious sites, and the site is often quoted by other media, portals, and chat rooms, not only in Arabic. At the same time, the users appear to be principally interested in religious questions, because they come to the site after having visited the webpages of other ulama.

Despite the disappearance of English as the site's main language in the move from For Islam to the 'Amr Khaled official website' (which took place paradoxically when Khaled arrived in England), some episodes of the television programmes *Sunnaᵉ al-hayyat* and *Hatta yughayyiru ma bi-anfusihim* – 'Until they Change what is in their Souls'[42] – have been translated by the *Dar al-tarjama* into nineteen other languages, ranging from English to Chinese. This renewed interest in a non-Arabic-speaking public seems to reflect a desire to open up to the Muslim world in its broadest sense, even though English definitely remains the second language of the website. After reading certain passages in the discussion forum dedicated to the *Dar al-tarjama*[43] and exchanging e-mails with the person in charge of the Italian section and another co-ordinator,[44] I discovered that the translations are done by volunteers eager to participate in spreading Khaled's message, who coordinate their activities through the discussion forums. The translation project came into being in October 2003 with a group of ten people; by August 2004 they had become 269 including translators, administrators, and editors, with ages ranging from 14 to 65, all of them volunteers working for free. This change in editorial strategy, from audio files in Turkish and Malay, to written texts in European and oriental languages, increases the usability of the site and avoids the risk of confusing Khaled's voice with that of interpreters/voice-over speakers.

The impression we get, if we consider how it has evolved, is that the young Egyptian preacher has decided to sink ever-greater investment in his site. Originally, *ForIslam.com* was a simple showcase site in English, probably because the software needed to write and publish in Arabic was harder to come by and more expensive. Later it became possible to supply e-mail addresses and chat rooms, which meant higher running costs. The first version of the site *AmrKhaled.net* dedicated more space to chat rooms and audio files than For Islam did, and to this must be added the free translations done in Turkish and Malay.[45] In its latest edition, the site was developed by an Egyptian firm Zad Solutions (<http://www.zadsolutions.com>), the programme archives and the chat rooms are getting ever bigger and the mammoth project of translating his lessons has begun. Calculating the cost of these sites is extremely difficult because part of the services come from Egypt, part from Europe, and so on. Furthermore, we do not know how much of these services were paid, and how much supplied free by fans and supporters. The only thing that is certain is that Amr Khaled is investing a great deal of energy in his site, perhaps because his audience uses it as a means of communicating with him.

Even in cyberspace Khaled does not forget (nor is he forgotten by) his female public. His writings and interviews are available in Arabic and English on the site Wasfa Sahla, run by a group of 'energetic Egyptian women' who, via the Internet, address themselves to young brides and mothers – and not only Arabs, which explains why their site is also in English.[46] They describe their mission in these terms:

> Our goal is to make our customers happily thrilled at finding much easier ways in taking care of their cooking and elegantly serving their family's favourite dishes, while taking care of their health and their children, and saving more time for their beauty care. Wasfasahla.com is aiming to help women in our society satisfy their ego by addressing endless enormous demands of having a good health, happy family, and a successful career.[47]

Through his websites and television programmes Khaled has always encouraged his audience to send him ideas that he would transform into feasible projects. Thus in January 2003 Amr Khaled opened up Right Start Foundation in Birmingham as a concrete result of his TV programme Life Makers. Right Start Foundation is

> a charitable organisation committed to building bridges between civilisations and nurturing constructive and positive co-existence. … It is an advocate for the voices of the youth and plays a developmental role in addressing the concerns and challenges faced by this important part of our future.[48]

This foundation has promoted several campaigns that are not specifically Islamic like the one against drug addiction and smoking, therefore quite successful in gaining the recognition of non-religious international organizations like the United Nations.

During his brief and unconventional carrier Amr Khaled has gained rapidly important international recognitions. In April 2006 he was described by *The New York Times Magazine* as 'the world's most famous and influential Muslim televangelist', and in 2007 he was ranked 62nd in *Time Magazine's* famous list of the world's most influential people, and 13th in the category of 'heroes and pioneers'.

Omar Bakri, leader of a transnational community?

Sheikh Omar Bakri Muhammad (OBM as he likes to call himself) was born in 1958 to a large and wealthy family of Aleppo. He was chosen by his father to follow a religious education.[49] Up until the age of 17 he studied in Syria, but because of his religious and political ideals he was forced to move to Lebanon, where he continued to study privately, joined the Hizb ut-Tahrir movement, and got married. In 1976, following the Syrian intervention in the Lebanese war, he went to Egypt, where he spent about eight months, during which time he sought unsuccessfully to enter the University of al-Azhar. He also came into contact with the Muslim Brotherhood, although he was not an active participant in the movement. Later he moved to Mecca in Saudi Arabia, where he continued his studies at the Sultaniyya University with a thesis on the Caliphate. Some time later he moved to Jeddah where, on 1 March 1983, he founded his own organization, al-Muhajiroun, which was initially associated with Hizb ut-Tahrir. Because of his political activities, he was arrested and expelled from Saudi Arabia in 1985.

Finally, Shaykh Bakri arrived in London, 'and because I was quite rich, Great Britain welcomed me without making any problem'.[50] There he lived until August 2005, unable to leave because the Syrian government had withdrawn his passport and the British authorities had given him neither political refugee status, nor citizenship. He finally received a residence permit in 1993 and requested citizenship in 1996, though it had not yet been granted him by the time he was obliged to leave. He left Hizb ut-Tahrir definitively in 1996, and dedicated himself exclusively to his own transnational organization, al-Muhajiroun, which is ideologically close to the al-Qaeda movement. In August 2005 he was strongly urged by the British authorities to leave the country and moved to Lebanon, where he lives almost in retirement.

Omar Bakri's theological position defies definition, for even during his lectures on Islamic law he spent more time discussing international and local politics rather than doctrinal issues. But when asked by journalists, students, and myself about his ideological affiliation he would affirm clearly that he followed the Salafi tradition, 'just like Ben Laden!' (as he used to say to impress his audience).[51] Al-Muhajiroun coordinated various political, cultural, and economic activities aimed at the restoration of the Muslim Caliphate. On various occasions he has collaborated with 'The International Islamic Front for Jihad against the Jews and the Crusaders' (IIF), gathering funds and recruiting volunteers (Thomas 2005).

Apart from his ambiguous dealings with the nebulous al-Qaeda organization, Shaykh Omar Bakri claimed to work above all for the 'cultural change' that must precede the creation of an Islamic State, because 'I don't believe force and violence can change society, and culture is at the base of the Caliphate'.[52] Indeed, it is in the field of culture that we find most of his public and professional activities. These can be subdivided into three categories: *da*ʿ*wa* (propaganda/the call to Islam), transmission of knowledge, and care of the community.

Omar Bakri's communication strategy until 2005

Sheikh Bakri used all means of communication available in order to awaken the conscience of Muslims and non-Muslims alike (i.e. for *da*ʿ*wa*): DVDs, audiocassettes, videotapes, CDs, Internet, lectures, and press releases. He also published *fatwas* in order to stimulate media attention in his activities. Communication was officially in the hands of *Alm Publications* (which belonged to al-Muhajiroun and also dealt in multimedia materials) and of *OBM Publications* (which belonged to an independent group that would like to publish all Bakri's works).[53] Both of them published above all brochures and pamphlets in various formats, because they are cheap to produce, have a wide circulation, and can be printed at very short notice, thus enabling Shaykh Bakri to coordinate the publications with his lectures and various important events.[54] The Internet played an important role in his communication strategy: by means of his various websites, Shaykh Bakri publicized his activities, spread his message, and maintained a dialogue with his supporters and with the Islamic intellectual community. His websites have been the target of continual attacks by hackers; and servers have often refused to host his violent proclamations, which can border on the illegal. In response to these problems, OBM has constantly had to change URLs and servers (nine URLs and six servers in two years), as well as to develop computer systems to defend himself from hackers.[55] All this has led to a low level of usage – according to Alexa its traffic ranking in 2004 was 457,830th – and to long periods of absence from cyberspace.[56]

In 2004 al-Muhajiroun's websites network was reduced to only one website and it was mainly in English, with part of the information available in Arabic.[57]

The English homepage presented the most recent publications, press releases, articles, latest opinion polls, and upcoming lectures (it is interesting to note how the structure of the homepage was very similar to that of the BBC).[58] In the header and footer of the homepage were links to the twelve sub-pages of the site: '*deen*' (the Arabic word for religion), letters, books, activities, leaflets, non-Muslims, Islamic topics, media, audio, video, about us, and links. At the top of the homepage, as downloaded on 25 August 2004, was an advertisement for a forthcoming lecture: 'REMEMBER, REMEMBER 11th September'. On the English site, it was possible to download extracts from books (most of them written by Shaykh Bakri himself), as well as audio and video material that could be purchased by contacting the association directly. It was also possible to send in e-mails on religious matters or contemporary political questions.

The Arabic version of the site appeared to be unfinished and was updated less frequently. Of the fourteen sub-pages presented in the header and at the foot of the homepage, only the links to the English site and to the homepage itself were active. The announcement of the lecture on 11 September was not visible either. Apart from the homepage, the graphics of which were identical to those on the English site, the second pages were all text-only on a white background. The Arabic site did not have the same propaganda and teaching material as the English site, almost certainly because the target audience was different, but it did contain political articles analysing the situation in the Arab world, and other material celebrating the struggle against the infidels – *kuffar* – who, according to Omar Bakri's political interpretations, persecute Muslims wherever they may be.

In order to attract media attention, Bakri tended to make violent statements and issue unconventional *fatwas*.[59] According to his own testimony, he had around ninety addresses of press agencies, freelance journalists, and newspapers at his disposal, and he contacted them personally when he wanted to pass on one of his messages.[60] An Italian journalist, who has been contacted by Omar Bakri on various occasions, summed up the Shaykh's ability in dealing with the press:

> he gives us the headlines of the articles! And I'm certain that when I write something about him it gets on the front page, because my magazine believes that his proclamations make us sell around 20 percent more than we usually do.[61]

In order to pass on his knowledge, Shaykh Bakri gave courses at the London School of Sharia, as well as numerous public lectures at small Islamic cultural centres throughout the UK. The lessons and lectures I attended dealt with Islamic law or commentaries on certain verses of the Qur'an. Omar Bakri Muhammad was always to be seen wearing traditional white robes, and he used to begin his lectures and classes with the phrase, *bi-sm allah ar-rahman ar-rahim*, before going on to read the notes from his laptop. His language was very simple and easy to understand, even for a little-educated public, and to explain the most important concepts he used examples taken from current political affairs. He also tended to pepper his speech with jokes and a little sarcasm. His lessons, in fact, became moments for reflection and cordial exchanges of views, and Bakri was always ready to answer questions and to give advice on any subject. Often, food and drink were served, all strictly *halal* of course.[62] His lessons at the London School of Sharia were often recorded on videotape and DVD and subsequently sold as educational material in order to support the association.

I feel that Bakri was seeking to consolidate a local Islamic community with strong transnational ties. Through the Sharia Court of Great Britain the Shaykh answered the questions of the faithful, issued *fatwas*, acted as mediator in marriage problems, dispensed divorces (from 1993 to 2004 he has issued 185), celebrated weddings (975 in the same period), and intervened in social prob lems.[63] He also occasionally acted as a consultant for British courts and gave advice on how to divide up inheritances. The al-Muhajiroun association also functioned as a solidarity network offering material assistance to needy members of the community: for example young women converts to Islam who had prob- lems in practising their new religion within their own families were given accom- modation by members of the association, and often ended up marrying into the community. In order to create transnational links, Shaykh Bakri maintained a continuous dialogue with the 'international Islamic scientific community' by means of modern communication techniques. He particularly used the Pal Talk chat room for direct discussions with other ulama and with anyone else who wanted to communicate with him.[64] Finally, al-Muhajiroun also presented itself as an international organization with branches in Pakistan,[65] in various Gulf coun- tries – Kuwait, Bahrain, and Saudi Arabia – and in the USA.

After he moved to Lebanon in 2005, OBM remained almost silent; since then he has not publicly managed any organization in the UK or elsewhere. The community of his closest supporters, such as the lawyer Anjem Choudary (who is of Pakistani origin), are attempting to take up his legacy but not with the same degree of success, because the political situation in Britain after the bombing of 2005 is completely different, and extremist talk is no longer tolerated.

Omar Bakri's audience, supporters, and legacy

Al-Muhajiroun's image as a movement contrary to Western values and family traditions (Thomas 2009) has generated much interest, not only from local and international media, and the British police, but also from many young Britons of Asian origin or with Muslim backgrounds, as well as a few converts.[66] It is difficult to define exactly who the audience and supporters of OBM and his al-Muhajiroun were, because the movement had a very flexible and open structure (there does not appear to be any kind of formal membership), although it is clear that there is a select group of people close to the leader. Furthermore, many activities were held in public, and journalists and researchers (such as the author), as well as the merely curious, were always well received. It is difficult, though, to establish who were the 'activists' and who the 'occasional spectators', or to distinguish those people who turned to him as a judge of the Sharia Court because he was quicker and more effective than others from those who shared his theological and political views.

In order to evaluate how many supporters and how large an audience he had, and what kind of people they were, I will consider the people who frequented his lessons, public lectures, and the sessions of the Sharia Court of Great Britain.

The lessons were held twice a week, on Tuesdays and Thursdays, from 9 p.m. to 11 p.m., and the number of students varied between fewer than ten to around twenty (no attendance record is kept). They were usually of Asian origin (Pakistani and Bangladeshi), aged between 18 and 30, and they often came with their wives and children (some just a few months old). The women and children were separated from the men by a screen, and to ask the Sheikh questions, they had to write them on pieces of paper which were then given to him. The people who participated in the lessons were very different from one another, and apart from a small number of assiduous participants, the others changed from one lesson to the next. The public lectures, on the other hand, might be attended by as many as 150–200 people. On these occasions too the public was usually made up of young people of Asian origin: men, women, and children separated by the usual screen. The lectures were held in a hotel, at the offices of *Alm Publications* in White Hart Lane in North London, or in rooms rented from local Muslim associations.

As for the Sharia Court, it was generally women who turned to OBM to ask for the annulment of their marriages. According to Omar Bakri, the activities of the Sharia Court were almost exclusively occupied by divorce cases.[67] The fact that there were more women than men is due to a legal issue since, according to Islamic law, a man can repudiate his wife simply by pronouncing the word *itlaq* – literally 'I divorce you' – three times in the presence of two witnesses. Women, on the other hand, have to explain their case before an Islamic judge who has the power to annul the marriage if he finds justified reasons to do so. During the course of my research, I followed five cases of annulment of marriage, all involving young women of Asian origin who, while still very young, married distant relatives.[68] The men, once they had arrived in the UK and obtained a British passport, either disappeared or refused to carry out their conjugal duties, such as providing for their wife and children. In these cases, Omar Bakri Muhammad's role was to make *de facto* separation and civil divorce acceptable to Muslim families. It should also be noted that in some cases Omar Bakri's interpretation of Islam acted as a modernizing force among the family traditions that survive in Muslim communities in Britain, as he opposed arranged marriages and marriages for economic interest.

After the London bombing of 7 July 2005, OBM's closest supporters opened up several organizations (like Ahl al-Sunnah wa al-Jamaʿah, al-Ghurabaa, and The Saviour sect, or the Saved Sect) that were all shut down under the Terrorism Act, approved by the British Parliament on 30 March 2006. There are still some websites where it is possible to read Bakri's texts and *fatwas*, but under the Terrorism Act it is no longer possible for an extremist organization to implement a complex communication strategy which comprises conferences, publications of booklets and websites, managing a sharia school, and even a court.

Fatwas: new definitions and transformations

The popularity of *fatwa* literature is not limited to the printed word but there have been online 'fatwa banks' or databases since the beginning of the World Wide Web in the mid-1990s.

A *fatwa* (pl. *fatawa*) is a precise juridical opinion given by a Muslim expert, *mufti*, who has no coercive power (Tyan 1999). Reading the specialized literature on the subject, it emerges that there are various ways to request, issue, and record *fatwas*, and that these vary depending on the cultural or political situation of the *mustaftis*, (i.e. those requesting the *fatwa*) and of the *muftis* (Messick 1986, 1993), as well as on the means of communications used (Messick 1996; see also Caeiro in this volume).

The service is also available on the Internet, where it has various forms and names. A close study of cyberspace reveals that a large number of websites in Arabic offer visitors free access to religious and other experts, giving them the possibility to discuss matters concerning morals, religion, and everyday life. This 'service' can have very different names: 'fatwa bank', 'ask the scholar', 'counselling', 'questions & answers', and 'dialogues'. From a study I conducted on the 100 most-visited Arab websites it emerged that nine of them offer a service they define as *fatwa*, though with various interesting variations.[69]

Of these, Islam Online (www.islam-online.net, the third most-visited site), offers visitors the chance to put questions to two kinds of experts: the *ahl al-dhikr* (scholars) and the *mustashar* (cyber counsellors). The former are ulama with a background of classical religious education, while the latter are simply good Muslims, with no particular religious qualifications, but are experts in family and social counselling, or in psychology. This is an orthodox separation of roles (Messick 1993; Tyan 1999), but it should be noted however that the English translation of the names reflects a very widespread Internet 'profession'; that of cyber counsellor, for example, is the person who seeks to respond to Internet users via the Web, offering career plans and advice on how to solve family and personal problems, etc.

Another site, Islam Questions and Answers (<http://www.islam-qa.com>), provides a large online databank of *fatwas* in ten languages.[70] However, though the name of the website is 'Questions and Answers' or *su*ª*al wa jawab* in Arabic, there are only *fatwas* on that site. Moreover, on the website dedicated to the soft drink Mecca Cola (<http://www.mecca-cola.com>), one may see how *fatwas* are also used to serve commercial ends, guaranteeing that the beverage in question is *halal*.

Self-definition of interpreters

A definition of what *fatwas* are implies also a definition of the authors of Islamic knowledge on the Internet. Here we may note the two different approaches of Omar Bakri Muhammad and Amr Khaled.

Studying the development of the latest version of the al-Muhajiroun website, we may see that the page '*fatawa*' has been replaced with one named 'letters', on which unidentified shaykhs answer e-mail messages from visitors. On the Arabic version of the site, there was no longer any page dedicated to *fatawa*, but it was possible to communicate directly with Shaykh Bakri on Pal Talk. In earlier versions, the site was in English and Arabic and, apart from the propaganda material, there was a page dedicated to *fatawa*. As Bakri explained to me, the publication of *fatawa*s served to express his own juridical and theological views, to help his readers (Muslims and non-Muslims) answer their questions on Islam, and finally to 'provoke the international Islamic scientific community'.[71] In order to explain this point, he took the example of the *fatwa* on Musharraf, issued on 16 September 2001, in which he affirmed:

> Question: What is the *fatwa* regarding those who assist or allow the US to carry out military action from Pakistan in order to attack Muslims in Afghanistan? – Answer: … herefore we ask Muslims with the capability, especially the army of Muslim countries, to move quickly and to capture those Apostates and criminals involved in these crimes, especially the ruler of Pakistan, King Fahd of Saudi Arabia and Rabbani of Afghanistan and his followers. … We call upon Muslims worldwide to support Muslims in Afghanistan, whoever can support them physically must do so, whosoever can support them financially must do so and whosoever can support them verbally must to do so according to his capacity.[72]

The aim was 'to tell to my dear ulama colleagues that, if they want to follow the principles of Islam they should condemn Musharraf', or as he wrote at the end of the *fatwa*: 'We have indeed a responsibility to inform the Muslim Ummah of this Hukm [decree], and let Allah (SWT) be our witness that we have indeed delivered the message'.[73]

The replacement of *fatawa* with 'letters' and 'live dialogue' may indicate a lack of desire to use this medium to participate in the religious debate, and a preference to maintain continuous contact – either real or fictitious – with the visitors to the site. Moreover, reading the contents of these pages it is clear that they have an important propaganda function. The letters come from various parts of the world, as well as from non-Muslims, particularly Christians, and the replies were written by authors using the names of Abu Ibrahim and Abu Osama, who are not further identified on the site. Subjects varied from religious questions to international politics and the tone of the letters was fairly calm, even though the religious stance was decidedly radically Islamist.

Finally, Omar Bakri did not refuse the titles of *shaykh*, *ʿalim*, and *mufti*, but when I asked him how he preferred to define himself, he replied smiling: 'as a *talib al-ʿilm* (seeker of knowledge), … like the Taliban'.[74]

Amr Khaled, on the other hand, expressly declared that he has no wish to 'undertake political action, support any party or issue *fatwas*'.[75] In keeping with this position, he never describes the replies he gives on his website as *fatwas*, nor does he present himself as a *mufti*. Nonetheless, Gn4me placed him on the site dedicated to *fatwas*, Gn4Fatawa, then put his replies to 'questions of the youth' in the *fatawa* category (though avoiding any explicit indication of him as a *mufti*), and have recently given him a personal page. Moreover, he remains in the *fatawa* page in the online version of the weekly magazine *Kull al-Nas*, which belongs to the same group. We have found the same text on his personal website, though presented with the title 'questions from the youth' to which he replies 'from a religious and social point of view in his weekly dialogues, *hiwar*, in *Kull al-Nas*'.[76]

As the examples we have given show, Khaled's preference to avoid the *fatwa* label, an uncomfortable label for him, while at the same time replying to questions on religion, is shared by other webmasters on the other websites (Islam Online, Islam Q&A, and al-Muhajiroun). The Egyptian preacher's decision probably stems from his wish to distinguish himself from traditional *ulama* and to avoid participating in political and religious debates (based on the exchange of *fatwas*). Indeed, what he wants is to address young Arabic speakers with words that 'come from the heart' and that help them to 'build their lives' on the basis of love for Allah.

The choice of the Gn4me group, on the other hand, may derive from the fact that *fatwas* have become a widely offered service, one easily recognizable by visitors to Arab websites, both Islamic and non-Islamic. Therefore, in order for a web portal to have a full range of services, it needs to offer the possibility of interacting with well-known figures on subjects involving morals, daily life, and religion. This service is generically defined as *fatwa*, even without entering into theological discussions. Recently, perhaps to avoid losing him and to give him greater exposure, Amr Khaled has been given a personal page, with no explanatory description (he no longer needs one!). At the same time, the *téléqoraniste* seeks to avoid overly rigid and limiting descriptions of his 'profession'. He refuses the title of *mufti*, and does not like to be called *daʿi* (preacher), *shaykh,* or *ʿalim*. He prefers the neutral title of *ustadh*, but considers himself to be a *muslih*, 'reformer', stressing his religious and social function more than his profession.[77]

Is Europe a new market or a golden exile?

What Amr Khaled and Omar Bakri Muhammad have in common is the fact that they arrived in London because they were considered as disruptive influences in their own countries. However, in their new home they operate according to different forms of logic and with very different aims, though both were adapting to their new context.

Despite the fact that the majority of Amr Khaled's public is made up of Arabs, and more specifically of Egyptians, I have the impression that he is preparing to conquer a European audience (though without neglecting his followers in Egypt, which remains his most important public, as well as his homeland); in other words Muslims and non-Muslims who do not speak Arabic.[78] Until 2004, his website contained audio files with Turkish and Malay translations of some of his television programmes. Subsequently, these languages were replaced with written translations in nineteen other languages of his TV programmes *Sunnaʿ al-hayat* and *Hatta yughayyiru ma bi-anfusihim*. This operation goes hand in hand with his participation in lectures and meetings organized by various Islamic communities in Europe and North America, events which are also presented on his website. Over the last few years, he has delivered public lectures in Germany, Canada, and England, Italy, as well as in Paris, where he participated in the meeting of the Union des Organisations Islamiques de France (UOIF), which is held every year at Le Bourget. On this subject, the president of the UOIF, Lhaj Thami Breze, told me that Khaled was invited because of his great popularity with the public and because his moderate positions and openness to dialogue reflect the stance of the UOIF.[79] According to Breze, Khaled's success is largely due to his style and his rhetoric: he is capable of talking about religion with a passionate and yet ironic style. Furthermore, in Breze's view, Khaled has communicative abilities that enable him to pass on his message in any circumstances, overcoming even linguistic barriers and capturing his audience's attention thanks to his theatrical skills.[80]

As for the al-Muhajiroun website, the part in English was far larger than the part in Arabic. This was probably due to the fact that OBM's audience was made up, above all, of Muslims living in the UK, while the use of Arabic served more than anything to maintain contact with the branches of his movement in the Arab world (especially Kuwait and Saudi Arabia), and to keep up a dialogue with the international scientific community. Since he moved to Lebanon in August 2005, Omar Bakri has had no official websites and he does not manage, at least openly, any religious community or intervene in public debates. His closer followers are somehow active in the British territory as well as online, but as the 'covenant' that enabled Omar Bakri to communicate widely and manage an association is broken, their presence in the public sphere is reduced.If we compare the relationship that Amr Khaled and Omar Bakri each had between 2001 and 2005 with the British and European Islamic communities, we may see they used different ways of exploiting the European public space. Shaykh Omar Bakri's aim was probably to create a community based in the UK but with strong international ties, and to this end he used associative networks, his school, and the Sharia Court, though without the support of large and well-consolidated Islamic institutions. Especially after 2005 it is clear that Europe was for Omar Bakri a golden exile, and now that it is over he is enjoying a more silent one in Lebanon. On the other hand, Amr Khaled does not seem to be interested in forming a local community but – thanks also to the support of important Islamic groups in Europe (such as the UOIF and the Muslim Association of Britain), his foundation, and that of the international media – is seeking to conquer a European audience; for the moment an Arabic-speaking one even though he is starting to spread his message in European languages. He himself said that, 'the next years are strategic' because he wanted 'to learn English good enough for giving public lectures, and to understand the western society and culture'.[81]

The motives driving Khaled to conquer an ever-larger audience are also to be sought in the market for religious commodities. In fact, because of demographic, legal, and commercial reasons, the Western market is far more interesting than that of the Arab world. Muslims living in Western Europe and North America have more economic might than others and live in an environment where the market is protected by a more secure, though by no means perfect, legal framework. In other words, the sale of audiocassettes, videotapes, CDs, DVDs, and books is more profitable in the West than in the Arab world where copyright is not defended. Moreover, communicating in English also opens the door to Southeast Asia, a market Khaled currently merely 'touches' with his translations in Malay, and where English is more widely understood than Arabic.

Conclusions

The cases we have considered give us a a basis upon which to found certain hypotheses about the consequences for the production of Islamic knowledge on the Internet and of the context in which that production takes place, as well as about how the role and definition of the *mufti*, *ʿalim*, and preacher (*daʿi*, in Arabic) is changing.

This reconstruction of the careers and personal histories of Amr Khaled and Omar Bakri Muhammad in the universe of global communications, seen in the light of the experience of other shaykhs and websites, would seem to support the theory of Anderson and Eickelman (Eickelman and Anderson 2003), who see the emergence of new interpreters of Islam who stand out for their innovative language, a largely self-taught religious education and, above all, for their great visibility in the transnational media. Yet the novelty of these new interpreters is more evident if one considers the evolution of Islamic debate on the Internet (Anderson 2003–4), which is reflected fundamentally in their education, career, and language.

Amr Khaled and Omar Bakri Muhammad did not emerge from the Muslim diaspora in Europe among which they worked, nor were they the classical ulama educated in the great universities of Islam. Both arrived in London when their political and professional activities were already well consolidated, they had unconventional careers, and maintained strong transnational links. In this sense, it is highly symptomatic that Amr Khaled's website should continue to be hosted by an Egyptian server, administered by a team based in Cairo and designed by an Egyptian company, despite the fact that he lives in London and works in Lebanon.

Living in Europe, and specifically in London, enabled both men to address a new public and to benefit from greater freedom and facility to communicate. However, Omar Bakri Muhammad and Amr Khaled developed very different relationships within the European context: while Omar Bakri was building a local community with strong transnational ties, Amr Khaled has maintained a strong link with his Arab public, dealing with subjects that interest them, and has sought to attract the attention of Muslims and non-Muslims who live in the west, propagating his message in various languages through the potentially universal channels of satellite TV and the Internet. London continues to offer Muslim thinkers and activists the facilities to organize a global communication strategy, but after the 2005 bombing only moderates and representatives of 'Islamism light' (Haenni 2005) have access to these facilities.

The comparison between the two different communication strategies also shows that the Internet is not yet sufficient by itself to maintain a strategy of global communication, but that it works well as an additional means of communication, alongside more traditional channels such as lectures, sermons, TV, books, DVDs, CDs, videotapes, and audiocassettes. The main reason for this is that the Internet is not economically profitable and cannot substitute direct contact with the public. Lessons, audiences of the Sharia Court, and lectures are the moments in which the 'producers' of religious knowledge create a strong link with their 'consumers/clients'. Amr Khaled appears to use his site and the online discussion forums in order to maintain contact with his public, to promote initiatives, and to spread his message. Thus, the Internet also becomes a way in which to publicize his own image, apparently more effective and definitely cheaper than advertising on the mass media.

What also emerges from this brief presentation is that various operators in the communication sector (owners, sponsors, and authors, as well as web designers and web masters) also participate in the process of defining and presenting the content of the sites and the role of men of religion in cyberspace. These choices are made with a view to the public one wishes to reach and the channel one uses. In fact, the Internet is beginning to have its own style, with a jargon that characterizes it, and all producers of Islamic knowledge, whether they like it or not, must come to terms with these factors.

Notes

1 VoIP -Voice over Internet Protocol – is a transmission technology for delivery of voice communications over the Internet.
2 Cyberspace is liquid. Liquid cyberspace, liquid architecture, liquid cities. Liquid architecture is more than kinetic architecture, robotic architecture, and architecture of fixed parts and variables links. Liquid architecture is architecture that breathes, pulses, leaps as one form and lands as another. Liquid architecture is an architecture whose form is contingent, on the interest of the beholder; it is an architecture that opens to welcome me and closes to defend me; it is an architecture without doors and hallways, where the next room is always where I need it to be. Liquid architecture makes liquid cities, cities that change and shift of a value where visitors with different backgrounds see different landmarks, where neighbourhoods vary with ideas held in common, and evolve as the ideas mature or dissolve. (Novak 1991: 250)
3 Using the sites: Easy Who Is <www.easywhois.com> and All Who Is <www.allwhois. com>, which give the name and addresses of owners, the name of the person who made the registration, the administrator, the ISP address, the date of purchase or renewal of the URL, and the date until which it is held.
4 Having identified the name of the ISP, I visited the site to see who they are and where they work.
5 I used the site Alexa <http://www.alexa.com>, which presents the traffic rank, based on three months of aggregated historical traffic data from millions of Alexa Toolbar users and is a combined measure of page views and users.
6 Information supplied by Alexa and by the search engine Google.
7 A visible site is easy to find, in other words it appears in the first pages of a search or it is publicized on other sites. Many sites are deliberately hidden, while others do not have the resources necessary to promote themselves. I used Google to define this parameter,

because in sorting search results it compares the relevance of the pages with the key words and the number of links out that the pages in question have. Cf. Google technology overview <http://www.google.com/corporate/tech.html> (accessed 4 March 2009).

8 For this I relied on 'Wayback Machine' <http://www.archive.org>, a free archive of websites, as well as on my own personal archive.

9 Internet portal exclusively in Arabic, with ISP in Egypt, URL <http://www.gn4me.com>.

10 During his religion courses, organized by Egyptian women of the upper middle class in private salons, he met Yasmin al-Khayyam. Al-Khayyam is a member of the 'group of penitent artists' and leader of the al-Hussary association, which is dedicated to the memory of her father (a famous reciter of the Qurʿan) and runs two mosques in Cairo: one in Agouza and the other in Madinat 6 October.

11 Dream TV is the first Egyptian satellite television station owned by a private financier, the Egyptian businessman Ahmad Bahgat (Hamdy 2002).

12 I have borrowed this French expression from Patrick Haenni (Haenni 2003).

13 Iqra TV is the religious channel of the Arab Radio and Television (ART) group, founded by the businessman Salah ʿAbd Allah Kamil who, in 1982, also founded the al-Baraka Investment and Development Company, one of the biggest Islamic finance groups. ART website <http://www.art-tv.net>.

14 Amr Khaled, personal interview, London, 17 July 2003.

15 Ibid.

16 *Kalam min al-qalb* is the title of a series of his programmes on Iqra TV.

17 Cf. <http://www.amrkhaled.net/acategories/categories24.html> (accessed 4 March 2009).

18 Amr Khaled, personal interview, London, 26 June 2003.

19 The Egyptian preacher often makes affirmations of the kind:

> Let's look now at the Japanese experience: The destruction in Japan was even worse. The American military forces dropped the atomic bomb over Japan and hundred of thousands were killed in seconds. ... Yet, similar to their German counterparts the Japanese people were directed by an idea that was deep in their hearts, even though it represented a wrong belief. The Japanese believed in the atheist Buddhist religion, they followed the commands of their atheist 'god' Buddha, these commands were: 'to please Buddha ... you should work ... and work ... and work'. So after the war millions of Japanese left the battlefield to join the work force, in the factories, in the farms, in the laboratories ... They toiled, they innovated, they invented, they fulfilled their nation's hope to rise from the bottom to the top, making the phrase 'Made in Japan" spread all over the world.' <http://www.amrkhaled.net/modules.php?name=News&file=article&sid=217> (accessed 18 May 2004). Incidentally, the official religion of Japan until 1945 was Shintoism, not Buddhism.

20 On the website Asfory Gift <http://store.giftsegypt.com/amrkhtaco.html> (accessed 3 March 2009), one can buy a CD with thirty-five hours of lectures in MP3 format for $14.99 (five CDs per customer only) and a collection of ten tapes for $11, or three videotapes for $9 each. For a certain time an Arabic weekly magazine, *al-Ahram al-ʿArabi,* gave out one of Khaled's cassettes as a gift to its readers (Bayat 2003).

21 Amr Khaled, personal interview, London, 17 July 2003.

22 The very name of the company expresses its intention to produce a new type of information: free of government control, and not necessarily 'bad news'.

23 Date of the site's launch retrieved from <http://www.archive.org>.

24 Shaykh Sayyid Al-Sabah received a classical religious education. He became a *hafiz al-Qurʿan* in his infancy, and later graduated from the University of al-Azhar in Cairo. Having worked for a number of years for the Ministry of Waqf (Islamic endowments), in 1996 he became *imam* of the Salah el-Din Mosque in Al-Manyial, Egypt.

25 Party Radio <http://www.gn4partyradio.com>.

26 Gn4me on YouTube <http://www.youtube.com/user/gn4me>.
27 In order to discover who emitted the *fatwa*, I signed onto the service and explicitly asked the name of the *mufti*, because this is not explained on the webpages.
28 In order to obtain *fatwas* it is necessary to register, but the service is free of charge.
29 Thanks to the simplicity of the design, and the absence of Java and Flash technology, the site remains compatible with older browsers, which are more widespread in the Arab world. On the other hand, if one does not have an Arabic operating system, interaction with the site is limited because it is not possible to access the chat rooms, undertake searches, or send e-mails in Arabic.
30 Amr Khaled affirms that he accepted by virtue of his personal friendship with the famous journalist (Personal interview, London, 26 June 2003).
31 Amr Khaled, personal interview, London, 17 July 2003.
32 Amr Khaled, personal interview, London, 26 June 2003.
33 For Islam was run by an Egyptian religious association 'al-Hussari', named after the homonymous mosque in Madinat 6 October in Cairo where Amr Khaled used to preach.
34 This is how his name is transcribed by the site Easy Who Is <http://www.easywhois.com>. No other information has been found about him.
35 Amr Khaled, personal interview, London, 17 July 2003.
36 Ibid.
37 In reality, this problem depends on the quality of ICT in Egypt, and is not specific to the server used by Amr Khaled.
38 Data retrieved at <http://www.alexa.com/siteinfo/www.amrkhaled.net> (accessed 19 February 2009).
39 Amr Khaled, personal interview, London, 17 July 2003.
40 Ibid.
41 Translations are available in: English, French, Spanish, Italian, Malay, Dutch, Albanian, Chinese, Japanese, Rumanian, Jewish, Danish, Russian, Urdu, Turkish, Czech, and Norwegian.
42 This is the translation given on the website.
43 Dar al-Tarjama Forum: <http://forum.amrkhaled.net/forumdisplay.php?f=51> (accessed 11 August 2004).
44 Both these individuals were extremely polite and obliging and gave me all the information I wanted, though they prefer to remain anonymous 'as a sign of modesty', August 2004.
45 Amr Khaled, personal interview, London, 26 June 2004.
46 Wasfa Sahla <http://www.wasfasahla.com>; this URL was registered in Heliopolis, a middle-class neighbourhood of Cairo in February 2001.
47 So it says under the heading 'About Us' <http://www.wasfasahla.com/docs/about. cfm> (accessed 14 September 2008).
48 Right Start Foundation 'About us': <http://www.rightstart.org.uk/index.php?option= com_content&task=view&id=19&Itemid=37> (accessed 20 February 2009).
49 I have found a number of biographies of Omar Bakri Muhammad. The brief summary presented here was done for me by Omar Bakri himself, personal interview, London, 25 February 2003.
50 Omar Bakri Muhammad, personal interview, London, 25 February 2003.
51 I was present at several journalistic interviews and he always gave this answer.
52 Shaykh Bakri stressed this point in most of our meetings.
53 Omar Bakri Muhammad, personal interview, London, 25 February 2003.
54 In 2003, with a view to the anniversary of 11 September, Bakri was preparing a lecture on how Muslims in the west should behave, as well as a pamphlet on the 'Land of the Covenant'.
55 My own study of his presence on the Internet has revealed the following addresses: <http://www.obm.clara.net> on the English server Clara, <http://www.clara.net>;

<http://www.al-muhaajiroun.com> on the Scottish server ScotReg, <http://www.scotreg.com>; <http://www.al-muhajiroun.com> on the Canadian server New.net, <http://www.qsrch.net>; <http://www.almuhajiroun.com>, <http://www.almuhajir-oun.org>, <http://www.muhajiroun.org> and <http://www.obmpublications.com> on the British server, Fast-host <http://www.fast-host.org>; <http://www.almuk.com> on the German server Schlund, <http://www.schlund.de> (now www.1und1.com); and finally <http://www.muhajiroun.com> (the last active website) on the British server One And One, <http://www.1and1.co.uk>.

56 <http://www.alexa.com/data/details/traffic_details?q=&url=http://www.muhajiroun.com/Arabic.html> (accessed 11 August 2004).

57 These were two distinct and different sites, not the same site in two different languages.

58 <http://www.bbc.co.uk> (accessed 25 August 2004).

59 Following the first night of McNally's musical about the life of Jesus Christ, Bakri issued a *fatwa* affirming that Jesus was also a Muslim prophet, and that whoever insults a prophet can be condemned to death in an Islamic State. 'This *fatwa* drew media attention to us at a time in which we needed it' (Omar Bakri Muhammad, personal interview, London, 5 June 2003).

60 Omar Bakri Muhammad, personal interview, London, 5 June 2003.

61 Personal interview with Ahmed Rafat, editor-in-chief of the Spanish weekly *Tiempo*, London, 5 June 2003. On that occasion, Bakri referred to the Spanish King Juan Carlos as 'the King of the Crusaders'.

62 On 5 May 2003, I attended what was supposed to be a press conference. In the end, following the refusal of the hotel to host the event, it became a lecture-cum-party in the al-Muhajiroun central headquarters at White Hart Lane in London. The hall was packed for the occasion, with around 200 people present. The men were separated from the women and children by a screen, mobile phones were ringing everywhere, children playing, and towards the middle of the address (in other words after about an hour) 150 kebabs arrived, with fried potatoes and drinks. At the back of the hall was a table where one could pick up a leaflet, or buy the multimedia material used to finance the association.

63 Clearly, none of the decrees and sentences handed down by the Sharia Court have any legal or coercive value; their power rests on the social recognition of the court within the community. Omar Bakri's main assistant Anjem Choudary provided me with the statistics about the activities of the Sharia Court.

64 Shaykh Bakri Muhammad was hosted in two different chat rooms on Pal Talk, one organized by Ansaar Publications <http://ansaar.ca.cx> every Monday and Friday on the meaning of Jihad and Tawhid, and another organized by al-Ansar <http://www.al-ansar.biz> every Friday.

65 Up until 23 June 2003, there are traces of the al-Muhajiroun website in Pakistan <http://www.almuhajiroun.com.pk> in the online archive <http://www.archive.org>.

66 Many young Muslim women turn to OBM in his capacity as judge of the Sharia Court in order to annul marriages organized by their families; or new converts turn to the al-Muhajiroun movement in order to find the Muslim environment lacking in their own families.

67 Omar Bakri Muhammad, personal interview, London, 10 March 2003.

68 Sharia Court of Great Britain, London, 10 March 2003.

69 A list of 100 most-frequented Arabic websites was compiled on the basis of Alexa statistics, retrieved, 10 March 2004.

70 English, Indonesian, Japanese, Chinese, Uygur, Turkish, Spanish, Arabic, Urdu, and French.

71 Omar Bakri Muhammad, personal interview, London, 5 June 2003.

72 'Fatwa or Divine Decree Against General Musharraf-USA', 16 September 2001, 'Supported by Juristic Muslim scholars from various countries such as: Syria, Lebanon,

Kuwait, Emirates, Saudi Arabia, Pakistan, Afghanistan and UK'; downloaded from the website <http://www.almuk.com>, 26 September 2003.
73 Omar Bakri Muhammad, personal interview, London, 10 June 2003.
74 Omar Bakri Muhammad, personal interview, London, 5 June 2003.
75 Amr Khaled, personal interview, London, 26 June 2003.
76 Website <http://www.amrkhaled.net/modules.php?name=News&file=categories&op =newindex&catid=5> (accessed 11 August 2004).
77 Amr Khaled, personal interview, London, 17 July 2003.
78 The subjects he deals with in his television transmission concern the situation in Egypt and the Arab world in general, even though the examples used to illustrate his ideas are often taken from European history.
79 Lhaj Thami Breze, personal interview, Paris, 18 January 2004.
80 In fact, Amr Khaled usually speaks in the Egyptian dialect whilst the majority of Arab-speaking Muslims in France are of North African origin.
81 Amr Khaled, personal interview, London, 26 June 2003.

Bibliography

Anderson, Jon W. (2003–4) 'Des communautés virtuelles? Vers une théorie "techno-pratique" d'Internet dans le monde arabe', *Maghreb Machrek*, 178: 45–58.

Anderson, Jon W. (2008) The Internet: Shaping the Post-Modern Public Sphere of Islam', in Kazuo Ohtsuka and Dale F. Eickelman (eds), *Crossing Boundaries: Gender, the Public, and the Private in Contemporary Muslim Societies*, Tokyo: Research Institute for Languages and Cultures of Asia and Africa, pp. 119–34.

Atia, Samir (2003–4) 'Internet en langue arabe: espace de liberté ou fracture sociale?', *Maghreb Machrek*,178 : 29–44.

Atia, Tarek (2001) 'Thinking Big', *Al-Ahram Weekly Online*, 537 (7–13 June) Online: <http://weekly.ahram.org.eg/2001/537/it1.htm> (accessed 18 February 2009).

Barthes, Roland (1985) *L'aventure sémiologique*, Paris: Éditions du Seuil.

Bayat, Asef (2003) 'From Amr Diab to Amr Khaled', *Al-Ahram Weekly* 639 (22–28 May). Online: <http://weekly.ahram.org.eg/2003/639/fe1.htm> (accessed 18 February 2009).

Benedikt, Michael (ed.) (1991) *Cyberspace: First Steps*, Boston: Massachusetts Institute of Technology.

Bunt, Gary (2003) *Islam in the Digital Age: e-jihad, Online Fatwas and Cyber Islamic Environments*, London: Pluto Books.

Chartier, Roger (1990) *Les origines culturelles de la Révolution Française*, Paris: Seuil.

Eickelman, Dale and Anderson, Jon (eds) (2003) *New Media in the Muslim World: The Emerging Public Sphere*, Bloomington and Indianapolis: Indiana University Press.

Galloux, Michel (1997) *Finance islamique et pouvoir politique: le cas de l'Egypte moderne*, Paris: PUF.

Gonzalez-Quijano, Yves (2000) 'Cheikh Shaarawi, star de l'islam électronique', *Réseaux*, 99: 240–53.

Gonzalez-Quijano, Yves (2007) 'La renaissance arabe au XIX siècle: médium, médiations et médiateurs', in B. Hallaq and H. Toelle (eds) *Histoire de la littérature arabe moderne*, Paris: Sindbad Actes Sud, pp. 70–113.

Gräf, Bettina (2007) 'Sheikh Yussef al-Qaradawi in Cyberspace', *Die Welt des Islams* 47(3–4): 403–23.

Gräf, Bettina and Skovgaard-Petersen, Jakob (eds) (2009) *The Global Mufti: The Phenomenon of Yusuf al-Qaradawi*, New York: Columbia University Press.

Haenni, Patrick (2002) 'Au-delà du repli identitaire ... les nouveaux prêcheurs égyptiens et la modernisation paradoxale de l'Iislam', *Religioscope*, November. Online: <http://www.religioscope.com/pdf/precheurs.pdf> (accessed 18 February 2009).

Haenni, Patrick (2003) 'Amr Khaled le téléqoraniste', *Le monde des religions*, 1 (September/October): 46–7.

Haenni, Patrick (2005) *L'Islam de marché*, Paris : Seuil.

Haenni, Patrick and Holtrop, Tjitske (2002) 'Mondaines spiritualités ... 'Amr Khalid, shaykh branché de la jeunesse dorée du Caire', *Politique Africaine*, 87: 45–68.

Hamdy, Naila (2002) 'A dream TV come true', *Trans national Broadcasting Journal*, 8. Online. Available: <http://www.tbsjournal.com/Archives/Spring02/sirhan.html> (accessed 18 February 2009).

Kepel, Gilles (1984) *Le prophète et pharaon: les mouvements islamistes dans l'Egypte contemporaine*, Paris: Le Seuil.

Kepel, Gilles (1994) *A l'ouest d'Allah*, Paris: Le Seuil.

Kovach, Gretel (2002) 'Moderate Muslim voice falls silent: charismatic young leader leaves Egypt as his popular sermons come under government scrutiny', *Christian Science Monitor*, 26 November. Online: <http://www.csmonitor.com/2002/1126/p06s01-woaf.htm> (accessed 18 February 2009).

Lewis, Philip (1994) *Islamic Britain*, London: I.B. Tauris.

Mariani, Ermete (2003) 'Youssef al-Qardawi: pouvoir médiatique, économique et symbolique', in F. Mermier (ed.) *Mondialisation et nouveaux médias dans l'espace arabe*, Paris: Maisonneuve & Larose, pp. 195–204.

Mariani, Ermete (2005) 'Dal Corano al Web, la carriera mediatica di Amru Khaled', *Meridiana*, 52: 117–38.

Mariani, Ermete (2006) 'The Production of Islamic Knowledge on the Internet and the Role of States and Markets: The Examples of Yussef al-Qaradawi and Amru Khaled', in G. Larsson (ed.) *Religious Communities on the Internet*, Uppsala: Universitetstryckeriet, pp. 131–49.

Mariani, Ermete (2007) 'Les oulémas syriens à la recherché d'une audience virtuelle', in Yves Gonzalez-Quijano and Christophe Varin (eds) *La société de l'information au Proche-Orient: internet en Syrie et au Liban*, Beyrouth: Presses de l'Université Saint-Joseph, pp. 93–115.

Messick, Brinkley (1986) 'The Mufti, the Text and the World: Legal Interpretation in Yemen', *Man, n.s.* 2: 101–19.

Messick, Brinkley (1993) *The Calligraphic State*, Berkeley: University of California Press.

Messick, Brinkley (1996) 'Media Muftis: Radio Fatwas in Yemen', in M. Khalid Masud, Brinkley Messick and David S. Powers (eds) *Islamic Legal Interpretation: Muftis and their Fatwas*, Cambridge, MA and London: Harvard University Press, pp. 310–20.

Moore, Philip (1997) *Islamic Finance: A Partnership for Growth*, London: Euromoney Books.

Novak, Marcos (1991) 'Liquid Architecture in Cyberspace', in Michael Benedikt (ed.) *Cyberspace: First Steps*, Boston: Massachusetts Institute of Technology, pp. 225–54.

Shahine, Gihan (2002) 'Preacher on the Run', *Al-Ahram Weekly*, 616 (12–18 December). Online: <http://weekly.ahram.org.eg/2002/616/eg7.htm> (accessed 18 February 2009).

Thomas, Dominique (2005) *Le Londonistan: le djihad au coeur de l'Europe*, Paris: Michalon.

Thomas, Dominique (2009) 'Britain – Rejecting Western Modernity?', in S.J. Hansen, A. Mesøy and T. Kardas (eds) *The Borders of Islam: Exploring Huntington's Faultlines, from Al-Andalus to the Virtual Ummah*, London: Hurst & Company.

Tyan, Emile (1999) 'Fatwa', in *The Encyclopaedia of Islam*, CD version v. 1.0, Leiden: E. J. Brill.

8 Guénonian Traditionalism and European Islam

Mark Sedgwick

This chapter deals with an intellectual movement, Guénonian Traditionalism, which I will refer to for short merely as 'Traditionalism' (with a capital T, in order to distinguish it from the many other forms of traditionalism that exist).[1] Traditionalism was one of the earliest European producers of Islamic knowledge, with publications appearing in Paris and Cairo before the First World War. It is not, however, a form of Islam, but rather a Western philosophical and religious movement that often expresses itself in Islamic terms.[2] It appears at first sight to be a movement calling for a return to true religion in general, and to Sufi Islam in particular, in reaction to the evils of the modern world. It was developed by a French philosopher – René Guénon – who was active in Paris before and after the First World War, and who moved to Cairo in 1930. He died there in 1951, a respected Muslim, cited as a model of Sufi piety by no less an authority than Abd al-Halim Mahmud, supreme shaykh of the Azhar (Mahmud 1974). As we will see, however, there is more to Traditionalism than at first meets the eye.

An examination of Traditionalism shows how Islam in Europe can be modified by extra-Islamic European discourse, both directly and indirectly. Traditionalism is a European movement in its origins, and one of the two forms of Islamic Traditionalism considered below was also primarily Western. The other two forms of Traditionalism we will examine, however, developed partly in Europe and partly in the Muslim world. Their influence on European Islam is indirect – from Europe to the Muslim world, and back again.

An examination of Traditionalism also shows quite how global contemporary Islamic discourse has become, and thus warns of the possible dangers of examining Islam in a purely European context. Although Islam is surely becoming localized in Europe today, and although examining Islam in a purely European context permits many valuable insights, the twenty-first century promises to be a century of ever increasing globalization. The Islamic discourse currently taking place in languages such as English is not limited to any particular region of the world.

The European origins of Traditionalism

Traditionalism's earliest origins lie partly in the Renaissance and partly in the eighteenth century. The Renaissance origins are the Platonic Academy established in Florence by Cosimo de Medici in the fifteenth century. The director of that academy was a leading Neoplatonist, Marsilio Ficino, a Catholic priest who concluded that all religions – from Christianity and Platonic philosophy to Zoroastrianism – were expressions of a single *Urreligion* [earliest, original, essential religion], later called the *Philosophia Perennis* or 'perennial philosophy' (Sedgwick 2004a: 23–4). Since the term 'philosophy' is used in this phrase in a sense very different from that which is current today, I will refer not to 'the perennial philosophy' but to *Urreligion*, even though that term is not used by Traditionalists themselves. The term they use is 'perennialism', which might be defined as belief in the *Urreligion*.

Ficino mistakenly believed that the works of Hermes Trismegistus – in fact a collection of early post-Christian Alexandrine writings – dated from the time of Moses or before, and were an expression of this *Urreligion*. Ficino's theory enjoyed a brief vogue until the correct dating of the Hermetic texts was demonstrated in 1614 (Hanegraaff 1996: 390). Since the supposedly great antiquity of the Hermetic texts had been the most important evidence for Ficino's theory, that theory was discarded by serious scholars after the seventeenth century. Both the Hermetic texts and the idea that an *Urreligion* had once existed, however, remained popular among Freemasons and more marginal groups, from where it reemerged into the general intellectual discourse during the nineteenth century (Sedgwick 2004a: 40–7).

The origins of Traditionalism also include eighteenth-century Deism which, present in restricted if important circles in Europe in the 1770s, had become widespread by the 1830s, not in its original form, but in the form of Romantic-Deistic misreadings of Hinduism and Sufism. Deists such as Sir Henry Colebrooke and Rammohun Roy promulgated a Deistic understanding of Hinduism as a 'simple primitive monotheism' (Kopf 1969), and similar understandings of Sufism can be found in Europe after the publication in 1815 of Captain Sir John Malcolm's monumental *History of Persia*, which contains one of the earliest detailed examinations of Sufism to be published in a European language. Quasi-Deistic understandings of Sufism seem to have been partly a result of the same forces that produced Deistic understandings of Hinduism, and partly the result of Malcolm's own misunderstanding of Sufism. A soldier-diplomat from Bengal, Malcolm does not seem to have spoken to any actual Sufis, and understood Sufism as a possible survival from the ancient Greeks, supporting this supposition with the philologically dubious derivation of *sufi* from the Greek *sophoi* ['wise men'] (Sedgwick 2007b). Whether or not Malcolm knew of Trismegistus, his *History* implicitly subscribed to a view of Sufism as a form of *Urreligion*, a view that became popular in Europe (Sedgwick 2008), even though later Orientalists and other scholars attempted to corrected initial misreadings.

The European discovery of the Hindu Vedanta during the nineteenth century provided an alternative source for humanity's *Urreligion*, a source on which Helena Blavatsky drew. After a period of extraordinary success, Blavatsky's Theosophical Society collapsed in scandal (Campbell 1980 and Washington 1995), but not before it had transmitted its version of Ficino's Renaissance theory to other groups. In Paris, the search for the *Urreligion* was continued by the followers of Dr Gérard Encausse, a physician with various esoteric interests, for a while the leading occultist in France, and perhaps all of Europe (André and Beaufils 1995). Blavatsky's Theosophical Society had wanted only to recover the *Urreligion*, but Encausse wanted to go further. Probably as a result of his interest in Freemasonry, he sought to practice the *Urreligion* through initiation into what might survive of it. Among his followers was the young René Guénon, and the 'tradition' to which 'Traditionalism' refers is, in essence, the *Urreligion*.

Guénon soon left Encausse's circle, and joined another Parisian religious group whose members included a European convert to Islam, the Swedish painter Ivan Aguéli. Aguéli had converted to Islam some years before and had spent several years in Egypt, where he had acquired an interest in Ibn al-Arabi from an Egyptian Sufi and political activist, Abd al-Rahman Illaysh (Sedgwick 2004a: 59–63). Illaysh was an early Islamist (in the sense that his concerns and motivations seem to have been more political than spiritual), but of a different variety from the more familiar school that was then emerging in Cairo. His father had studied in the circle of one of the century's most noted interpreters of Ibn al-Arabi, the Amir Abd al-Qadir al-Jaza'iri, and Sufism was central to Illaysh's approach. Ibn al-Arabi featured prominently in the earliest Traditionalist publication, the journal *Il Convito/Al-Nadi* published in Cairo around 1906.[3] Guénon's encounter with Illaysh's former associate Aguéli was his first contact with Islam and with Sufism.[4]

Another associate of Guénon's in the same group was a prominent French commentator on colonial affairs, Count Albert de Pouvourville. De Pouvourville, a colourful character, was not a Muslim and had no real interest in Islam, but is important as the main source of Guénon's (and so Traditionalism's) 'cultural pessimism' (Sedgwick 2004b: 56–8). De Pouvourville warned against the 'yellow peril', arguing that – in order to survive the inevitable clash of civilizations – the 'white race' needed to exploit not only the East's material resources, but also the East's religious and philosophical resources (Pouvourville 1906: 11–16).[5] Although Guénon soon came to dismiss the 'yellow peril' as 'chimerical' (Guénon 1924: 115), he kept de Pouvourville's view that European culture and civilization were in imminent danger of collapse unless Europe could learn the spiritual wisdom of the East. Modern European civilization was, in Guénon's view, a fragile shell, empty of the necessary spiritual core.[6]

After the First World War, Guénon developed the philosophy of Traditionalism on these bases, initially under the patronage of the leading Catholic philosopher Jacques Maritain. When the anti-Christian implications of Guénon's work became fully apparent, however, Maritain turned from being one of Guénon's most important supporters to being one of his firmest opponents (Boulet 1962: 24–5),[7] although at least one Catholic cardinal remained an enthusiast of Guénon's work (Daniélou 1984: 138–9 and James 1981: 88–9). Guénon's mature Traditionalism retains Ficino's and Blavatsky's search for the *Urreligion*, Encausse's conviction of the need for initiation into it, and de Pouvourville's vision of the spiritual destitution of modern Europe contrasted with the spiritual riches of the East. Guénon replaced de Pouvourville's East (Taoism) with Blavatsky's and

Encausse's East (Vedanta), and followed Aguéli in seeing Sufi Islam as the most accessible of the surviving expressions of the *Urreligion*. He also developed de Pouvourville's cultural pessimism into something more powerful, drawing on Hindu conceptions of cyclical time. To the standard European conviction of the possibility and the desirability of progress, Guénon replied that progress was an illusion masking regression. Changes that most Europeans saw as improvements were actually degeneration. The growth of individualism, for example, did not bring any real freedom, but rather the atomization and homogenization of society, and so the reduction of real freedom (Guénon 1945). The decline that Guénon saw everywhere was, he argued, inevitable. The true direction of humanity's movement was not ascent but descent. Modernity constituted the last and lowest stage of this descent.[8]

Early Traditionalism, then, is European in that it addresses European rather than non-European concerns. As a reaction to modernity, it in some ways resembles the Romantic Movement or the Arts and Crafts Movement.[9] Second, non-European systems (Neoplatonism and Hinduism) acted as catalysts in its development, and Islam was little more than a passive provider of elements used in a distinctively European construction.

We can also identify a second important characteristic of Traditionalism at this point. It is that Traditionalism is an intellectual movement – not in the sense of being more about thought than action, but in the sense of being a system that appeals almost exclusively to intellectuals. This is as true today as it was in the 1920s, when a small circle of followers first began to form around Guénon. What has changed since the 1920s is the nationality of those intellectuals. At first they were all French or Francophone; then they came to include other Europeans and also Americans. Today they include Turks, Iranians, Arabs, Pakistanis, and Malays. Born Muslims have been especially prominent among Traditionalists in recent decades. This is probably because the intellectuals to whom Traditionalism has appealed most have always been those who feel most alienated from Western modernity, and there are today even more Muslim than European intellectuals who feel alienated from Western modernity.

Traditionalist intellectuals are producers of knowledge of two kinds: 'hard' Traditionalism aimed at other Traditionalists, and 'soft' Traditionalism aimed at a more general public. 'Soft' Traditionalism is usually not overtly Traditionalist, and often only an informed reader can see that discussion of other matters (usually religions, and very often Islam) follows perspectives and interpretations taken from 'hard' Traditionalism. The appeal of 'soft' Traditionalism has generally been much wider than that of 'hard' Traditionalism, but even so 'soft' Traditionalism has no appeal for the typical first-generation Muslim immigrant to Europe, to whom many Traditionalist tenets would appear scandalous when they are not merely incomprehensible. In the same way, no variety of Traditionalism appeals much to the non-Muslim European working classes, though for slightly different reasons.[10] The typical consumer of the knowledge produced by Traditionalists ('soft' Traditionalism) is someone with a reasonably good modern (i.e. Western) education, someone who is spiritually and aesthetically interested or 'aware', whatever their religion of origin or place of birth. The politically conscious, on the other hand, are rarely attracted to either hard or soft Traditionalism. Traditionalists mostly aim to change individuals, not societies.[11] There have been few Islamist or 'fundamentalist' Traditionalists, and those few Traditionalists who are politically active are seen by most others almost as heretics.[12]

The emergence of Islamic Guénonianism and of Traditionalist Islam

Guénon's Traditionalism and its early followers, then, constituted a European movement, but one with links to Islam – through Guénon's early associate Aguéli to the Amir Abd al-Qadir, and in the form of Guénon's own choice of Sufi Islam as the best available instance of the *Urreligion*. Despite these links, it was not an Islamic movement. Although Guénon lived in Cairo as a devout Muslim, he maintained that he had not 'converted' to Islam. Anyone who truly understood the *Urreligion* was (in Guénon's view), by virtue of that understanding, incapable of being converted to anything. Guénon had, in his own words, 'moved into' Islam ('s'y est installé') rather than converted (Guénon to Alain Daniélou, 27 August 1947, quoted in Zarcone 1999; Laurant 1998: 139). Although he followed the *sharia* of Islam scrupulously, Guénon was never just a Muslim. His primary interest, as can be seen from his contacts and correspondence, continued to be in his project for the rediscovery of the *Urreligion* (which he termed 'tradition'), and in all possible projects for the realization of that *Urreligion* in the modern world. He had no significant contact with the Egyptian *ulama* or participation in any Egyptian discourse, and was as interested in projects for realizing the *Urreligion* in a Catholic context or in the form of Freemasonry as in an Islamic context (Sedgwick 2004a: 75–80). The main Catholic project soon collapsed, but the Masonic project continues, and another Christian project – in the context of Orthodoxy – has come into being since Guénon's death.

After Guénon's death, however, the Traditionalist movement split and developed in a number of directions. Some of these directions were Islamic, properly speaking, and it is those that we will consider in the remainder of this article, under three headings: European, Muslim, and Euro-Muslim.

The first Islamic form of later Traditionalism was purely European: Sufi orders in Europe (and then America) whose members were exclusively European converts to Islam. As we will see, only one of these orders was even in communication with the (admittedly, then small) wider Muslim community in Europe, and none of these European forms had much impact on Islam in Europe. The second Islamic form of Traditionalism was Muslim rather than European. It dates from the 1960s and 1970s, when Traditionalism began to emerge in the Muslim world – first in Iran, and then in Turkey and (to some extent) in Malaysia. These two Islamic forms of Traditionalism have had some impact on Islam in Europe through the role they have played in transnational Islamic discourse, but have not resulted in the creation of any distinct religious communities, in Europe or elsewhere. Both the first (European) and second (Muslim) forms were cases more of

Islamic Traditionalism than of Traditionalist Islam, in the sense that the emphasis remained on Guénon's theories, and Islam was always in some sense incidental.

Finally, since the 1980s, a Euro-Muslim form of Islamic Traditionalism has emerged. This third form is the most interesting development for our present purposes, because the emphasis switched from Guénon to Islam, and also because distinct religious communities began to emerge.

These three forms of Islamic Traditionalism have very different degrees of legitimacy for contemporary European Muslims. The European form has little legitimacy, partly because it has been peopled exclusively with European converts. The Muslim and Euro-Muslim forms have greater legitimacy, partly because they involve born Muslims, and partly because their leading figures are in some cases not just intellectuals but also have something of the authority of the *ulama*.[13]

Purely European forms of Islamic Traditionalism

The earliest instance of the European form of Islamic Traditionalism was a Sufi order established in Switzerland and France shortly before the Second World War by a Swiss enthusiast of Guénon's work, Frithjof Schuon. Schuon had converted to Islam in the 1930s and had travelled to Algeria to join the Sufi order of Ahmad al-Alawi, and on his return to Europe opened branches of the Alawiyya first in Basel, and then in Amiens and Paris. At the time of Schuon's death in 1998, his order had long become independent of its Algerian origins, and was known as the Maryamiyya. By then it had more than a thousand members worldwide.[14]

The Maryamiyya is little known because, until very recently, its existence was secret. It was however an important producer of knowledge. Its members wrote hundred of books in various languages, sometimes about Islam and sometimes about other religions, and taught at various universities, especially in America.[15] Its most widely read adherent, Huston Smith, is little known in Europe, but is widely known in America, where he published twentieth-century America's best-selling book on comparative religion, *The Religions of Man* (later retitled *The World's Religions*), a book that has sold over one and a half million copies (Sedgwick 2004a: 163–5). No European Maryami has achieved such success, but the works of Martin Lings and Gay Eaton, Titus Burckhardt, and Roger du Pasquier have all been widely read.

The Maryamiyya is important not only in its own right but also because it was the source of several other Traditionalist Sufi orders. One of the earliest of these was that led in Paris by Michel Vâlsan, a former Romanian diplomat who was originally a member of the same pre-war Bucharest Traditionalist group as the late, great scholar of religions, Mircea Eliade.[16] Vâlsan's order was a small one in comparison to Schuon's Maryamiyya and never spread far outside France, but its followers – who included several distinguished French scholars – were facilitators if not producers of Islamic knowledge, being in large part responsible for introducing the French public to the works of Ibn al-Arabi (Elmore 1999: 101). A later order established by another former Maryami is the Ahmadiyya of Abd al-Wahid Pallavicini, located in Milan. Again, this is a relatively small order, but Pallavicini was a prominent figure in the Italian press during the 1980s, and again became prominent in Italy during 2001 in connection with his project for building a mosque in Milan.[17] His interpretations of Islam have, as a consequence, reached a wide public (Sedgwick 2004a: 136–42).

The extent to which these three Sufi orders resemble Sufism as found in the Muslim world varies considerably. Vâlsan's followers were the closest to the norms of the Muslim world, and were on friendly terms with many born Muslims in Paris. Vâlsan even married the daughter of the imam of the Paris Mosque. His order transmitted a distinctly standard understanding of Sufism.[18] In contrast, although the practice of Pallavicini and his followers is broadly that of devout Muslims in the Muslim world, the understanding of Islam that Pallavicini has transmitted to the Italian public has been widely criticized by other Italian Muslims as heterodox. This criticism has at times been without any real justification, but the views that Pallavicini presents as Islamic sometimes owe much more to Guénon than to the Prophet Muhammad.[19] Schuon's followers' representations of Islam are more subtly influenced by Guénon than Pallavicini's, but their practice departed from the Islamic norm in a way that neither Vâlsan's nor Pallavicini's did. Schuon localized Islamic practices to fit more comfortably with European norms, allowing his followers to delay the ritual prayer until they got home, to ignore the Ramadan fast if they were busy at work, and to drink beer. Even extramarital sexual relations may sometimes have been permitted on a case-by-case basis, though always with restrictions on the actual activities allowed.[20] These modifications of fundamental aspects of the *sharia* to conform with Western culture constitute a rather striking variety of localization of Islam.

In general, these instances of the European form of Traditionalism lack legitimacy and authority for born Muslims in Europe and elsewhere. As we have seen, Vâlsan was accepted by the North African Muslim community in Paris, and born Muslims would occasionally attend the *dhikr* sessions he held, but none joined his order or followed him as a shaykh.[21] Their visits to Vâlsan's *dhikr* may have been prompted by no more than a mixture of courtesy and curiosity. Vâlsan received various invitations to speak in public, which – had he accepted them – might have led to his becoming a more influential producer of Islamic knowledge and with time might have given him legitimacy and authority, but he invariably refused such invitations. He was by nature a retiring man.[22]

That Pallavicini and Schuon lack legitimacy among born Muslims may be deduced from the absence of born Muslims from their followings (with one or two exceptions in the case of Schuon). This absence partly reflects their own lack of interest in recruiting such followers, and partly the distance between Pallavicini's and Schuon's interpretations and/or practice and those that are commonly accepted as orthodox among born Muslims.

One exception to this lack of legitimacy is found among the children of Vâlsan's followers, who are not converts, and are closer to Islam than to Traditionalism. Some of them have become accepted, if minor, figures in Islam in France. Yacoub Roty, for example, has written a number of books on Islamic subjects for Muslim children (Roty 1994), and has taught at the Paris mosque.[23] Pallavicini's order is of too recent origin for its followers' Muslim-born children[24] to have reached adulthood, with the single exception of Pallavicini's own son, Yahya. Yahya Pallavicini shows signs of being more generally accepted than his father, and may one day become a significant producer of Islamic knowledge for born Muslims. No children of Schuon's followers are known to have played any significant part in any capacity, for reasons which this chapter does not afford space to discuss.

Another exception is Martin Lings, one of the earliest Maryamis and author of a well-received biography of the Prophet Muhammad (Lings 1983). Lings was respected among sections of the Muslim community in England and elsewhere both for this book and for his piety. After his death in 2005, *Q-News*, which describes itself as 'Britain's leading Muslim magazine' and might be described with justice as Britain's leading intellectual Muslim magazine, dedicated an issue to him under the title 'we shall not look upon his like again',[25] giving almost half the issue's pages to testimonies. Some were by other Maryamis, but one was by Hamza Yusuf, an American convert to Islam described by *The Guardian* as 'arguably the West's most influential Islamic scholar' (O'Sullivan 2001).[26] Even if this is an exaggeration, Yusuf is certainly important, and a leading figure in a rather different sort of traditionalist movement, which has been described as consisting of

> Muslims who adhere to 'traditional' modes of Islam as exemplified in the 'traditional' *hadith* of islam-iman-ihsan. Taken to a proper conclusion: *ᶜaqidah* according to the Ashᶜaris, Maturidis (and according to some, the Atharis), *fiqh* according to the four Sunni *madhahib*, and *tasawuf*, whether it is *tariqa*-based or not.
>
> (Anonymous 2008)

Discussion of this movement, which is an increasingly important source of Islamic knowledge in the West, lies beyond the scope of this chapter. It resembles Traditionalism in some ways, but differs most importantly in that it has no interest in an *Urreligion*. Some of its members are extremely critical of this aspect of Traditionalism. Another American convert who is also a leading figure in this movement, Nuh Ha Mim Keller, rejected the Traditionalist view of the *Urreligion* as

> something that has waited for fourteen centuries of Islamic scholarship down to the present century to be first promulgated in Cairo in the 1930s by the French convert to Islam Rene Guenon, and later by his student Frithjof Schuon and writers under him. Who else said it before? And if no one did, and everyone else considers it *kufr* [disbelief], on what basis should it be accepted?
>
> (Keller 1996)

In his *Q-News* article, however, Yusuf warned gently against the dangers of *takfir* (accusations of *kufr*) and wrote of Lings as a man of great piety and learning whose views on the *Urreligion* might be excused given his other admirable and inspiring qualities (Yusuf 2005). Yusuf was in effect arguing that Lings should be respected *despite* his Traditionalism, suggesting that his influence on European Islam, like that of Yacoub Roty and Yahya Pallavicini, was inversely related to his Traditionalism.

Lings was also influential in two royal families, one Muslim and one non-Muslim. He headed a (probably small) Maryami *zawiya* in Jordan, and three members of the Jordanian royal house provided testimonies to him included in the *In Memoriam* section of a posthumous volume: Prince El Hassan bin Talal (the brother of the late King Hussein and for a long time Jordan's Crown Prince), Princess Wijdan Ali (a prominent artist with a PhD from the School of Oriental and African Studies in London, married to the private chamberlain of King Abdullah II), and Princess Wijdan's daughter (Lings 2005). There was some Traditionalist inspiration behind a very successful aspect of official visits that King Abdullah paid to the United States in 2005 and 2006: dialogue with Jewish and Baptist leaders, arranged by the king's then Special Advisor for Interfaith Affairs, an American Maryami academic (Duin 2006).[27] The *Urreligion* can be an excellent basis for interreligious dialogue, and so for improving Arab–Western relations.

The other royal family in which Lings was respected was the British one. Prince Charles has spoken of his respect for Lings, who used to visit the prince regularly, and reads at least one Maryami journal (Wales 2006).[28] It has been suggested that the prince may be a 'secret convert to Islam' (Pipes 2003), but this is almost certainly not the case. Traditionalism, however, plays a significant role in his personal spirituality (Sedgwick 2007a), and is an important factor behind the unusually sympathetic view of Islam often promoted in his public speeches.

Prince Charles's speeches are not, strictly speaking, 'Islamic knowledge', and neither are King Abdullah's speeches at Baptist prayer meetings in Washington D.C. Both, however, have an impact on Islam in Europe, as well as having an impact on non-Muslim views of Islam, as do the works of Lings and some other Maryamis. Writers and speakers who are Traditionalist or Traditionalist-inspired can do little to lessen the hostility towards Islam of the general public in Europe, but they can and do present Islam in terms that makes it more respectable among well-educated Europeans, whether non-Muslim or Muslim-born. This is important: Muhammad Abduh wrote in the nineteenth century of the risk that Muslims educated in the modern Western sciences and humanities might be tempted to turn away from Islam as one might turn away from an old garment in which it was embarrassing to appear in public (Abduh 1897: 127). This was one reason why Muhammad Abduh attempted to construct an Islam that was compatible with the intellectual world of those with modern educations. In exactly the same way, many of the forms of Islam available in contemporary Europe hold little appeal for the Muslim who is well educated in the humanities. Islamic Traditionalism, like the Islam promoted by Hamza Yusuf and Nuh Ha Mim Keller, holds more appeal for such Muslims than does neo-Salafism or the Islam of the Muslim Brothers.

Muslim forms of Islamic Traditionalism

The first and most important Muslim-born Traditionalist was an Iranian, Dr Seyyed Hossein Nasr. Nasr was born into the pre-revolutionary Iranian elite, the son of a prominent Pahlavi courtier and one-time minister of culture, and went to high school in the West (not in Europe but in America) before studying at the Massachusetts Institute of Technology and at Harvard. He discovered Traditionalism in America, and joined Schuon's Maryamiyya (Sedgwick 2004a: 154).

Nasr established in Tehran the first branch of a Traditionalist Sufi order (the Maryamiyya) in the Muslim world, a branch which still exists, though it is now small and based in Shiraz.[32] The Maryamiyya itself was a European form of Islamic Traditionalism, but Nasr operated largely independently, giving rise to a Muslim form of Islamic Traditionalism. More important than the Iranian Maryamiyya were Nasr's scholarly and organizational activities. As well as making a success-ful career at Tehran University, where he became dean of humanities, he used his excellent relations with the court to establish a well-funded and prominent Imperial Iranian Institute of Philosophy. The philosophy in question was that which is in Persian known as *hikma* and in English might be termed 'sapiential philosophy': the Iranian mystic school deriving in part from Ibn al-Arabi and whose best-known exponent is Mulla Sadra al-Din al-Shirazi. Nasr was an influ-ential producer of Islamic knowledge in Iran, with the legitimacy of a senior and recognized scholar coupled with something of the legitimacy of the *alim*. Though he lacked the full training of an *alim*, after his return from America he had studied *hikma* under some of the leading *ulama* of the time, and was closely associated with two respected ayatollahs.[33] One indication of Nasr's impact on Iran is that of the seven members of the Council for the Cultural Revolution established after the revolution by Ayatollah Khomeini to Islamize Iran's universities, three had at some point been either Traditionalists or semi-Traditionalist members of Nasr's institute.[34]

The Imperial Iranian Institute of Philosophy was also a Traditionalist training school, dedicated to the revival of the traditional religious sciences. It frequently hosted figures such as the distinguished French scholar Henri Corbin and the distinguished Japanese scholar Toshihiko Izutsu, who were Traditionalist fellow-travellers though not Traditionalists, and trained future scholars such as William Chittick, who is now arguably the leading scholar of Ibn al-Arabi writing in English. In addition to producing Islamic knowledge for consumption in Iran and abroad, then, Nasr's institute also educated future producers of knowledge. These would later carry Traditionalist Islam around the world.

Nasr's activities in Iran ended with the revolution. Although he was on good terms with some of the leading figures in the revolutionary regime on a personal and scholarly level, he was far too closely associated with the previous regime to be safe (Radji 1983: 270),[35] and went into exile in America, where he has since continued his academic career. He is today well known in America, but has never achieved there the prominence he once enjoyed in Iran – that would have been almost impossible.[36]

As a producer of knowledge, Nasr is most important for his books, the most important of which were written (in English) in Tehran. These all deal with Islam from a Traditionalist perspective, but are much more 'Islamic' than the books of any other Traditionalist writer, addressing Muslims as well as non-Muslims.

This both makes them more accessible to born Muslims and increases their perceived legitimacy.[37] Other Traditionalist writers have addressed only Westerners, and so have limited appeal for Muslim-born audiences, though they have sometimes been translated into Muslim languages. Nasr's works, in contrast, have almost all been translated into Persian and Turkish, and have sold well in both countries, and to a lesser extent in Malaysia. Translations of other Traditionalist writers have often followed translation of Nasr's books, riding on the interest in Traditionalism generated by Nasr (Sedgwick 2004a: 255–6).

In both Iran and Turkey, Nasr has introduced Traditionalist views and even Traditionalism itself into the general intellectual discourse, and there are indications that Nasr's impact in Malaysia is also significant. More research is required to confirm the extent to which Nasr's impact in Turkey and Iran has spread to Turks and Iranians in Europe. There are, however, strong indications that Nasr's books appeal even more to Muslims who are familiar with European modernity through residence at its source than they do to Muslims who are familiar with extra-European forms of modernity. For European Muslims, Nasr's dual legitimacy as scholar and part-*alim* – as a modern and as a traditional (in the usual sense of the word) figure – gives him an authority that few others have. His status as a respected commentator on Islam in the US media adds to this authority, and also has an impact similar to that of King Abdullah and Prince Charles, discussed above.

Euro-Muslim forms of Traditionalist Islam

The earliest Euro-Muslim Traditionalist was Dr Najm al-Din Bammate, an Afghan national of Daghestani origin who met Guénon in Cairo, was one of the three persons who attended Guénon's funeral,[39] and who then for many years lived in Paris, first working at UNESCO and then teaching Islamology at the University of Paris VII (Lisieux). Bammate's background was similar to Nasr's: he was a highly educated member of the elite (his father was Afghan ambassador to the United Nations), a cosmopolitan intellectual (Sellam 2000: 13–15). Unlike Nasr, however, his impact was more in Europe than in the Muslim world. More research needs to be done into his years in Paris, but early indications are that from the 1970s until his death in 1985 Bammate was the leader of a group of Muslims in France, some French converts and some of North African origin, a group that still exists in some form today.[40] The size and importance of this group remains to be established, but it seems that it departed from the Traditionalist norm in that it was not, formally, a Sufi order. It is not known to what extent Bammate's Islam was a localized form, but given the presence of European converts among Bammate's followers and Bammate's interest in Muslim–Western relations, it seems unlikely that no varieties of localization occurred.[41]

The most important Euro-Muslim Traditionalist group was established a decade later than Bammate's, also in France. This group was headed by Dr Faouzi Skali, a Moroccan. Skali resembles Nasr and Bammate in being well-educated and cosmopolitan, though he was the son of a hospital administrator rather than of a minister or an ambassador. He discovered Guénon's works while a student in Paris during the 1970s, rather as Nasr had discovered Guénon and Schuon in America. Skali's attention was initially drawn by Guénon's work to non-Islamic non-Western religions, especially Taoism. In this, Skali reacted to Guénon as did many non-Muslim Europeans. He then began to read about Islam and Sufism, however – a French translation of Rumi, a book by Henry Corbin, and similar works – and finally returned to Morocco in search of a Sufi shaykh. There he encountered and joined the Boutchichiyya [*Budshishiyya*], a remarkably successful Sufi order of Qadiri and Darqawi origin which had already attracted an unusual following among Moroccan Francophone intellectuals (Haenni and Voix 2007). The Boutchichiyya, despite the unusually high proportion of university professors among its *muqaddam*s [local section heads] in Morocco, is in essentials a classic Sufi order.

After joining the Boutchichiyya, Skali returned to Paris to complete his graduate studies, and has remained based in France ever since. He has a dual identity there as a Traditionalist and as a Sufi, but the Sufi (and so the Islamic) identity predominates, as it seems to have done for Bammate. This was not the case with Schuon or even Vâlsan, and is not the case with Pallavicini. In private conversation, Skali stresses that Traditionalism is not a spiritual path, even though many who have never found a true spiritual path have tried to turn Traditionalism into a spiritual path.[42] Skali's own path is not Traditionalism but the Boutchichiyya and the *sharia*, and his ultimate human authority is not Guénon but his shaykh in Madagh, on the Beni Snassen plateau, near Morocco's border with Algeria.

Skali is a man of remarkable energy and considerable talents, and as a consequence was for a while an important producer of Islamic knowledge in Europe. By 2007, for reasons that are not entirely clear, Skali had become less active; what follows describes his activities as they were in 2003, when he was the *muqaddam* of the Boutchichiyya for France, overseeing *zawiya*s in Paris, Strasbourg, Nantes, Montpellier, Aix, Nice, and Marseilles. He also had responsibility for a small number of Boutchichis in some other parts of Europe.

Skali's followers were predominantly French residents of North African origin and French converts to Islam; I do not know in what numbers or proportion. Skali was clearly a figure with much legitimacy – as a Boutchichi *muqaddam*, as the holder of a French PhD in anthropology, and as (as we will see) a cultural figure of international standing. Like Nasr, he combined the authority of the intellectual with much of that of the *alim* – in this case, as the *muqaddam* of a well-known Sufi order.

Skali's influence was decisive within the European Boutchichiyya (Voix 2004), and also extended beyond it. He was active in Traditionalist circles in France, and author of a number of books and articles addressed to Traditionalists[43] – and in this context he was less explicit about the futility of trying to turn Traditionalism into the spiritual path which it is not. Understandably, he did not want to cut himself off from his audience. Skali also addressed even wider circles, participating in and organizing a variety of alternative-religious and cultural events, none of which were overtly Boutchichi or Traditionalist. These included a café-bookshop in Marseilles (Le Derviche), a magazine (*Soufisme d'Orient et d'Occident*), and a cultural association (L'Isthme) that specialized in 'Oriental' music and 'Sufi singing'. He organized two annual events: the 'Rencontres Méditerranéenne sur le soufisme' in France (a series of meetings, films, exhibitions and concerts), and the Fez Festival of Sacred Musics of the World, established in 1994.[44] This event is by now one of the major cultural events of the year in Morocco, attracting ever larger numbers of visitors from Europe. All these activities reflected a keen understanding of contemporary European conditions. It is hard to think of better ways through which to present Islam to a somewhat hostile audience than in terms of cultural achievement, music, and handicrafts, in terms of 'the transformation of being' (Skali 2000: 2) rather than of Allah's will.

All these 'outreach' activities served to attract recruits to the Boutchichiyya, and paralleled the Boutchichiyya's successful approach to recruiting from among the Francophone elite in Morocco itself (Sedgwick 2004b). Occasions such as the Fez Festival or performances of 'Sufi singing' in France have no direct impact on Islam in Europe but, like the speeches of Prince Charles and King Abdullah, and the books of Lings and Nasr, may have an indirect impact through their impact on general perceptions of Islam.

Skali implemented a conscious policy of localization which might be termed 'the localization of inessentials'. The assumption and hope was that in time all his followers would become devout Muslims on the standard Sufi model, but in the meantime Skali followed the Moroccan Boutchichis approach in not stressing the details of the *sharia* as ends in themselves. The *sharia* is the *sharia*, eternal and absolute, but female headscarves are not the most important part of the *sharia*. Skali was keenly aware of the potential for cultural conflict between the three main groups with which he was dealing: socially conservative Moroccan Muslims, French residents of North African origin, and French converts. He was more concerned to help integrate immigrants from North Africa into the French cultural milieu than to maintain a traditional Moroccan environment, and – in his own words – did not want 'to dress Frenchmen in turbans'.[45]

A second variety of localization was the way in which Skali's interpretations combined Islam, Sufism, and Traditionalism. They were attractive to a certain type of French resident, irrespective of origin. The typical French Boutchichi might be described as reasonably intelligent and somewhat adventurous, educated to at least BA level, and dissatisfied with the superficialities and selfishness of contemporary secular European culture. The religion of origin varies more than do these characteristics. Skali, then, led and expanded an established community that may serve as an interesting model for one of the future shapes of Islam in Europe.

Another Traditionalist Muslim who has increasing authority as an intellectual, if not as an *alim*, is Dr Bruno Guiderdoni, an astrophysicist at the CNRS. Guiderdoni is a follower of Pallavicini, but he operates largely independently in France, and both his intellectual powers and his diplomatic abilities are of a higher order than is the norm among Pallavicini's Italian followers. Pallavicini's audience consists predominantly of non-Muslims and of converts; in contrast, Guiderdoni – like Skali – also addresses born Muslims in Europe. For several years he presented what was then French television's sole Islamic television programme, 'Connaître l'Islam', which had a significant audience among French Muslims. Traditionalist emphases and slants were often visible in this programme,[46] though neither Traditionalism nor Sufism was promoted openly.[47] Guiderdoni no longer presents 'Connaître l'Islam', but remains a popular speaker on Islam both in France and abroad. Guiderdoni, like Skali but to a lesser extent, is an interesting producer of Islamic knowledge in Europe.

One obvious test of my contention that these Euro-Muslim producers of Islamic knowledge have had an impact on Islam in Europe would be to look for that impact. This is a difficult task, given the shortage of data on European Muslim behaviour and attitudes, and a task that remains to be completed. There is clearly a minority stream within European Islam, however, a stream that is to be found among better-educated Muslims and does not share the radical political or neo-Salafi preoccupations of many, that emphasizes the spiritual aspects of Islam more than is the norm in Europe or, indeed, in the contemporary Muslim world.

Conclusion

Traditionalism is in origin a European intellectual movement, and has more in common with the Renaissance than with the Muslim world. Its origins in the alternative religious milieu of late nineteenth-century Paris are clear, and significant in determining its later tenets. The movement's subsequent development, however, has brought it increasingly close to Islam.

Guénon, Schuon, and the Maryamiyya are more a part of Western intellectual history than of Islamic intellectual history, but they are read today by Muslims from Los Angeles to Cairo and Jakarta, and – of course – in Paris. The *Q-News* special issue on Martin Lings is indicative of the respect in which he personally was held, and of the role played by Traditionalist Muslims in Europe today, a role similar to that played by non-Guénonian traditionalists such as Hamza Yusuf and Nuh Ha Mim Keller. Nasr's form of Islamic Traditionalism was generated partly in Tehran, and partly in a global discourse that included Europeans and Iranians, and also Americans and Japanese. Its impact is also felt globally, by those – Muslim and non-Muslim – whose experience of modernity has made them receptive to Traditionalist views.

The final form of Traditionalism examined in this article is truly Euro-Islamic, the property of intellectually sophisticated European Muslims such as Skali and his followers. Once again, however, we are reminded that we are dealing with global phenomena. Skali may be a French resident, but his activities take place in the context of a Moroccan Sufi order. He is read in Morocco as well as in France. The crucial division, it seems, is not a regional one, but an educational and experiential one.

This phenomenon may not be entirely new. Centuries before the internet was imagined, long before English had become a global language, intellectual movements were already trans-regional. Luther was not merely of importance for Germany, and Ibn al-Arabi was not merely of importance for Syria. The difference today, perhaps, is that the linguistic and other divisions between the intellectual worlds of Syria and Germany, of Iran and Italy, are falling.

Notes

1 This chapter is based on a paper, 'The Renaissance Returns to Europe by Way of Tehran: Traditionalism and the Localization of Islam', presented at the Fourth Mediterranean Social and Political Research Meeting, Florence and Montecatini Terme, 19–23 March 2003, organized by the Mediterranean Program of the Robert Schuman Centre for Advanced Studies at the European University Institute. For the history of Guénonian Traditionalism, see Sedgwick 2004a, on which this chapter draws heavily for its factual basis. What is new and specific to this article is the analysis of Traditionalism's impact and significance for Islam in Europe, an analysis made in 2003 and brought up to date in various ways – notably with regard to literature – for the current publication.
2 Throughout this article, I use 'Islamic' to denote the religion, and 'Muslim' to denote the people(s) or culture(s).
3 It is of course problematic and in some ways anachronistic to describe a journal published without Guénon's involvement as 'Traditionalist', but Aguéli's early writings have since become part of the Traditionalist canon.
4 Some date Guénon's conversion to Islam from this encounter. In Sedgwick 2004a, I argue that Guénon's 'initiation' into a Sufi order did not involve conversion to Islam, and that Guénon's Muslim period started only in the early 1930s. Anyhow, as we will see below, Guénon himself denied ever having actually 'converted' to Islam. The real significance of this encounter was the transfer into Traditionalism of the central position taken by Ibn al-Arabi in Damascus.
5 De Pouvourville did not actually use the term 'yellow peril', but rather wrote of the threat constituted by the 'yellow race'. His 'clash of civilizations' was actually an earlier variety of clash, that of races.
6 I am here and below summarizing very briefly an entire philosophy, and of necessity my summary involves some distortion. The best starting place for those interested in Guénon's work is Guénon 1927.
7 Maritain's later hostility is deduced from the evident breach between the two men, and from persistent (but unconfirmed) rumours that Maritain tried to put Guénon's work on the Index of Prohibited Books. On the other hand, when towards the end of his life Maritain met an active (though undeclared) French Traditionalist, Henri Hartung, on a flight from Montréal to Paris, the two men found much in common and subsequently kept in touch. Sylvie Hartung, interview, Switzerland, August 2001.
8 Technically, the *kali yuga* or fourth age. The *kali yuga* is discussed in almost all of Guénon's later work, and plays a central part in the analyses of every Traditionalist I have ever read or interviewed.
9 Ananda Coomaraswamy in fact provides a loose link between William Morris and René Guénon.
10 I am here paraphrasing the views of several Muslim-born North Africans familiar with Guénon's work (various interviews), views that my own experience of the Arab world confirm. No member of the European working classes has ever played any part in the history of Traditionalism save, very occasionally, as an adherent of a Traditionalist Sufi order, and – more frequently – as a member of a rightist political organization inspired by Julius Evola. My general rule holds more for mainstream, spiritual Traditionalism than for political Traditionalism, discussed in Sedgwick 2004a.
11 They recognize, of course, that changing a sufficient mass of individuals may indirectly change a society, but changing societies is a possible outcome rather than a primary objective.

12 Again, this comment applies to mainstream, spiritual Traditionalism. Followers of Evola and of his most notable contemporary exponent, the influential Russian political commentator Alexander Dugin, are very active politically.

13 My comments on the varying legitimacy of the three different forms are based more on deduction and on impression than on hard data, but are even so almost certainly correct.

14 Schuon and the Maryamiyya are dealt with at length in Sedgwick 2004a (see chapters 4, 7, and 8). The estimate of the size of the Maryamiyya's membership is a very rough one.

15 The books published by these authors are listed and analysed on my www. traditionalists.org.

16 Eliade's debt to Traditionalism has been much debated, and my contribution to the debate is contained in Sedgwick 2004a: 189–92. Eliade was perhaps the most important Traditionalist of all, but as a non-Muslim falls outside the scope of this article. Vâlsan's order is considered in chapter 6 of *Against the Modern World*.

17 There had of course been many mosques operating in Milan for years, but none of them was formally regarded as a 'mosque'. Pallavicini's project to build a small but formal mosque therefore attracted much attention.

18 These comments are based on my reading of the work of Vâlsan and of his followers, and of interviews with Michel Chodkiewicz and with Vâlsan's son Muhammad in France in 2000.

19 For some of the criticisms, see Sedgwick 2004a: 140–1. I would like to thank Stefano Allievi and the late Ottavia Schmidt for their help in placing Pallavicini within the complex map of Italian Islam. Pallavicini's critics are often opposed to Sufism as such, and so accuse him of departures from Islam which are in fact only departures from their own understanding of Islam, and with which any Sufi in the Muslim world could equally be charged. More problematic is, for example, Pallavicini's understanding of the relationship between Islam and Catholic Christianity, which is purely Guénonian, and differs significantly from the mainstream Islamic view.

20 These points are all very controversial. They were established through numerous interviews with former Maryamis, most of whom wished to remain anonymous, and also through review of documentary evidence, including correspondence from the 1950s and sworn affidavits prepared during the 1990s for use in a US investigation. For a full discussion, see Sedgwick 2004a, chapter 8.

21 Chodkiewicz and Muhammad Vâlsan, interviews.

22 Chodkiewicz, interview.

23 Roty's former association with the Paris Mosque was confirmed by a telephone interview with a mosque official, 2000.

24 In the sense of being born into Muslim families and brought up as Muslims. According to standard Islamic belief, of course, all humans are Muslim-born.

25 The quotation from Hamlet is a slightly modified one. Hamlet in fact says (of his father): 'He was a man, take him for all in all, / I shall not look upon his like again'.

26 Also described by an irreverent American Muslim blogger as 'the great goeteed demigod of traditional Islam' (Eteraz 2006).

27 That the king's then Special Adviser, Joseph Lumbard, was a Maryami is not reported in the *Washington Times*. It is a conclusion based on interviews in Cairo in 2004.

28 The Prince of Wales indicated that his favourite Traditionalist reading is the journal *Sacred Web*, and suggested that he also reads *Sophia*.

32 I did not visit the Maryamiyya in Shiraz, and so only have second-hand information on its size and activities. These seem to be less significant than other aspects of Traditionalism in Iran today.

33 These were Ayatollah Mortada Motahhari at Tehran University and Ayatollah Jalal al-Din Ashtiyani at Nasr's institute. Motahhari was a prominent Islamist ideologist as well as a respected scholar, but Ashtiyani was broadly apolitical (he retired from Tehran to the shrine city of Mashhad after the revolution). Neither man was a Traditionalist.

34 Nasrullah Pourjavadi, Reza Davari Ardakani, and Abdolkarim Soroush.
35 Nasr, for example, went to London to attempt to dissuade the BBC from transmitting material hostile to the Shah; an alternative plan was to use Iranian commandos to blow up the BBC relay station in Cyprus.
36 Iranian academic and intellectual life was and remains far more compact than American academic and intellectual life. I can think of no American equivalent of Nasr in Iran in terms of prominence.
37 These comments are based on interviews with Muslim-born readers of Nasr in Turkey, Egypt, and Iran.
39 This seems to be the case, though according to other accounts there were only two people, neither of whom was Bammate. S. Katz, letter to Swami Siddheswarananda, February 6, 1951, printed in Accart 2001: 241–2, and Perry 1999: 90–1.
40 Preliminary discussions in Paris, 2000.
41 Bammate was much concerned with issues relating to Islam in Europe, on which he delivered numerous speeches and papers. See his posthumous *L'Islam et l'Occident*.
42 Interview, Fez, 2001.
43 His most important book is probably Skali 1995. The second half is more readable, and in many ways more impressive, than the first half.
44 By 2007, Skali no longer directed this festival. He started instead an annual Fez Festival of Sufi Culture. The third of these festivals, in 2009, mixed concerts with round-table discussions involving Sufis, academics, a French senator, and the president of the Hermes foundation.
45 Skali, interview.
46 This was my own view after watching some transmissions in 1996. The slants might have been less obvious to another viewer.
47 Guiderdoni, interview, Milan, 1996.

Bibliography

Abduh, Muhammad (1897) *Risalat al-tawhid*, Cairo: Matbaʿa al-kubra al-amiriyya.
Accart, Xavier (ed.) (2001) *L'Ermite de Duqqi: René Guénon en marge des milieux francophones égyptiens*, Milan: Archè.
André, Marie-Sophie and Beaufils, Christophe (1995) *Papus, biographie: la Belle Epoque de l'occultisme*, Paris: Berg International.
Anonymous (2008) Comment on 'Traditionalists and Traditionalists', on Mark Sedgwick (ed.) 'Traditionalists: A Blog for the Study of Traditionalism and the Traditionalists', 6 October 2008. Online: <http://www.blogger.com/comment.g?blogID=29711878&postID=6944575914152717475> (accessed 15 March 2009).
Boulet, Nöele Maurice-Denis (1962) 'L'ésotériste René Guénon: souvenirs et jugements', *La pensée catholique: cahiers de synthèse* 77: 17–42.
Campbell, Bruce (1980) *Ancient Wisdom Revived: A History of the Theosophical Movement*, Berkeley: University of California Press.
Daniélou, Alain (1984) 'René Guénon et la tradition hindoue', in Pierre-Marie Sigaud (ed.) *René Guénon* [Dossier H], Lausanne: L'Age d'Homme, pp. 136–40.
Duin, Julia (2006) 'Breakfast to Have Interfaith Flavor; King of Jordan Guest of Honor', *The Washington Times*, 1 February.
Elmore, Gerald T. (1999) Islamic Sainthood and the Fullness of Time: Ibn al-ʿArabi's Book of the Fabulous Gryphon, Leiden: Brill.
Eteraz, Ali (2006) 'Hamza Yusuf and Haram Sex Music.' Online: <http://eteraz.wordpress.com/2006/07/23/hamza-yusuf-and-haram-sex-music> (accessed 26 May 2007).

Guénon, René (1924) *Orient et Occident*, Paris: Payot, 1924; reprint, Paris: Guy Trédaniel, 1993.

Guénon, René (1927) *La crise du monde moderne*, Paris: Bossard.

Guénon, René (1945) *Le règne de la quantité et les signes des temps,* Paris: Gallimard.

Haenni, Patrick and Voix, Raphaël (2007) 'God by All Means ... Eclectic Faith and Sufi Resurgence among the Moroccan Bourgeoisie', in Martin van Bruinessen and Julia Day Howell (eds) *Sufism and the 'modern' in Islam*, London: I.B. Tauris, pp. 241–56.

Hanegraaff, Wouter (1996) *New Age Religion and Western Culture: Esotericism in the Mirror of Secular Thought,* Leiden: Brill.

James, Marie-France (1981) *Esotérisme, occultisme, franc-maçonnerie et christianisme aux XIX et XX siècles: explorations bio-bibliographiques*, Paris: Nouvelles éditions latines.

Keller, Nuh Ha Mim (1996) 'On the Validity of All Religions in the Thought of Ibn Al-ʿArabi and Emir ʿAbd al-Qadir'. Online: <http://masud.co.uk/ISLAM/nuh/amat.htm> (accessed March 14, 2009).

Kopf, David (1969) *British Orientalism and the Bengal Renaissance*, Berkeley: University of California Press.

Laurant, Jean-Pierre (1998) 'La "non-conversion" de René Guénon (1886–1951)', in Jean-Christophe Attias (ed.) *De la conversion*, Paris: Cerf, pp. 133–9.

Lings, Martin (1983) *Muhammad: His Life Based on the Earliest Sources*, London: Allen & Unwin.

Lings, Martin (2005) *A Return to the Spirit: Questions and Answers*, Louisville, Kentucky: Fons Vitae.

Mahmud, Abd al-Halim Mahmud (1974?) 'Al-ʿarif biʾLlah shaykh Abd al-Wahid Yahya', in Mahmud, *Al-madrasa al-Shadhiliyya al-haditha wa imamha Abuʾl-Hasan al-Shadhili*, Cairo: Ahmad Hamdy, pp. 230–341.

O'Sullivan, Jack (2001) 'If you Hate the West, Emigrate to a Muslim Country', *The Guardian*, 8 October. Online: <http://www.guardian.co.uk/world/2001/oct/08/religion.uk> (accessed 14 March 2009).

Perry, Whithall (1999) 'Aperçus', in Bernard Chevilliat (ed.) *Frithjof Schuon, 1907–1998: études et témoignages*, Avon: Connaissance des Religions, 1999.

Pipes, Daniel (2003) 'Is Prince Charles a Convert to Islam?' Daniel Pipes blog. Online: <http://www.danielpipes.org/blog/2003/11/is-prince-charles-a-convert-to-islam.html> (accessed 14 March 2009).

Pouvourville, Albert de (1906) editorial, *Le Continent* [Paris and Berlin], 1 (1): 11–6.

Radji, Parviz (1983) *In the Service of the Peacock Throne: The Diaries of the Shah's Last Ambassador to London*, London: Hamish Hamilton.

Roty, Yacoub (1994) *L'attestation de foi: première base de l'Islam*, Paris: Maison d'Ennour.

Sedgwick, Mark (2004a) *Against the Modern World: Traditionalism and the Secret Intellectual History of the Twentieth Century*, New York: Oxford University Press.

Sedgwick, Mark (2004b) 'In Search of the Counter-Reformation: Anti-Sufi Stereotypes and the Budshishiyya's Response', in Charles Kurzman and Michaelle Browers (eds) *An Islamic Reformation?* Lanham, Md: Lexington Books, pp. 125–46.

Sedgwick, Mark (2007a) 'Prince Charles and Rumi', in Mark Sedgwick (ed.) 'Traditionalists: a blog for the study of Traditionalism and the Traditionalists', 2 December 2007. Online: <http://traditionalistblog.blogspot.com/2007/12/prince-charles-and-rumi.html> (accessed March 15, 2009).

Sedgwick, Mark (2007b) 'Quelques sources du dix-huitième siècle du pluralisme religieux inclusif', in Jean-Pierre Brach and Jérôme Rousse-Lacordaire (eds) *Etudes d'histoire de l'ésotérisme: mélanges offerts à Jean-Pierre Laurent*, Paris: Editions du Cerf, pp. 49–65.

Sedgwick, Mark (2008) 'European Neo-Sufi Movements in the Interwar Period', in Nathalie Clayer and Eric Germain (eds), *Islam in Inter-War Europe*, London: Hurst, pp. 183–215.

Sellam, Sadek (2000) 'Un frère des hommes', in Najm-oud-Dine Bammate (ed.) *L'Islam et l'Occident: dialogues,* Paris: UNESCO, 2000), pp. 13–6.

Skali, Faouzi (1995) *La voie soufie*, Paris: Albin Michel.

Skali, Faouzi (2000) editorial, *Soufisme d'Orient et d'Occident*, 5: 2.

Voix, Raphaël (2004) 'Implantation d'une confrérie musulmane en France: mécanismes, méthodes et acteurs,' *Ateliers*, 28: 221–48.

Wales, Charles Prince of (2006) speech to a conference on 'Tradition in the Modern World', University of Alberta, Canada, September 23–4.

Washington, Peter (1995) *Madame Blavatsky's Baboon: A History of the Mystics, Mediums and Misfits who Brought Spiritualism to America,* New York: Schocken Books.

Yusuf, Hamza (2005) 'A Spiritual Giant in an Age of Dwarfed Terrestrial Aspirations', *Q-News*, 363: 53–58.

Zarcone, Thierry (1999) 'Relectures et transformations de soufisme en Occident', *Diogène*, 187 (47): 110–21.

Glossary

[A: Arabic; T: Turkish; U: Urdu; where no language is indicated, the terms are given in their Arabic form]

adhan (A), *ezan* (T)	the call to prayer
Ahl-i Hadith	South Asian reformist movement that strictly rejected all practices that cannot be documented in authentic hadith. Strong opponents of Sufism and traditionalist *fiqh*-based scholarship, much like the Wahhabis
ᶜalim, pl. *ᶜulamaᶜ*	(Islamic) scholar
Barelwi	Blanket term for South Asian mainstream traditionalist and Sufi-flavoured Islam. Named after Bareilly, the residence of leading nineteenth-century apologist of traditionalist Islam, Raza Ahmad Khan
batil	falsehood (often used in opposition to what is right and true, *haqq*)
daᶜi	preacher, Islamic missionary (literally, a person carrying out *daᶜwa*)
dars-i nizami	the traditional curriculum of South Asian madrasas, named after the eighteenth-century scholar Mulla Nizamuddin of Farangi Mahall in Lucknow
dar al-ᶜaqd	'House of Convenant', i.e. non-Muslim territory with which peaceful contractual relations have been established.
dar al-daᶜwa	'House of Predication': non-Muslim territory open to Islamic propagation
dar al-harb	'House of War', i.e., the parts of the world dominated by the enemies of Islam
dar al-islam	'House of Islam', i.e. the parts of the world where Islam is the dominant religion
dar al-ᶜulum	college-level Islamic school ('house of sciences')

da^εwa	the preaching and propagation of Islam
Deobandi	one of the two mainstream movements of South Asian Islam, named after the moderately reformist madrasa of Deoband. Critical of Sufi orders and strongly opposed to saint worship and other 'popular' practices condoned by the more traditionalist Barelwi movement
dhikr	'remembering': reciting the names of God or other simple formulas
dini ta^εlim (U)	religious training
faqih, pl. *fuqaha^ε*	specialist of Islamic legal thought (*fiqh*)
fatwa, pl. *fatawa*	opinion on a matter of religious importance, usually issued in response to a specific request
fazil, pl. *fuzla* (U) (A: *fadil, fudala^ε*)	(in South Asia) graduate of college-level madrasa
fiqh	Islamic jurisprudence, legal thought
fiqh al-aqalliyyat	branch of Islamic legal thought that takes account of the special situation of Muslim minorities in countries with non-Muslim majorities
firqa najiya	'the saved sect' (reference to a well-known *hadith* according to which the *umma* will be divided into 72 sects, only one of which will be saved)
fitna	dissent, internal conflict
fuqaha'	pl. of *faqih*
furu^ε	'branches': the body of positive rules derived from the sources of legal knowledge
fuzla (A: *fudala^ε*)	pl. of *fazil* [q.v.]
hadith, pl. *ahadith*	'Prophetic tradition': a report on what the Prophet said or how he acted in a specific situation
hafiz, pl. *huffaz*	memorizer of the Qur^εan
halal	licit, allowed by Islam
haqq	right, truth (cf. the common term for its opposite, *batil*); in Sufi discourse, the term often refers to God
haram	illicit, forbidden by Islam
hifz	memorization, especially of the Quran
hijab	Islamic 'covering' of women
hikma	'wisdom': philosophy and the (ancient) sciences
Hizb ut-Tahrir	'Liberation Party', Islamist movement striving to unite the entire *umma* under a new Caliphate

ʿibada, pl. *ʿibadat*	(act of) worship
idara	'office, bureau'; the name by which the mosques and Islamic centres of the Minhajul Qurʿan movement are known
ʿidda	the waiting period a woman has to observe after divorce or death of her husband (to be certain she is not pregnant)
iftaʿ	the act or process of issuing fatwas [q.v.]
iftar	breaking of the fast
ijaza	diploma or permission to teach a certain subject
ijmaʿ	consensus, agreement – especially, consensus among the leading scholars of Islam, which is traditionally ocnsidered as a source of Islamic law
ijtihad	solving a problem of Islamic law, for which no immediate scriptural answer is available, by individual reasoning
ikhwan	brethren, brothers (term often used to denote fellow members of a Sufi order or other religious movement)
al-Ikhwan al-Muslimun	the Muslim Brothers: the first major Islamist movement, established in Egypt in 1928 by Hasan al-Banna
imam	leader;- among Sunni Muslims, the prayer leader in a mosque;- among the Shiʿa, the legitimate successors of the Prophet, Ali b. Abi Talib and his descendants
imamat (A: *imama*)	the charismatic leadership of the imam (in the Shiʿa tradition)
istiftaʿ	the requesting of a fatwa [q.v.]
jamaʿa (A), *jamaʿat* (P, U), *cemaat* (T)	congregation (especially, of a mosque, but also of a religious association)
Jamaʿat-i Islami	South Asia-based Islamist movement and political party, established by Mawlana Abu'l Aʿla Mawdudi
kafir (pl. *kuffar*)	unbeliever
kalam	systematic theology
khalifa	deputy or successor of a Sufi shaykh
khatib	preacher, the person who pronounces the sermon at the Friday prayer. The position of imam and khatib in a mosque are commonly (but not necessarily) combined
khutba	sermon (especially the sermon pronounced at the Friday service in the mosque)
kufr	unbelief
kurban (T), *qurban* (A)	sacrifice, sacrificial animal

madaris	pl. of madrasa
madhhab, pl. *madhahib*	school of Islamic law (Sunni Islam recognizes four madhhab: the Hanafi, Shafiᶜi, Maliki and Hanbali; sometimes the Shiᶜi Jaᶜfari madhhab is accepted as the fifth school)
madrasa, pl. *madaris*	school teaching religious subjects
mahram	[a woman's] close relative of the opposite sex, with whom marriage is forbidden and who may act as her chaperone
maqasid al-shariᶜa	objectives of the divine law (a category in Islamic legal theory)
maslaha	what is beneficial to the umma, the 'common good'
maslak	'denomination' [term used in South Asia to denote the main streams in Islam]
milad	(commemoration of) the birth of the Prophet
Milli Görüs	'the National View': the major Turkish Islamist movement, which in Turkey gave rise to various Islamist parties; in Europe, the major Turkish Muslim association independent of the official Diyanet
Minhajul Qurᶜan	Pakistani traditionalist Islamic movement, rooted in the Qadiri Sufi order
muᶜamala, pl. *muᶜamalat*	worldly activities; Islamic legal thought distinguishes between ᶜibadat, acts of worship, and *muᶜamalat* or interaction between human actors
mufti	expert of Islamic law who issues fatwas [q.v.]
muhaddith	scholar specialized in hadith studies
al-Muhajiroun	'Migrants': a radical Islamist movement that branched off from the Hizb ut-Tahrir
muqaddam	leader; especially the spiritual leader in certain Sufi orders
mushrik	'idolater': a person who associates anything or anyone with God, polytheist
mustafti	person who requests a fatwa [q.v.]
mustashar	counsellor
naji	saved [*firqa najiya*: 'the sect that will be saved']
pir	Sufi master
qarar	decision
qari, pl. *qurraᶜ*	reader, reciter (of the Qurᶜan)
qawwali	devotional songs of the South Asian Sufi tradition

qurban	sacrifice, sacrificial animal
qurra'	pl. of *qari*
al-salaf al-salih	'the pious predecessors', i.e., the first three generations of Muslims
Salafi	Muslim who adheres to what he believes to be the faith and practice of *al-salaf al-salih*, rejecting all later developments in Islam
shirk	associating anything with God, 'idolatry'
tabligh	spreading the Faith, preaching
Tablighi Jamaʿat	revivalist piety movement, established in British India in the 1920s, that became Islam's most successful transnational missionary movement
tafsir	Qurʿanic exegesis
takfir	declaring someone to be an unbeliever
talfiq	combining rulings of different schools of Islamic jurisprudence
taʿlim	teaching [*dini taʿlim*, 'religious training']
taʿwidh	protective amulet
taqlid	following the rulings of a recognized religious authority or school of Islamic jurisprudence
tarbiya	training, disciplining
taysir	'making things easy': a principle in fiqh allowing one to opt for the less onerous of several interpretations of specific religious obligations, based on the conception that God has made religion easy for mankind
umma	religious community (incorporating all believers)
ʿurf	customary practices
ʿurs	(in South Asia) death anniversary of a saint
usul al-fiqh	Islamic legal theory
waʿz	admonitory preaching
wuduʿ	ritual ablutions
zakat	obligatory religious tax, one of the five 'pillars' of Islam
zawiya	Sufi lodge

Index